D1733186

Living in
Two
Worlds

Living in Two Worlds

Addressing Humanity's Greatest Challenge

By
Ian McCallum and Ian Michler

Quickfox

Published by Quickfox Publishing
PO Box 50660, West Beach, 7449
Cape Town, South Africa
www.quickfox.co.za | info@quickfox.co.za

Living in Two Worlds: Addressing Humanity's Greatest Challenge
ISBN Print: 978-0-639-70629-0
ISBN Epub: 978-0-639-70630-6
ISBN Kindle: 978-0-639-70631-3

First edition 2022

Copyright © 2022 Ian McCallum and Ian Michler

All rights reserved.

The rights of Ian McCallum and Ian Michler to be identified as the
authors of this work have been asserted by them in accordance with
sections 77 and 78 of the Copyright, Designs and Patents Act, 1988.

No part of this book may be reprinted or reproduced or utilised in
any form or by any electronic, mechanical, or any other means, now
known or hereafter invented, including photocopying, and recording
or in any information storage or retrieval system, without permission in
writing from the authors: ianmichler@mweb.co.za

Publishing director: Vanessa Wilson
Edited by Peter Borchert and Michelle Bovey-Wood
Book interior and cover design by Vanessa Wilson
Cover images by Ian Michler
Typesetting and production: Quickfox Publishing
Traffic and print manager: Adele Wilson
Printed by Shumani RSA, South Africa

All attempts have been made to reference and secure relevant permissions
to publish extracts of printed materials. In the event of any omissions, please
contact the authors at ianmichler@mweb.co.za who will attempt to rectify
the situation as soon as possible.

CONTENTS

"It's the beginning of something else, and the end of something that's done with. I know and there's no altering it, that I've got to live differently."

DH Lawrence, *St. Mawr*

FOREWORD

{ *By Andrew Muir* }

I have known the two Ians, as we affectionately call them, for practically my entire conservation career. In fact, Ian McCallum gave me my first job. He was a board member of the globally renowned Wilderness Leadership School in the mid-80s when he convinced his great friend Ian Player to employ me as a field guide for its Western Cape operations. I subsequently went on to take over the running of both the Wilderness Leadership School and Wilderness Foundation Africa from Ian Player. McCallum introduced me to the 'other' Ian in the early 90s. Since then our paths have all crossed and interwoven through the many conservation projects and adventures we have taken on across the continent and world. I have always been in awe of Ian McCallum's ability to communicate and explain, in both the written form and orally, complex processes and the interconnectedness between humans and nature in a way that inspires us to want to learn more and get involved. Ian Michler is truly authentic in everything he does and is one of the bravest conservationists I have ever met; his investigative journalism and exposure of the true horrors of the captive lion industry in the 90s and commitment to ending this practice is an example to us all.

We exist at a time in the earth's history when we are facing unprecedented environmental challenges. We are one of more than 13 million species that make up our planet. It is commonly accepted that by the year 2050, 20% of the species that currently inhabit the earth with us will either be extinct or on the brink of extinction. This is due in part to the perfect storm of biodiversity loss, unsustainable resource utilisation and the human impact on climate change.

When the two Ians approached us in 2010, we were instantly intrigued about their idea to follow ancient elephant migration routes on foot, bike and kayak across Southern Africa, to highlight awareness about transboundary conservation, traditional wildlife tracking skills, leadership and important conservation issues such as climate change, water and habitat fragmentation. For us as a movement we believed 'Tracks' would illustrate the importance of large, interconnected wild areas to wildlife and human communities. As such we agreed to run their Tracks of Giants project under the auspices of Wilderness Foundation Africa, and together we embarked upon two years of planning and fundraising to make this happen. They assembled an amazing team of people to support them and act as a backup team, and along with Sharon McCallum, became immersed in planning every aspect of this expedition. By April 2012 we were ready to embark on this epic journey.

Living in Two Worlds is, on the one hand, a story of two great friends, master guides and brothers-in-arms for the cause of nature. It is also a story of two brilliant writers and critical thinkers who, with their other skills of investigative journalism, tracking spoor, guiding, and psychiatry, are able to immerse the reader and take us on this trek with them, and in so doing, enthral us with vignettes and stories that show the interconnections of life on earth and how our only way forward as a species is to tread lighter and commit to sustainable living.

Clearly, the answers to the many challenges they illustrate so clearly in this book cannot come from one discipline or sector alone, but rely on multi-sectoral collaboration and the critical need to put the environment at the top of the political agenda. A faint hope we may say. Yes, but as Ian McCallum and Ian Michler continually illustrate through both their ground-truthing journey and actions examined in this book, it is the duty of each and every one of us to continue to remind those in power that the environment, that our interconnectivity and dependence on it, must come first.

Andrew Muir is the CEO Wilderness Foundation Africa and Wilderness Foundation Global, Rolex Laurette and Schwab Foundation Social Entrepreneur.

{ PART A }

NOTES FROM THE AUTHORS

GETTING THE MESSAGE ACROSS

{ *Ian McCallum* }

'This has something to do with me …'

This book contains the writings and voices of two men among the many individuals globally who are concerned about and committed to addressing the environmental crises of our time – more especially, the threatened future of the wild habitats and animals of the world. My voice and that of Ian Milcher may speak with different tones and styles, but we essentially speak the same language. In a friendship spanning more than 35 years, we have opened our hearts to each other and have uncovered not only our shared love of the wild, but also our love of teaching.

This collection of essays is the result of a non-motorised journey that Ian and I, along with an extensive support team, undertook in 2012: Walking, kayaking, cycling and connecting elephant migration routes and clusters through six countries across southern Africa. From the Atlantic Ocean in the west to the Indian Ocean in the east, the 5 000 km transect would take a little over four months to complete.

Upon completion, our intention had been to write a book titled *In the Tracks of Giants,* about our goals; the physical, social and mental challenges that arose on our journey; the role of the managerial and back-up crew; the guides, and not least of all, our encounters with wild animals. However, in the days and months following our journey, ruminations and reflections – subtle yet important insights – began to consolidate. Those insights shaped the way this book was to be written and emerged in the form of questions that will demand an answer from all human beings in the years to come. To Ian and me, answering these questions serve as the greatest ecological challenges of our time.

The first question concerns the need for a profound renewal of our present, economic definition of the concept of environmental sustainability: 'If it pays, it stays.'

What is it going to take to question our current values, lifestyles, beliefs, perspectives and understanding of a biosphere in which we co-exist with all living things, that the wild animals in the world are in our blood and in our psyche ... that we need them more than they need us? Who and what would we be without them?

The next question arose from the realisation that the story of our journey needed to be told within the context of the intertwined environmental crises of our time: The human contribution to climate instability, global warming, our exponential population growth, and with it the increasing threat to the future well-being of wild habitats and wild animals worldwide.

Could it be that elephants are not only one of many keystone species of the wild, but rather, large, grey mirrors of the fate of all wild animals, including us? Could it be that without wild animals in our lives we would die of a lonely spirit?

Finally, if it's not too late:

How are we going to communicate the environmental message in a way that promotes action?

This will not happen unless those who hear it or read the message are left with a deepened sense of personal accountability ... that the challenges we are facing have 'something to do with me'.

There is no escaping the human contribution to the environmental crises of our time. However, developing a willingness to examine ourselves and to face up to our complicity in the unfolding of these global climatic events is not an easy task. The truth is that we don't really want to know. The subject is either too depressing or too distant – it is not affecting us or our neighbourhoods ... yet. Despite the wealth of scientific papers, facts, figures and documentaries on this subject over the past 20 years, getting this message across continues to be a frustrating challenge for environmental activists, conservationists and climate and biological scientists.

Apart from the psychological motivations for switching off to the environmental realities of our time, there is another reason why our message so often falls on deaf ears. I would suggest that this has something to do with the disconnecting way that our written and spoken language comes across. For a start, let's address the way we speak about ourselves in relationship to Nature. How often do we hear of, or speak about, 'getting back to Nature', as if Nature is something 'out there', to be visited, photographed, protected or tamed for human purposes? We are Nature. We are in it and of it. Each living thing is an expression of it.

Another example of an albeit unintentional language of disconnection is that of science itself. The language of science, as essential as it is, can be both daunting and alienating to the layperson. Perhaps this is not only because of its sometimes cold, academic terminology, heady acronyms, facts and figures, but also because of its reluctance to acknowledge the value of subjectivity or, if you prefer, feelings or emotions, in its discourse. This is a pity. The environmental issues of our time are emotional ones –and so they should be. Anger, outrage, despair, grief and joy cannot be measured, but they cannot be denied, either. Much like the feelings of awe, wonder and 'terrible beauty' (W.B. Yeats) evoked by science.

Our bond to the natural world – to rivers, mountains, forests and animals – is as much emotional and immeasurable as it is physiological and measurable, subjective *and* objective. Many of the questions leading to some of our greatest scientific discoveries were born and nurtured in the 'hard-wired' crucible of human intuition and emotion. We cannot live without them.

'I believe in intuitions and inspirations. I sometimes feel that I am right' said Albert Einstein, adding: 'The important thing is not to stop questioning.'

For me, this includes questions like: 'What do we need to do to be more effective in the way that we share and teach the environmental message?'

If we are serious about getting our message across to a wider audience, we need to focus on a language that is inspiring; that celebrates the feelings of beauty, awe and wonder; that does not turn a blind eye to tragedy, and that carries within it seeds of hope. I will wager that most people who did not enjoy biological science when they were at school, did not enjoy the uninspiring way the subject was taught to them. If we cannot inspire, we're in trouble. We have to be able to engage with people. As Molly Steinwald, a PhD graduate in Conservation Genetics at the University of Tennessee, puts it: 'If you can't engage your audience, you don't have an audience.' It's not about showing how clever we are as scientists, but about sharing our passion, bringing the best out of our audiences, and not underestimating their intelligence.

For me, this is what this book is about. It is not a biography, but it has 'something to do with me'; with my early life; with my training in psychiatry and analytical psychology; with my fascination for cosmology; evolutionary biology; and with the wilderness trails I undertook with Ian Player of the Wilderness Leadership School. Most importantly, it has to do with the pivotal time I spent with Ian Michler as a co-guide in Botswana in the late 1990s. It is something of these experiences with Ian that I would like to share.

In 1998, my wife Sharon resigned from her position as partner in a Cape Town law firm, and I took what would become a two-year sabbatical from my work as a psychiatrist. With Sharon taking on the role of manager and Ian and I doing the guiding, we headed to Botswana and Wilderness Safari's tented camp in the north-eastern Linyanti region of the country. It didn't take long for me to realise that I had not turned my back on my work as a therapist and psychiatrist. Instead, as a wilderness guide, I was alerted to the way various guests regularly voiced a sense of homecoming … a rediscovery of themselves in that ancient setting. For many, the experience was not only unforgettable, but therapeutic, too.

The theme of 'homecoming' – the rediscovery of a sense of Self – is another way to describe the goal of analytical therapy. My responsibilities as a wilderness guide were essentially no different from those of a therapist. As a guide, one's main concern is the safety of one's guests.

Animal encounters are treated with a deep respect. What I call a 'critical distance' is maintained between you and the animal – a safe distance or boundary between the observers and the animals in question. If you get too close, the animal takes flight. If you're too far, you'll lose the details of the event. The same approach and attitude apply to the therapist as a guide into the sometimes-unfamiliar wilderness of the psyche. Encounters with the emotion-charged images of the imagination and dreams need to be handled with respect.

A guide must know how to listen, to be sensitive to the timing of explanations of animal sightings. Sometimes it is better to keep silent … to let the experience of the event speak for itself. A little later, perhaps, the guide can enhance the experience by offering a different perspective – the bigger picture by, for example, describing the dynamics of the day's events in terms of ecosystems and food chains in which the animal and plant kingdoms co-exist. Again, this is no different to formal therapy, where the realisation of a 'bigger picture' in the concerns of the patient can be immensely helpful. Explanations are not always necessary. Sometimes all that is needed is to listen, and to do so with an empathic ear. For me, the wilderness setting: The land, the river, the trees, the birds, the insects and the animal life, became the most dynamic and beautiful extension of my consulting room back in Cape Town.

However, something else happened to me during that time in the Linyanti. Poetry came in search of me. Determined to keep a diary of everyday happenings, I struggled to find a way to capture the tension and excitement of the various animal encounters. However, with pencil to paper, what I began to write was distinctly poetic. Where it came from, I do not know, but I wrote it down. My pages came alive with a heightened sense of respect for the wild animals. But there was more … a deepened sense of resonance with them. They were alive in me … an ancient kinship. For example, the spotted hyaena, a long-standing target of negative human projections of callousness, cowardice and brutality, are anything but. '*Great, blemished beasts of the night*,' I wrote, '*we, too, have our spots.*'

Considering the snakes and the seasonal shedding of their skins, I realised that so it is with human beings. We, too, need to shed outdated attitudes, '*and that even a god must shed his skin*'. The co-existence and dependency of the animals on other species within that wild habitat, forced me to write questions like: '*Who is looking at who? ... Do I not speak for you, or is it you that speaks for me?*'

Recognising the interwoven fabric of the wild, the baobab became the '*elephant tree*'. Vultures became '*midwives of new life*', and in the wild, '*to be abandoned, is to grow*'.

Increasingly aware of the threat to the future of wilderness areas worldwide, I wrote: '*... have we forgotten that wilderness is not a place but a season, and we are in its final hour?*'

It was there, in the Linyanti region, and through a poetic lens, that I began to understand what it means to live in two worlds simultaneously, and that it is inescapable and necessary. Like the two separate, yet interconnecting threads of DNA, we live in an interconnected world of subjects and objects; measurement and metaphor; the wilderness without and the wilderness within. For me, poetry had come to the rescue of an embattled scientific message. Through rhyme and resonance, I found within me a voice and source of hope; a voice, among many others, that could speak for the threatened wild habitats and animals of the world – and possibly for the Earth itself.

Let's get our language right. Let's give the Earth and Nature the capital letters they deserve. Let's find a place for the word 'sacred' in our language and conversations about our planet. Treat it as a living church – which it is – in which all living things are worthy of our concern, understanding and gratitude.

THE PRIVILEGE
TO ROAM

{ *Ian Michler* }

All of my appreciation, thanks and love to Tessa and Liam for their support, leeway, and patience.

I guess the urge to roam, explore and then ask probing questions about life, our universe and the nether world is driven for many by what Steven Tyler, frontman of rock band Aerosmith, referred to as 'the noise in my head'. Throughout his raucous career, Tyler had plenty of noise with which to contend, which makes the title of his memoir, *Does the Noise in My Head Bother You?* particularly apt.

I started my journey because I had noise going on in my own head, but over time I realised that the essence of inquisitive and meaningful writing, as well as the activism that goes with it, is to drill down into what emerges as the loudest of the noise. I hope that at least something in this book will bother you.

Of all the privileges I have been fortunate to enjoy, my life in the wilderness has been one of the most meaningful. Being able to undertake the Tracks of Giants journey, along with Ian, which sparked this book, and having the chance to share some thoughts on the stories linked to it, is in some way a culmination of that experience. I still spend plenty of time exploring Africa's wild places, but it certainly has influenced my understanding of what is at stake and how humanity's current trajectory is playing out.

This book is more than a record of vignettes gathered along this journey; it is a collection of essays that attempt to record, comment on, and understand the dynamics of our relationship with this astonishingly rich and diverse continent, as well as with the wider world.

Perhaps a little background might add some insight to the chapters that follow.

I grew up on a farm along the southern Cape coast of South Africa. My early years offered a solid foundation for what I now do. The greater part of my pre- and early teens was spent amid some of the country's most magnificent biodiversity. However, it was the world of birds that grabbed me. Often alone but sometimes accompanied by family and friends, I would go in search of sightings and nesting locations, never tiring at the delight of new discoveries. At other times, we would simply roam the fynbos-covered mountains and the strikingly rugged coastline that was our home. Those wholesome surroundings and immensely enjoyable times defined our lives. It was there, among the Cape sugarbirds, African fish eagles, bontebok, common dolphins and giant proteas that my deep appreciation for wilderness, and the inspiration to get to know it, was fostered.

During these pursuits, I began to develop a greater sense of what life and being were all about. With that came a sense of my personal place in the world. There was no defining moment and no epiphany, just a gentle emergence and growing realisation that my own roots, spirituality, and interpretation of symbolism were centred in the natural world. Despite my church-school education, and the best efforts of some decent enough men, religious ramblings never provided much vision or sense to me. It was the processes of science and biology that offered fascination. While certain concepts in these disciplines were somewhat baffling to my young mind, they would eventually provide all the explanations, understanding and insight I needed.

Then came those mid- to late-teenage years – the period in which I came to realise that I would soon be tossed from the nest. It is around that time that young people are expected to make crucial life decisions without any appropriate tools to do so. Like so many young white South Africans coming of age in the 1970s, my uncertainty was clouded by the horrors of Apartheid. I was sensitive to the brutality and injustices that brought such anguish, pain and suffering to the vast majority of South Africans. It also brought fear to my own protected living. However, I was not perceptive or committed enough to make bold or ethical decisions.

As I recall, back then, doing what I now do was not evident in the cards I held – nor was it an obvious option on my wish list. Nothing changed when I left school. Uncommitted to the regime and its military, after an initial call-up I flirted with the options of fight or flight, before opting to duck out of university to embark on lengthy travels across Europe and Africa. However, the lure of my home and a sense of belonging brought me back. Eventually, I settled on another privileged path: A diversionary career that took me into the world of stockbroking and finance while continuing my part-time studies.

During the day, I donned my suit and tie with gusto. At night, I retreated to my 13th-floor haven in Johannesburg's Hillbrow. During the 1980s, that high-density suburb was one of the more exhilarating cultural and political melting pots in South Africa. It was a life of never-ending experiences, enriched by the juxtaposition of cultures, communities and individuals. I got to explore and understand more than one reality, including a much-heightened awareness of the Apartheid government's illegitimacy, while witnessing the immense fortitude and wisdom of those against whom it discriminated.

Initially, the status and trappings that came with my work were gratifying, but my daily dealings, based almost entirely on the culture of money, soon began to erode my enthusiasm. Seeing the corporate enclave from the inside raised many more questions within me. At that stage of my life, those concerns outweighed any need for financial security. Disenchantment set in around the nature of broking and banking, obscene remuneration levels, and the ethical standing of what was nothing more than a closed club. I sensed that those aspects, together with the other key drivers of the economy, were doing as much as the political regime to erode our chances of achieving a just and genuinely democratic society. I felt increasingly ill at ease with my place in all of that, but I couldn't figure a way out.

Growing up, and during my working life, I also spent a fair amount of time in the wilderness, for occasions that marked family and work vacations to a host of Africa's most enthralling destinations. Once home or back at my desk, those trips lingered with me, often for months. I guess I was straddling different worlds but trying to reconcile them by finding space for them both. However, as my broking career progressed, I found myself in the process of planning another life. Those plans were playful at first, but as my career path demanded greater responsibilities, and with a growing unease at having to make new commitments, the yearning grew to step out of it.

Round about then, I also got to experience and understand both the power and deceit of the state. As a family, we lost our home to expropriation. It went to the thuggish brutes that propped up the Apartheid-era government – that self-same military regime that was still harassing me and other white kids to comply with their vile ideology. Not only had my extended family, which included our cousins, lost their home, but I had also lost that personal and intimate access to the natural world that had been so instrumental in forging my brittle being.

On reflection, I now suspect it must have been around then that I made a subconscious decision to seek out a life in the wilds – one that excluded any proximity to the system driving the brutality and inequality. I knew what was making me so uncomfortable, and I knew what I needed to do. But would anyone else understand my reasons for giving up such a coveted and lucrative career?

With the burdens of both eagerness and a fear of change in my head, I continued to drift. But it was only a matter of time before I quit my job. I emerged after eight years in the city with great relief and few regrets.

Still without a clear life map, and joined by Tessa, now my beloved life partner, we eagerly sought refuge in the wilds of Botswana. Nxama-seri Lodge, a tiny enclave of magic in the upper reaches of the Okavango Delta, became my starting point. What a wondrous wetland it was. There was no greater wilderness in which to enter a period of apprenticeship.

After two years on the waterways of the Panhandle, I got into the saddle, and two or so adventurous years of riding horses with great friends and mentors across the floodplains followed. I then ventured further into the heart of the Delta in my first foray as a full-time guide and part-time photographer and writer.

Those were extraordinary years that reinforced my decision to alter course. For those of us fortunate enough to have lived and worked in the fledgling ecotourism industry across northern Botswana and its neighbouring states in the 1990s, there could surely have been no less inhibited time. Looking back, those stories seem so implausible, so far-fetched in their joys, wonder and freedom. It was also a time of discovery and learning, and a growing awareness of the ever-present balance demanded to meet the needs of people and wildlife in the most responsible of manners. Above all, what stood out for me was my own pleasure and contentment at being immersed in a simple lifestyle, surrounded by the raw integrity and authenticity of wilderness.

That period was another defining interlude. It had dawned on me that such an indulgence was not going to be enough. I was fortunate to meet and work alongside, and under the tutelage of, many great guides; photographers; filmmakers; camp owners; researchers and naturalists, who all made vast contributions to the world of ecotourism, conservation and ecology. Fed by their knowledge and successes, and at times, our shared experiences, I began to feel the compulsion to make a greater and more meaningful contribution.

No doubt, that compulsion was also fed by a naivety that had begun to wear thin. Again, that realisation comes with hindsight. Upon arrival, I must have carried with me a whimsical hope, one that somehow suggested that my new life was going to be utterly different from everything else I had done. To a degree, it was, but after some time, I began to recognise two of the driving themes that had dominated my previous work: The crude pursuit of financial returns and the political playbooks that often emerge in support thereof. Although no less entrenched, they came insidiously cloaked in shades of the romance that tends to define living in the bush. Of course, those twin themes of profit and politics are principal drivers that define everything in our current world –

conservation, wildlife management and ecotourism included. It became apparent that I needed to understand them in that context, as well as my own role in the space.

During that time, I started an immensely stimulating and gratifying period of guiding, along with Ian McCallum. That work continues to this day. A great friend, mentor and work colleague, as well as my co-trekker and author of this book, Ian has too many attributes and accomplishments to list here. His immensely insightful and intelligent understanding and interpretation of what he refers to as the 'human/ animal interface' introduced me to a more profound appreciation of both human and animal behaviour. No one speaks or writes of this fascinating intricacy in the way he does. These nuances have woven themselves into much of my current work.

In exchange, I introduced him to the contentment that comes from birding, and the wonders of Bruce Springsteen – surely one of the most candid, intuitive, and inspirational singer-songwriters ever – as well as the excitement and frustrations that come with being a devoted Arsenal Football Club supporter.

I feel a massive sense of privilege to have shared so much time and so many discussions with Ian, often layered in dust, fireside smoke, and music. We speak with different tones and walk in distinctive ways, yet we share a common language and understanding based on a familiar interpretation of the natural world, the challenges it faces, and our places in it. It is impossible to think of my career path without Ian's contributions to it.

My wanderings were not yet complete: East Africa and selected destinations in west and central Africa were proving irresistible. So, I ventured out, not because I was done with the south, but because I was lured instead by tales of magical places, people, and wildlife further north. My primate and Great Migration sightings, and the road trips to Timbuktu, and beyond into the Sahara proved among my most thrilling ever. They have added immeasurably to my thinking and writing.

Many decades later, I still deal with noise. However, as I continue to grapple with specific tones and elements – particularly when it comes to global living patterns – I sense my roaming is beginning to complete its circle. To this end, I became a part-time student at the Sustainability Institute at Stellenbosch University, South Africa. I find the work absorbing. Here, among the most incredible array of curious and learned people, I found a home that responds to probing questions rather than simple smart answers, and inventive rather than conventional thinking. My time there is not done.

Working and writing with hope

Because wilderness guiding was my starting point, it made sense that the focus of my writing grew out of the issues and debates within the regional ecotourism and conservation sectors. At first, it was tough finding a way, and I recall labouring in the discussion rather than blossoming in the prose. But the process spurred me on, and with each piece I wrote, another ponderable appeared, adding to the growing fascination and quandary.

Then I stepped into my first experience of a predator breeding facility. I recoiled with a knotted stomach at the sight of rotting chickens being tossed at emaciated lions that mindlessly paced concrete cages. Those were such depressing events on squalid farms amid the kind of cruelty I had never before experienced. I knew I had found the end thread in my huge ball of questions about humanity and how we live and behave. It sparked a quiet rage in me, and a fierce commitment to start unravelling it all.

Since then, I have redirected my shock and anger at the distress I saw in those lions' eyes. That has allowed me to broaden my scope, to embrace the practices and philosophies of conservation, environmentalism, and our wider living paradigms that I now find more challenging. These all come with such contradictions, many of them personal that are exposed daily in my own life. In essence, it is the mess we have made, our duplicitous roles, and our shameless denial of responsibility that niggles me most. Often collectively referred to as the 'sustainability challenge' – and call that as you wish: A hoax, myth, or valiant attempt at survival – I sense it is the decisive narrative, our greatest test that still needs deciphering.

Ultimately, the story is about human behaviour and whether our selfish predispositions can be overcome to stabilise the environment and realise equitable societies at all levels. In the meantime, the global play continues to be driven by nations seeking supremacy through power and trade; a political and corporate world with its insatiable drive for greater growth and profits, and our obsessive individual pursuit of a take-and-waste consumerist lifestyle. It's as if we believe humanity is entitled to an open-ended contract with the planet, and if directed by the prophecy of smart technology and meaningless mantras, everything will work out. It all adds up to an explosive mix of confidence, deception and folly, and I find these incongruities and their consequences both fascinating and alarming.

Ignorance can no longer be an excuse; we have more than enough data on the state of our world to act upon. Despite this knowledge, widespread denial continues. We are seemingly unable to quell our addictions or to curb our selfish and destructive ways. It's as if the collective momentum of humanity's development has passed the point of reason, leaving our evolutionary destiny beyond any ability to influence or restrain it.

What then about writing and working with hope? I don't know of a writer or activist, or a concerned conservationist or academic for that matter, who does not grapple with this in some way. It is part and parcel of the territory. Most, however, would agree that becoming stifled by despondency should not be an option.

Stepping forward

To step forward into this space with hope, one needs to find the fire and spirit, a deep-rooted sense of meaning in what we are doing. This then drives passion and motivation, which fuels imagination, creativity and commitment.

The notion that 'life is not about finding yourself, but about creating yourself,' a sentiment expressed by George Bernard Shaw and Bob Dylan among others, rings with the greatest clarity here. So, be clear and honest about what you stand for and who or what you want to represent. Are you a storyteller, researcher, activist, or politician? Do you represent a vested interest, or a force for change?

It's also worth heeding the wisdom of Nelson Mandela: 'May your choices reflect your hopes, not your fears.' I suggest trusting a path that meanders, rather than setting some precise end goal that may well end up being fantastical. It also helps to tap into inspirational characters and organisations already doing incredible work. I have also learnt to fathom the reality, define my own contribution, and then accept what's at stake, but I do so without giving up on the belief that each of us must get involved in some way.

I also find it helpful to remember that the work is not about us; it's not about you or me. Our contributions reflect an ethic and an attitude, but the challenges and goals should always remain the focus. They are way more important. While it's acceptable to change your approach or to use a different strategy, be sure to stick to your underlying philosophy and principles.

I have also found that with time and knowledge, the path becomes less daunting. This is not because it becomes any clearer, but because you are trusting that a worthy and honest process is underway.

I like the way Bruce Springsteen, reflecting on age and maturity, sums it up. In an article by David Brooks for *The Atlantic* (October 23, 2020), Springsteen said:

'You learn to accept the world on its terms without giving up the belief that you can change the world. That's a successful adulthood – the maturation of your thought process and very soul to the point where you understand the limits of life, without giving up on its possibilities.'

In the end, we need to consider our exalted position on this planet. I have no idea if the megafauna, various ecosystems, or our societies and heritage will survive, but I am damn sure that Earth and some species will do so. While here, this privileged state we enjoy is another powerful reason – even an obligation – to give caring about what we have our best shot.

Keep going to the well

There is an immense wonderment and joy to be experienced from being in the wilderness with family and friends. Wild places have an uninhibited ambience, an honest embrace – qualities that are mostly absent in our day-to-day worlds.

We also go into the wilds for their immense beauty, and to experience the untamed excitement. It reminds me of a sentiment I have expressed before: 'Wilderness is the most secure place to measure our own personal maladies and levels of unease. Being there is like coming up for fresh air, and it's the only place that I know where we can exist for some time in that refreshed state of mind.' The spiritual calm and pleasure this bequeaths clears the mind and stimulates a refocus.

Being in the wild always brings me back to an ongoing fascination with the inter-relatedness of ecological functioning and how formidable these processes are. This, in turn, inspires endless thought as to when and how humanity became so detached from the natural world, and whether there is any way we could ever return in a beneficial way. My guess is: Probably not. Despite our cunning ways, I sense that we will never outsmart Nature. That is kind of reassuring. It also makes me wonder why we ever leave the natural calm of the wilds to re-enter the crazy and contrived world in which most of us live.

Of course, there is always time for birding, or the next Arsenal game, or an upcoming Springsteen concert to dream about.

In the tracks of giants

To walk in the wake of elephants,
to be small in a world of giants,
to learn the spoor of silence,
and the deep rumbling eloquence
of kin.

To move in the skin of elephants,
to feel the alliance of sand,
the contours of land
and the far-reaching pull
of water.

To be alive to the sway of elephants,
to remember the songs of seasons,
the ancient lines of migrations,
and loosen your reasons
for fences

To wake up to the web of intelligence,
to the wild origins of sentience,
to find your voice and raise it,
that others may raise theirs
for elephants.

– Ian McCallum

PROLOGUE

{ *Ian McCallum* }

The idea of following in the tracks of elephants was first voiced by Ian Michler in 1998. He, my wife, Sharon and I were sitting around a campfire at the Linyanti Tented Camp – a comfortable but rustic guest camp in the remote, beautiful region of northern Botswana.

The three of us were employed by safari organisation Wilderness Safaris. Ian and I worked as guides and Sharon took the role of camp manager. There were no guests in the camp that mid-November night and there we were, the three of us, sitting around the campfire: Ian and Sharon with a glass of wine, and me with a cold beer. The ritual night call of red-billed francolins began to sound, followed by another evening ritual: A resident flock of 30 or more helmeted guineafowl lined up one behind the other. Each in turn flew up to their chosen roosting position on the branches of the large jackalberry tree above us.

There was something missing in that ritualistic evening display. It was the dry season in Botswana, and each night we had feasted on the sight and sounds of countless elephant herds coming in from the forest to drink from the Linyanti River, which was a mere stone's throw from where we were sitting. The first early summer rains had fallen a day or two before, and with it had come the dramatic disappearance of the elephants. What had happened to them?

The answer was fairly simple: With the promise of the oncoming rainy season, it was as if the elephants had taken it upon themselves to rely instead on whatever water would fall and collect in the shallow clay-based pans that dotted the region. Their absence felt strange, and I was missing them. Then Ian spoke up: 'How about, one day, we do a circular walk ... following the elephant migration routes through the Caprivi, into Zambia, Zimbabwe and back to Botswana?' he asked.

My reply was almost immediate: 'Sounds great ... following in the tracks of giants ... Why not?' I asked, raising my glass to toast the fascinating idea.

The seed was sown. Little did we know that seed would take 12 years to grow and flourish, and that the eventual fruit would look a lot different from what we had imagined.

Our circular, four-country plan transformed into a 5 000-km transect – walking, kayaking and cycling – through six southern African countries: Namibia; Botswana; Zambia; Zimbabwe; Mozambique and South Africa. The original idea to follow international elephant migration paths was replaced by the more realistic notion of following elephant cluster groups within those six countries. In reality, for historical, political and social reasons, elephant migration routes no longer exist in the way they did in the early part of the century but identifying those cluster groups helped us to define the route of our undertaking.

You may well wonder why it took 12 years to take our first physical steps. The answer can be summed up in three words: Logistics, integration and imagination. First was the challenge of the logistics. Without a considerable degree of planning, permissions, and not least, the necessary financial and organisational support we received from various organisations and individuals, the expedition could not have happened. We needed a backup crew, along with two vehicles. One vehicle was to go ahead of the riders to find and set up campsites, buy food and drink, and prepare and sort out passport issues at national borders. The other was to come from behind with baggage, bicycles and repair equipment. For a high-quality record of the journey, we needed a professional filmmaker ... and so the list went on. To implement and integrate those requirements, we required a project manager. As reluctant as she may have been when her name was suggested, Sharon took on the role. With a background in legal conveyancing, she was familiar with extensive planning and had a sharp eye for detail. I don't know of anyone who could have done a better job.

As for imagination, we needed to keep the dream of the journey alive. It wasn't that difficult. I think there is a deep sense and longing for adventure in every one of us – a nomadic spirit if you wish. After all, who wouldn't leap at the opportunity to be part of an adventure like that? However, there was a more serious side to the stirrings of our imagination. In the years that followed that night around the fire in the Linyanti, Ian Michler, through his investigative research, public presentations, writings and skill as a wilderness guide, had become an increasingly respected and challenging environmental journalist. As a columnist and features writer for *Africa Geographic*, it was no secret that Peter Borchert, the founder and then-editor of the magazine, would sometimes suffer sleepless nights, wondering whether or not to publish Ian's findings. Ian had also committed to delivering a slate of five natural history and travel books to a well-known publishing house.

My voice for the wild came in another form: Through writing, presentations and conferences. During those 12 years I had put together two anthologies of wilderness poems, *Wild Gifts* and *Untamed*, as well as a book, *Ecological Intelligence – Rediscovering Ourselves in Nature*. It became the foundation of my work as a 'specialist' guide. While working with Ian, our friendship deepened. When integrating facts, figures and science with metaphors and poetry, as well as insights into the evolutionary and psychological significance of wild animals in our lives, we fed off each other. We knew what we wanted. We wanted to be advocates for the wild places and animals of Africa. Taking those thoughts further, in 2001 we formed a safari organisation, Invent Africa. Our intention and mission statement were clear: 'Dedicated to wilderness awareness.'

With that background and mission statement, the reason for the Tracks of Giants initiative became increasingly urgent. It was important to do something in the name of wild animals and their threatened habitats. The title spelt it out. Elephants would be the focus and flagship species of our journey. Our aim and purposes were as follows:

1. To promote the importance of transfrontier conservation corridors. These would allow wild animals, especially elephants, to move freely across both local and international boundaries.

2. To engage with local human communities living in or around protected areas on issues ranging from human-wildlife conflict to their living conditions and benefits from land use and ownership.
3. To explore and assess the contentious issue of hunting versus tourism as a way to ensure the future of all wild animals.
4. To meet and learn from some of the 'human giants'; those doing the invaluable work at the coalface of conservation.

The team

As mentioned, Sharon became the project manager, or rather, the conductor of the orchestra. Governmental permissions to transect national parks on foot and bicycle sometimes arrived at the last minute, and not without urgent emails and calls from her to the various officials involved. It was a stressful task. Reading through her file is a reminder of every transaction, piece of correspondence and contact necessary for the smooth running of the event. With regular satellite phone contact, she kept us abreast of what was happening, and told us what to expect regarding planned meetings and link-ups with personnel along the way. It was also good to have her with us in person at different stages of the journey. Her contributions made her one of the giants of our journey.

Our backup team comprised a permanent crew of willing volunteers: Johnny Frankiskos (60 years old), Anton Kruyshaw (21) and Frank Raimondo (71). To assist them, we also had a rotating support team of stalwarts from the Wilderness Leadership School: Mandla Buthelezi (48), Lihle Mabunda (34) and Martin Peterson (52). The latter three, in turn, joined us for three to four weeks at selected stages of the project. Without the backup team, the event would have been like a game of soccer without a goalkeeper. We have yet to find an adequate way to thank them for what, at times, must have been a tiring and thankless task. As a group, they were integral to our success.

Guides

We owe thanks to Chris Bakkes (Skeleton Coast and Horasieb River Valley); Garth Owen-Smith (northern Namibia); John Sandenberg and PJ Bestelink (Okavango Delta, Savuti Channel and Zambezi River); Dr Michael Chase and Kelly Landen (Savuti and Chobe National Park); Courteney Johnson (Hwange National Park); Rob and Lundi Burns (northern Kruger National Park); Billie Swanepoel (Greater Limpopo National Park), and Graeme Harman (Gaza province, Mozambique).

A special thank you goes to PJ Bestelink and John Sandenberg, without whom the expedition would have been very different. John heads up a kayaking safari organisation in Botswana. I first met him in Maun in 2011. When I explained to him what our 2012 expedition was about, and that kayaking the Okavango Delta and lower Zambezi River was an option for our journey, his response was immediate: He was in! What's more, he would do it without a fee. All we had to do was pay for the transport of the kayaks to and from designated starting and finishing/pick-up venues. PJ, a great friend of ours and a doyen of the Delta, gave a similar response. Having lived and operated across the Okavango since the 1960s, it was such a privilege to share that experience with PJ. Their expertise and experience as mekoro (dug-out canoe) and kayaking guides, along with their knowledge of the geography of the Okavango Delta, was immense. We all felt safe with them at the helm. Rich with elephant, hippo and other wild animal contacts, the mekoro and kayaking stages with PJ and John are indelibly carved into our memories. Thank you for that.

Film crew

The journey at various stages was recorded by four world-class filmmakers: Nick Chevallier for the opening and closing weeks of the expedition; James Brundige for the Zambezi River stretch; Michael and TJ Holding for the cycle across the Makgadikgadi Pans in Botswana, and Simon Wood for the walk, cycle and kayaking legs through the Greater Limpopo National Park of South Africa and Mozambique. In their absence, Anton Kruyshaw, our 'Mr Fix-it' of the backup team, and Ian Michler were in charge of the camera. Anton is responsible for the excellent footage of our elephant interaction in Hwange National Park.

Challenges

Our challenges were threefold: Physical, mental and social.

Physical

Since we were not in a competitive race, we took comfort in the knowledge that we were both reasonably fit and would get fitter as the journey progressed. The first week of cycling was the toughest. Negotiating long, upward inclines on sandy roads often resulted in us having to walk while pushing our bikes.

One particular stretch involved a 40 km steady, deceptive, uphill ride toward the top of the Etendeka plateau. We renamed that 'hill' four times on what seemed to be a never-ending ascent; each name a reflection of our 'bum-sensitivity-barometers'. To begin with we called it 'Relentless', then 'Deception', then 'Unprincipled' and finally ... 'Mother f****r'! We soon discovered that it was one thing to have natural fitness, stamina and leg power, but it was another to be saddle-fit. Less saddle-hardened than me, and despite copious layers of skin lubricant, Ian eventually resorted to strapping a pillow to the saddle of his bike. The lesson from that discomfort was swift: The realisation of the punishing difference between sitting on the saddle versus sitting in it.

With that challenge behind us, we grew increasingly cycling fit. We soon got used to covering more than 100 kilometres a day, sometimes for two or three days in a row.

On the 27th night of our journey, my 'wheels came off'. Soon after setting up camp outside the town of Grootfontein, my body began to ache. I spent most of that night shivering, sweating and ridding my bowels of whatever demon it was that had singled me out for that unwelcome episode. Come morning, I felt a little better, and with only 60 km scheduled for that day – including the promise of a full day's rest ahead – I chose to ride the distance.

By day 30, I felt rested and ready to ride, but the 222-kilometre gravel-road cycle to the eastern Namibian border village of Tsumkwe took its toll. When we arrived there, exhausted, I felt my pulse. The beats were irregular. In short, I was in dehydration-induced atrial arrhythmia. Thankfully, after two nights' rest and rehydration, the arrhythmia ceased. However, my physical condition did not go unnoticed by the team. Having crossed into Botswana, I was put under pressure to reconsider any further riding until I was completely better. By then on antibiotics, I promised to do so if I was not measurably better by the following day. Upon waking the next morning, I felt a tangible sense of recovery. It was a sense of the end of a rite of passage … I had come through. The lesson from that was clear: When exercising the body, do not wait until you are thirsty before drinking water. Drink to avoid thirst.

Social and mental

Four months is a long time to be away from friends and family. It was in that light that at our first team meeting in Windhoek on April 26, and without any attempt to dampen enthusiasm, I cautioned the back-up team against what I believed would be their biggest challenge – boredom. Imagine being part of an expedition where, for most of the journey, you drove an average of 80–90 kilometres a day while Ian and I cycled, or only 40 kilometres when we walked … and for multiple days on end? To minimise this reality, each of the backup team took turns cycling, walking and kayaking with us at pre-selected stages, or when they were free to do so. It made a huge difference to the depth of their participatory roles.

Not unexpectedly, another challenge involved the inevitability of occasional personality clashes. It took time to get used to each other's temperaments. We all like to have our way, but there's no doubt that the older one gets, the adventures we choose in life tend to be the ones that we would rather do on our own terms. I speak for myself. Meanwhile, all things considered, these natural and minor issues paled into insignificance when compared to the many highlights we enjoyed together.

THE JOURNEY: MEMORIES AND REFLECTIONS

{ *Ian McCallum* }

Namibia

On 1 May 2012, to the tune of *Ode to Joy* from Frank Raimondo's harmonica and the accompanying lens of Nick Chevallier's camera, we took our first steps along the rocky Atlantic coastline of Namibia's Skeleton Coast, and then headed south toward the mouth of the Horasieb River. From there, we followed the dune-surrounded riverbed along its winding inland course to the village of Puros. From there, we began our first cycle stage.

The five-day inland trek to Puros was one of amazement, not only at the dry harshness of the surroundings; of how different trees, shrubs, animals and insects adapt to these tough conditions, but to the realisation that after all the years of dreaming and planning, we were finally on our way. We had kept our promise.

Chris Bakkes, an intelligent, amiable and well-known author, ranger and wilderness guide, as well as a passionate voice for the endangered rhino population in Namibia, led the way. Chris is a giant of a man: Tall, powerfully built and with a below-elbow amputation of his left arm (the result of a crocodile encounter in the Kruger National Park of South Africa a few years prior). With him was his one-eyed Jack Russel named Tier (meaning 'Tiger'). The dog had lost his eye as a result of a snake bite! Sometimes, Tier would run along beside us, and at other times, when tired, or when the sand was too hot to walk on, Chris would lift him onto his left shoulder, where the dog cradled himself between Chris' neck, shoulder and the upper end of his rucksack. A one-eyed dog carried by a one-armed man. It is an image I will not forget.

Animal signs and sightings along the way included the night calls of a brown hyaena, the cough of a leopard we could not see but who we knew could see us, a small herd of curious springbok, oryx, as well as a lone desert-adapted elephant male. Each kept their own safe distance between them and us. There were other animals that we did not see, but whose footprint signatures around life-giving pools of brackish water along the riverbed were clear: Porcupines; striped pole cat; striped mouse; steenbok; grey heron and spotted thick-knees. And then there were the stars: Four moonless nights under a spectacular canopy of distant suns. Dominant in the eastern sky was the magnificent constellation of Scorpius (a sure sign that winter was on its way), and in the west, Orion and its brilliant companion star, Sirius.

The mountains and on to Etosha

Five days later, in baking heat, we arrived at Puros. The following day, flanked by the more-than-billion-year-old Etendeka Mountains – arguably the oldest mountains in the world – we set off on our bicycles. Rich in coarse-grained granite and topped by layers of sedimentary rock, it was hard to believe that those mountains were once covered by ocean. It was virgin territory for Ian and me, as well as the memorable first morning of a winding, 21-day, 1 800-kilometre cycle that would take us through the northern Kaokaveld, south to the lower boundaries of the Etosha Pan, and then eastwards through the savannah woodlands to the border crossing into Botswana at Tsumkwe.

Thanks to Garth-Owen Smith (who cycled with us for the first few days) and his long-time partner and co-founder of the Integrated Rural Development and Nature Conservation organisation (IRDNC) Margie Jacobsohn, we were able to meet with some of the elders of the indigenous Himba communities along the way. Recognisable by the red ochre-adorned women, the Himba of the Kaokaveld live in one of the last areas in Africa where human communities, without fences, co-exist with wild animals: Giraffes; cheetahs; jackals; honey badgers; mongooses; zebra, a variety of antelope; lions and not least, the flagship species of our journey, desert-adapted elephants. Three hours into our first day, we were treated to our first close, yet safe, encounter with a matriarchal herd of adults and calves.

As beautiful as it was, that arid mountainous region was physically and mentally demanding. We were guests in that landscape. We had to ask permission to know it.

Apart from a handful of pre-planned stops at selected campsites, which included two nights and a full day's rest, every other day became a routine of early rising, cycling, midday resting and bush camping. Along the D2964 dirt road skirting the southern edge of the Etosha National Park, we met farmers who spoke openly about human-wildlife conflict. Opinions differed. One farmer told us that he had to shoot five spotted hyaenas one night because they were hunting his cattle. 'I'm not a hunter ... I hate it,' he said.

Ian asked the man: 'Why don't you keep your cattle in a paddock at night?' There was no reply.

A neighbouring farmer was doing exactly that – corralling his cattle. I put a question to him: 'Can you imagine a situation when or if there were no longer wild animals in this area?' Shaking his head before speaking, his answer still echoes: 'What will we tell our grandchildren? We will be the poorer ... unthinkable,' he said.

After a gruelling 112-kilometre stretch along a hard, corrugated sand road, we rode into Tsumkwe, Namibia's most eastern outpost. This dusty hamlet is the administrative centre for the basic welfare of the Namibian Bushmen who, in a period of fewer than 30 years (1966–1990) – spurred on by the South African war against the then-anti-government army liberation fighters, the South West Africa People's Organisation (SWAPO) – were forced to trade their ancient hunting grounds, loincloths, bows and arrows for running water and the promise of an economic future that continues to evade them.

Today, with few employment opportunities available, the villagers rely on government grants and donations to survive. Some of them, to supplement their basic living grants, have turned to the promise of income from tourism. They have done so by creating a traditional Bushman settlement, where, through music, hand-clapping and dance, they re-enact their ancient way of life.

There is another reason for this re-enactment of their traditional lives: 'We do this to keep our stories and traditions alive,' said Jacobus Kolbooi, a young, proactive leader in the community. 'We must not forget where we have come from.'

Looking back on our journey through Namibia, exchanges like that remain indelible. As it is with indigenous societies worldwide, it was not difficult to draw a parallel between the futures of the traditional way of life of the Himba and Bushmen with the future of all wildlife. It was a reminder that hunter-gatherer communities are the last to live truly sustainable lives.

Botswana, Zambia and Zimbabwe

We could not have arrived in Botswana at a more opportune time to attempt the exciting challenge ahead of us: Kayaking the Okavango Delta, the Selinda spillway linking the Okavango system to the Linyanti River system in the north, and finally the 100-kilometre Savuti Channel linking the Linyanti River to the Savuti Marshes in the southern section of the Chobe National Park.

The Okavango and beyond

Owing to a combination of tectonic plate movement, as well as exceptionally high rainfall in the eastern highlands of Angola (the source and catchment area of the Okavango River) from January through to March 2012, it had been the first time in more than 30 years that those river systems would be navigable. Today, both the Selinda Spillway and the Savuti Channel are wild gardens of riverine reeds and grasses. We were lucky – and for more reasons than being blessed by a navigable water course. The flowing waters were a magnet to wildlife: Crocodiles, hippos, elephants, antelope and birdlife. However, there were other blessings, too. For the first four days of our 20-day adventure, we travelled in mekoros; two individuals in each vessel with our own local 'poler', steering us silently across the crystal-clear waters northward to the village of Sepupa, where our kayaks awaited us. Without PJ's knowledge and understanding of the directional flow, we may well still be trying to find our way out of there. After having endured a bout of infective gastritis, it was exactly what my body needed. To me, it felt like the equivalent to business-class air travel.

When we arrived at Sepupa, we were met by John Sandenberg, the leader and sponsor of that crucial stage of the journey. John gave us the all-important safety 'dos and don'ts' of kayaking in the Delta. While doing so, he drew attention to the absence of elastic and string beading on the kayaks. Such beading is normally used to hold and fasten equipment that can't be stored in the limited packing space within the kayak. It had been deliberately removed to prevent crocodiles' teeth from getting tangled up in it. That sometimes happens when the crocodile mistakes a kayak for a territorial-challenging suitor. John had learned this the hard way!

The following 16 days will be remembered for the long silences, the regular bird-watching tutorials by Ian, sub-zero night temperatures, guitar-strumming evenings around the fire, the night skies, and having Murray, my son, with me for the three-week adventure. I know that Ian Michler was thrilled to have his great friend, Clifford Toop, join us for that section.

During that time, we had some close encounters with wild animals. One particular encounter involved two adult hippos. It was in the very early, dark hours of the morning (Murray was on night watch) when two territorial male animals, one in hot pursuit of the other, charged through our campsite, on a path directly between two sleeping campers – Johnny Frankiskos and me! There was never a day on that stage without an elephant encounter, either. All of them were from relatively safe distances and never without a high degree of respect for those giant creatures.

Another unforgettable scene was our arrival at Wilderness Safaris' Duma Tau camp, at the junction of the Linyanti River and the Savuti Channel. Having seen us from a distance, staff members came out to meet and greet us in song, with a tray of cold beers opened and poured. What a welcome, and what a thirst-quencher! That night we slept in the comfort of a lodge unit. The following day, with Grant Woodrow (then-MD of Okavango Wilderness Safaris), we drove the winding, familiar 30-kilometre road from Duma Tau to the more rustic Linyanti Tented Camp, our old stomping ground. Like a waking dream, it was a deeply nostalgic return. That evening, we huddled around the very same fire where 12 years before, the idea of what we were then doing had been seeded. With elephants in sight of us, we toasted our hosts, our friends, our team and our journey.

The following morning, well rested and feeling positive, we were back in our kayaks, ready for whatever the channel offered us. It did not disappoint. Daily sightings of elephants, hippos and crocodiles slipping into the water from the banks were regular feasts. During the early hours of the morning, on my night watch on day three in the channel, I sensed the presence of a visitor. Turning slowly to my right, my flashlight caught the full face of a loan and curious hyaena a mere 10 metres away. Filled with a sense of privilege, I watched the animal turn and head off into the night.

On the final day, only a handful of kilometres from the destination in Savuti Marsh, we had to make a route choice. Did we risk navigating a large pod of hippos occupying a bend on the narrow channel ahead, or did we carry our kayaks across the bend to a safer re-entry point to the channel further down? We chose the latter, not because of a lack of a sense of adventure but because of a simple and important rule. It came in the form of a question: Who was there first? If it was the animal, then respect its presence. Give them a wide and visible berth. And so, to the sound of grunting hippos, we did just that.

Chobe National Park

Arriving at the Savuti Marsh in the south-western corner of the
11 700-square-kilometre Chobe National Park will be remembered for a
nostalgic farewell to Murray, Clifford and PJ, as well as a warm welcome
to Sharon and Frank, Martin Peterson (our new backup team member),
Marguerite McDonald (a close friend), James Brundige (filmmaker)
and not least, Dr Michael Chase and Kelly Landen (partners and co-
directors of the Elephants Without Borders organisation). A top-rated
scientist, Michael's work with Kelly is pivotal to the campaign to raise
awareness and understanding of the ecological importance of elephant
migration corridors across political boundaries.

Bordering Namibia in the north and Zimbabwe in the east, the
Chobe National Park is home to approximately 120 000 elephants – the
densest concentration of migratory African elephants on the continent.
Among the prime reasons for this is the abundance of vast woodland
forests of Mopane (one of the favourite food sources for elephants), as
well as the countless seasonal, rain-filled pans. In the dry season, the
elephants migrate to the more permanent water of the Linyanti, Chobe
and Zambezi Rivers in the north. It is hard to believe that the Chobe
region was once part of a great inland lake. Now, millions of years
later, beneath a thick but shallow layer of sand, the water-retaining clay
sediment accounts for the lifegiving, inland pans.

We started off our six-day walk on a sandy 4x4 track. It was hard
going, and we soon realised that because of the thickness of the sand,
not many animals used it. Those that did, did so for short stretches only.
We followed their example and moved into the forest where the ground
surface was much firmer underfoot. Wherever possible, we walked in
the tracks of elephants.

On one particular stretch, we tried walking like an elephant. The
slower pace accompanied by the lengthening of our stride was almost
automatic, leaving us with a strange, mirroring, yet calming sensation
of being in the skin of the animal. Apart from a few sightings, the only
close encounter we had with an elephant was toward the end of the

walk, within sight of the Chobe River. The animal was dead! It had been shot, not by poachers, but by a man from a local village whose new home had been built too close to a well-established elephant pathway. The large adult male was considered a threat to human life.

Michael took advantage of the situation and delivered an onsite and heartfelt 'tutorial' on human-animal conflict as one of the biggest ongoing challenges to their organisation. While filming his presentation, a swaying, inebriated man arrived on the scene and demanded money for filming the dead animal on his property. Whether he was the owner of the property or not, Michael, a citizen of Botswana, reminded the gentleman that elephants are the property of the government of Botswana. Michael's reply contained within it a thinly veiled message of concern for the welfare of those giant pilgrims. Their future was in the hands of politicians!

In 2012, the then-president of the country, Ian Khama, was highly protective of Botswana's wildlife. Things have changed since then. Today, the current leadership appears less inclined to protect Botswana's wildlife, and it shows. Since the removal of the military anti-poaching unit that had been established by Khama in the 1990s, the poaching of elephants and rhinos has significantly increased. Another telling observation was the visible difference in animal populations between designated hunting and photographic (non-hunting) concessions. Compared to the abundance of grazing antelope, zebra and warthogs on photographic concessions, there was not a single visible animal in the hunting concessions. Wild animals seem to know where they are safe.

Zambezi River

Getting to the Zambezi River town of Sesheke in Zambia involved a two-day cycle through the eastern Caprivi of Namibia. We were joined by Tessa van Schaik (Ian's beloved partner and the mother of their son, Liam), and five representatives from Avis, the sponsors of our back-up vehicle. It was good to be on the water again. As the fourth-largest river in Africa, stretching at least 200 metres across at our point of entry, it was easy to understand why the Zambezi is regarded as one of the great rivers of the world. From its humble beginnings in the north-western Zambian marshland at Mwinilunga, it winds its way through eastern Angola and back into Zambia where, fed by multiple tributaries, it gathers momentum to become an ever larger and forceful river on its 2 500-kilometre course, via the magnificent Victoria Falls, and the Kariba and Cahora Bassa dams, before ending as a huge delta on the Indian Ocean shores of Mozambique.

Going with the flow, it was easy to take the river for granted. Remembering the old philosophical saying: 'You never step into the same river twice,' was a reality. That is how we encountered the changing face of the Zambezi River on our six-day journey to the geologically recent (10 million-year-old) multiple-gorge phenomenon of the Victoria Falls. The current gorge and spectacular waterfall are roughly 100 000 years old.

Every day brought with it different curves, river speeds and rapids. Engraved on the mud-stained adjacent landscapes of fallen trees and vegetation was evidence of how high and wide the river could get following high-quantity rains in the catchment areas, . That was a mellow time to be on the water, but not without danger. Apart from a handful of testing, white-water rapids, pods of hippos and basking crocodiles, each day was a feast of riverine birds: African skimmers; white-crowned lapwings; whiskered terns and on one occasion, a lone flamingo.

Then, 126 kilometres west of Livingstone, and thanks to the efforts of Alan Sparrow of the Peace Parks Foundation, we met with Chief Inyambo Yeta at his Sesheke district home (some call it his palace) at Mwendi, on the north bank of the river. Ironically, 'Mwendi' means 'plenty of fish'. That is an image from times past. We came away from that meeting with some vital insights about the importance of community involvement in the care of the local environment.

Tracing the history of the role of poachers in the decline of the area's wildlife, fish population, and not least the denuding and burning of the forests for the sale and export of charcoal, Chief Yeta laid the blame on the disempowerment of his people by the seemingly good, yet disastrous, conservation policies of the newly-formed Zambian government in 1964. Instead of asking the local people to remain 'the keepers' of local resources, the government had decreed that they would be managed by the newly-established Departments of Wildlife, Fisheries and Forestry. With that historical responsibility removed, and with most of the local population surviving on less than a dollar per day, the doors opened not only for animal poaching, but for the locals who saw charcoal burning as a livelihood. 'Thankfully things have changed since then,' said the chief, adding 'We are now planting trees instead of burning them ... but we still have a long way to go.' I will not forget that visit.

After a week on the water, we arrived in Livingstone. The following day, we were back on our bicycles and crossed the Victoria Falls road bridge into Zimbabwe. A short visit to say: 'Hello and thank you,' for the work done by those at the Wild Horizons Research Centre (outside of the town of Victoria Falls), set the tone for the two-day, 205-kilometre ride to the Painted Dog Sanctuary close to Hwange National Park.

Hwange National Park

The name 'Painted Dog' is a poetic description of the patterns of colour on a wild dog. Threatened by mining prospecting in the region, the sanctuary is more than a research, rescue and relocation operation for this endangered species. Founded by Dr Greg Rasmussen, it is also an ecological education centre that links wild dog research to the care of local people who are HIV-positive. It is a parallel reminder that there is no such thing as a typical wild dog or a typical human being, and that each individual can do what they can to promote the dual welfare of these endangered animals, as well as those who benefit from donations and support of the centre.

Upon entering the Hwange National Park, and with thanks and appreciation to Courteney Johnson, we were treated to a two-day rest at Wilderness Safari's Davison's Camp, in the eastern section of the 14 651-square-kilometre park. Much like the Chobe National Park, Hwange is dominated by Kalahari woodland of Zambezi teak, baobab and flowering sand camwood trees in the east and central regions, and mopani forests in the west.

As for the animals, apart from close sightings of zebra, roan antelope, giraffe, hippos, buffalo, impala, as well as several bird species, including a rare, yellow-morphed, crimson-breasted shrike, the park belongs to the elephants. Joined by Anton and Martin, there was never a day on our five-day cycle to the western border of the park that we did not encounter elephants. On the fourth day, filmed by Anton, we stood in awe as we watched a herd of about a hundred elephants, one behind the other, crossing the road ahead of us on their way to a waterhole. We couldn't have asked for a better encounter or treat.

Makgadikgadi Pans and Tuli

With Zimbabwe's National Park behind us, we peddled the heavily corrugated road into the eastern Botswana town of Pandamatenga. There to meet us were my two daughters, Alison and Michelle, my brother, Roy, brother-in-law, Steve Moubray, and two great friends, Peter and Joan Berning. It was also a farewell filled with deep appreciation for our backup team member, Martin Peterson, and the welcoming of his replacement, Lihle Mabunda. Over the following two days, we cycled the long and straight, tarred road to the village and campsite at Nata, and from there into the dauntingly beautiful salt flats of a once ancient lake the size of Switzerland – the Makgadikgadi Pan.

The first night on the pan was unforgettable. Sleeping under the stars on a cold Botswana night and with only three days until it was full, the gibbous moon threw a delicate but haunting light across the vast expanse of white sand.

The following morning, looking out at the white expanse surrounding us, I wondered what it would be like to cycle with one's eyes shut. For a start, you would have to trust the surroundings to make sure there were no trees or humps or bumps to hinder you. I put the idea to the cyclists, all of whom were happy to give it a try. Unrestricted to any given path, we headed out into the great white plains, eyes closed and with nothing but the sound of the rubber tyres on the salted surface to assure us of our forward momentum and balance. Judging each full cycle of peddling to be the equivalent of 10 metres, I cycled for roughly two kilometres, opening my eyes only once. The exercise turned out to be a meditation of sorts; an acknowledgement of muscle memory and the body's capacity to adapt and to keep balance without visual assurance.

True to the nature of the Makgadikgadi, the stillness of the morning was short-lived. Suddenly the wind came up and within minutes clouds of fast-moving white powder moved in from the east. Pulling our buffs over our mouths and noses to protect us from inhaling the talcum-like powder, and with visibility reduced to a few metres around us, we alighted from our bicycles and regrouped.

Pushing our bikes in the powdered haze, we were suddenly confronted with a ghost-like apparition ahead of us ... something that didn't belong in that landscape. It was the notorious 'buffalo fence', a two-metre-high, barbed-wire barrier. Erected in 2004 for the sole purpose of reducing conflict between the wild animals in the park and livestock to the west of the pan, the nearly 500-kilometre-long fence has long been a constant source of contention between the government and conservationists. Stories abound about animals starving to death at the fence line. To us, the fence was the very antithesis of the 'corridor' theme of our journey ... to loosen our reasons for fences.

Lifting our bicycles over the fence, we headed south to Kubu 'island' – an ancient outcrop of granite boulders, baobab and wild chestnut trees. Breathtaking in its beauty and solitude, to me, the island is a monument to the resilience of living organisms to adapt to extreme environmental conditions. The more-than-a-thousand-year-old baobabs seemed to demand from us a moment or two of silence ... to remember that we are linked in time, space and biology to these huge, grey arboreal giants. What a sight! What a feeling! In the presence of those massive trees and harsh surroundings, it was not that difficult to understand the traditional, spiritual significance of silent spaces and sacred groves.

Ruminating on the stark beauty of Kubu Island, and with the wind behind our backs, we headed toward Botswana's southerly elephant cluster in the Mashatu Game Reserve in the Tuli Block. Taking three days to get there, I will remember that stage for three particular events. Firstly, thoroughly spoiled and with my two daughters and friends to cheer me on, I celebrated my 68th birthday. A line in my diary for that day reads: 'If anything untoward should happen to me now, I will die a happy man.'

The second event was saying goodbye to the family and fellow cyclists who would head for Francistown and then home. It was an event, not only because of the closeness of family and friends, but also because their laughter and sense of fun had added so much to the spirit of the team.

The third event was joyful. Awaiting us at the Tuli Wilderness Safaris concession in the Mashatu Game Reserve in the Tuli Block was Carole Frankiskos and Ida Raimondo, spouses of Johnny and Frank. It was the first time that Johnny had seen his wife in a little more than three months. Frank had been with Ida for the time we had been negotiating the Okavango Delta in our kayaks.

The timing of our arrival coincided with the eve of the annual ultra-marathon, cross-border (South Africa, Zimbabwe and Botswana) Tour de Tuli cycle event. It also marked the completion of 4 000 kilometres of our 5 000-kilometre journey. Excited to have us with them, David Evans, CEO of Mashatu and host of the bike rally, invited us to participate in the event. We agreed to ride the first 18 km, a narrow, winding and exhilarating stretch to the 'breakfast' stop, where tables heavily laden with croissants, cereals and fruit cake awaited the riders. I had to be pulled away from that table.

South Africa and Mozambique

Later that morning, we crossed the Limpopo River into South Africa. With a full month of cycling, walking and a short kayak ahead of us, it felt good to be back on home soil, to make local cellphone contact with friends and family, and to watch a televised rugby match at a nearby lodge. The next three days were spent cycling the busy, tarred road via the town of Musina to the next elephant cluster group in the northern Pafuri region of the Kruger National Park (KNP).

Arriving at Wilderness Safari's Pafuri Lodge, which is sensitively situated within the treeline above the banks of the seasonally shallow-flowing Pafuri River, we were reunited with Sharon, Tessa, Liam, Ida and Carole. The same lodge was all but washed away by an unexpectedly high summer flood in 2013 – a reminder that climate extremes have become a global-warming reality.

We celebrated Liam's fifth birthday at Pafuri. Combining harmonica and guitar, I sang Bruce Springsteen's *Devils and Dust* to Liam, who said: 'Wow!' I think he was the only positive respondent. Thank you, Liam.

Abundant in birdlife, antelope, giraffe and not least, elephants, the Pafuri is also home to spectacular groves of greenish-yellow fever trees. Until 2013, these trees were classified as acacias, but that genus is now reserved only for species indigenous to Australia. Its colloquial name dates back to the belief of colonial explorers that this riverine species was somehow responsible for tropical malaria. Only later was the female, water and blood-dependent female anopheles mosquito unveiled as the culprit.

It was in those surroundings, joined by filmmaker Simon Wood, that we rode to Crooks Corner in the far north of Kruger Park. Situated on the south bank of the Limpopo River, the corner is so named because of its geographical position – a small triangle of land where three countries (South Africa, Zimbabwe and Mozambique) meet. It was an ideal hideaway for those escaping the law, (gun runners and ivory poachers) who, with sufficient warning, could easily escape to another country. It was there, in that heavily-guarded no man's land that we were met and escorted by seven heavily armed game rangers to the Mozambique border, a mere three kilometres away. The reason for the company of rangers was to make sure that we did not wander off the designated path, where stumbling onto unearthed land mines from the Mozambican civil war (1977–1992) was a risk not worth taking. That short walk included the crossing of a small tributary into the Limpopo – a basking place for a huge group of some of the biggest Nile crocodiles we had ever seen. Close by, among a pod of hippos, a large male hippo announced himself.

Safely across the border, we were met by Peace Parks Foundation contact and ranger Billie Swanepoel, who would guide us through the

Mozambican side of the unfenced (since 2002) Limpopo National Park and the western border of the KNP. Together, these two parks are known as the Greater Limpopo National Park (LNP). However, unlike the Kruger Park, with its strictly monitored camping and lodge facilities, the Limpopo Nature Reserve is dotted with community villages. Entering the park at Mashatu Gate, we were welcomed by the sight of a suspended, bent and buckled bicycle with a sign below it that reads: 'Binged by an Elephant'. It was a telling reminder of which animal had the right of way! The sign gave no information regarding the fate of the rider of the bicycle. Ironically, apart from the buckled bicycle, occasional scatterings of dried-out dung and only one sighting of an elephant, there were no other signs of elephant life in the LNP. It was as if those creatures, sensitised to poaching and human warfare, knew that they were safer in the KNP.

Passing through the villages, we were warmly welcomed by curious and excited children, eager to know what we were doing, and had we brought them sweets or something to eat? Notably absent in the villages were young adult males. We were told that they were working in the cities like Maputo and Beira.

Day three in the LNP involved a memorable 15-kilometre hike to our evening campsite – not only because of the surrounding dense bushveld and Limpopo ironwood trees, but once again, and for good reason, we were obliged to stick to the designated narrow path. Along the way we passed a site where six people had died from a landmine explosion. A little further on, and untouched since the civil war, we passed a rocky outcrop scattered with multiple discarded and rusted mortar shells.

The following day revealed another chilling impact of war and poverty on the fate of wild animals in this region. Walking along the dry bed of the Shingwedzi River, a reedbuck sprinted across the sand a little ahead of us. Giving chase was a group of poachers with their dogs. Seeing us, they turned around and ran off, discarding what we believe was their only weapon – a single bow with a quiver of three arrows. Clearly, those men were not professional poachers but hungry hunters doing what their fathers and grandfathers had traditionally done for their families – hunting for the pot. Yes, they knew that it was illegal, but on reflection, if I had a family to feed, I think I would have done the same. Knowing that our route would take us through the village where those hunters lived, we decided not to make an issue of it and instead of displaying our 'weapons-find', Billie hid them away for collection on another day.

After three days, two bicycle wheel punctures, and a farewell at Lake Massingir (the southern border of the LNP) to Sharon and Lihle, we picked up the spoor and signs of a completely different category of poachers. Then out of the park, we faced the reality of poaching in private tourist/safari concessions. That time, we identified the day-old spoor of a black rhinoceros. Within metres of the spoor was the empty brass cartridge of a .303 rifle. Whew! It was serious. Looking around, we found no signs of any successful killing of the animal. That may have been a lucky escape for one of these highly endangered species.

Not surprisingly, the discussion around our campfire that night was the perennial challenge of poaching, poachers and syndicates. Figures show that South Africa at the time, and with Mozambican-based poachers playing a key role, was losing rhino at a rate of nearly one animal every 12 hours. In the next five years, those figures would reflect a different tally – one animal dying every eight hours. Suspecting that poachers and syndicate members lived in the village of Messingir itself, it was here that Ian's inquiring mind led him to glean new information and data on the operating procedures of the rhino poaching industry.

Then out of the LNP, it was a time to reflect on what we had witnessed. As beautiful as some of the regions were, more especially the river-carved cliff faces of the dry Shingwedzi River and spectacular views of the escarpment below, I will mostly remember the park for its paucity of wild animals. I could name the single sightings on one hand: a reedbuck, a kudu, a sounder of warthogs, a duiker and as mentioned earlier, a solitary elephant, as well as a large, dead crocodile in the bed of the dry river Shingwedzi. Those were all reminders of the cycles of birth, maturation, reproduction, ageing, dying, decay and rebirth. It was the natural, and ultimately necessary, fate of every living thing. From prey to predator, every creature is part of an ancient food chain. Every sighting had a story to tell.

Relatively untouched was the birdlife, which Ian Michler was always quick to point out and name.

Entering the Gaza province, south of the LNP, did not mean that our safety was guaranteed. We headed for the Sabie River Dam, where we kayaked the 14 km-wide body of water. Once we were out of the kayaks and had pulled our craft ashore, it was not difficult to miss the abundance of the bilharzia carriers, and the transmitters of human bilharzia (*schistosomiasis*). Anton would later test positive for the condition. Back on our bicycles again, we were joined by two delightful, uniformed Peace Parks officials, Rozero and Razia, both on their own bicycles. For two days, they escorted us from village to village, negotiating thick and sometimes badly corrugated surfaces en route. Every village we passed through triggered instant crowds of children fascinated by our presence and mostly by our bicycles.

From the bustling town of Magude, closely escorted by Johnny in the Avis backup vehicle, we took to the tarred but heavily used trucks and vehicle highway to the capital city and port of Maputo. We were also grateful to have the company of Wojtek Orzechowski, a long-time friend of Ian Michler. Wojtek, well-known for his skills and experience on the ocean, joined us for the last leg of the journey.

The home run

Determined to ensure that the entire journey (other than vehicle travel off the given route for meetings and landscape explorations) was non-motorised, while in Maputo, we pulled out the map to decide on the mode of travel to the coastal Maputo Elephant Reserve, and then on to the border town of Ponto do Ouro. Peace Parks has been supporting the development of that elephant reserve since 2002.

According to the map, it looked to be a long, circumventing gravel road. It then occurred to us: Why not hire a traditional dhow to take us from Maputo to the coastal settlement of Santa Maria on the Indian Ocean shores? We leapt at the idea, and the following morning we were at sea, on a 45-kilometre sail across the bay. The backup vehicles had to go the long way round on what turned out to be a slow, sandy and challenging drive to the coastline of the elephant park. When we met up, Frank's dark mood said it all.

Safely on the Indian Ocean coastline and looking at the open beach stretching into the southern horizon, we knew that we were on our way home. A day-and-a-half later, we arrived in the all-but empty tourist resort of Ponto Chirumkane. There to meet us was one the giants of conservation in Mozambique, Paul Dutton. Then 79 years old and still 'fighting on', as he put it, it was good to see him again. I first met Paul in 1987 and was both charmed and inspired by the man. The pilot of a two-seater aircraft named *Spirit of the Wilderness*, in which we had flown together, he was and remains, a free-spirited individual with a fierce dedication to his conservation cause. Ian had also flown with Paul, but under different circumstances. Paul's beloved plane had been all but written off in a potentially fatal crash-landing in Mozambique. Both men were lucky to escape unscathed.

Paul greeted us with great warmth. When I asked him what keeps him going, he answered: 'Waking up every day and doing something for the environment is my adrenaline.' It did not take long for him to speak of his concern for the elephant park. Also known as the Maputo Special Reserve, it is a highly sensitive centre that combines lakes, wetland, swamp forests, grasslands and mangrove forests with a pristine coastline, a marine protection area and not least, an inland elephant corridor that links the Maputo reserve with the unfenced Tembe Elephant Park in South Africa. It was exactly what our expedition had been attempting to promote.

As idyllic and attractive as the 'corridor' idea may sound, the Mozambican government had other ideas. They were going to transform the inland wetland area into a huge shipping port that would be deep and expansive enough to berth the largest of ships.

The following morning, we went inland to inspect the designated wetland area for the proposed shipping port. Meeting us at the site was Kenton Kirkwood, a knowledgeable and experienced ecologist, who expanded on Paul's concern. The pocket of land, which was cradled by the elephant corridor, the southern border of the reserve and the coast, is in the human settlement district of Techobanine.

According to Kenton and Paul, the hotly-debated economic-driven idea, not without considerable suspicion around the issue of corruption, would undoubtedly impact on the wetland areas and the adjacent greater land and marine reserve itself. As I write, and with great relief, this project has been abandoned. In 2018, the Peace Parks Foundation signed a partnership agreement with Mozambique's National Administration of Conservation Areas (ANAC) to jointly develop Maputo Special and Ponta do Ouro Partial Marine reserve and region, with Peace Parks providing technical and financial support for conservation and tourism development.

Bidding farewell to Paul and Kenton, we made our way back to the coast, hiking through a bird-rich forested area, with well-worn elephant paths and droppings as evidence of the presence of the grey giants. About 25 kilometres later, back on the coast, we set up camp on the shoreline. After a good night's sleep, we pushed on to Ponta do Ouro, from where, the following day, we crossed the border into South Africa.

Back on our bicycles for the last time, we cycled from the inland border post to Rocktail Bay on the shores of the iSimangaliso Wetland Park, now a world heritage site. It was here that we bade farewell to our backup team who would rejoin us four days later at Cape Vidal.

For that final stage, we were joined by another long-time friend and the CEO of the Wilderness Foundation, Andrew Muir, as well as five other members and associates of the Wilderness Foundation and Wilderness Leadership School. Among them were former back-up team members Mandla Buthelezi and Martin Peterson.

On the 2nd of September 2012, after a 5 164-kilometre trek across southern Africa, we arrived at Cape Vidal to a grand welcome from gathered family and friends. Among whom was one of the great giants and champions of conservation in South Africa: Ian Player. A long-standing friend and the founder of the Wilderness Leadership School in 1957, he presented us with a gift – a freshly cut trifoliate leaf of an African coral tree (*Erythrina africana*). The leaf is the emblem of the Wilderness Leadership School and its foundation. The three leaves serve as a compass and symbol, for what the organisation represents: Man to Earth, Man to Man and Man to the Great Spirit.

Looking back

It was only after the journey had been completed that two, critical reasons for undertaking the expedition – something that we could not articulate at the time – became clear. The first was the profound realisation that without an ecological renewal of our present understanding of the meaning of sustainability and human co-existence with all things wild, and that which goes with it – a radical change in human consumptive behaviour – the future of our remaining wild habitats and the creatures that depend on them is grim. The second realisation came in the form of questions that I believe will continue to be asked of human beings in the years to come: If we can't understand the significance of, or protect an animal as big as an elephant, how on Earth could we be expected to protect the little things?

To both Ian and me, those realisations, and the answers to our questions would be impossible without a willingness to open the 'corridors' of our minds ... to be willing to question our current values, beliefs, perspectives and understanding of the significance of wild animals in the world and in our lives. We need them more than they need us. It is also clear to us that another fundamental question we should all be asking of ourselves and our communities relates to current ways of living and the impacts this is having on the planet. How were we going to get this message across? Answering these questions is the reason why it took so long to put this book together. It simply could not have been done any sooner.

Travelling through some of the most diverse and beautiful landscapes in southern Africa, we learned a lot – not only about people and places, but about ourselves. I believe that for us both, the adventure was physically, emotionally and intellectually profound, and that it was an outer and inner journey that it continues to this day.

THE NATURAL WORLD

{ *Ian Michler* }

One of my all-time favourite bands is Tinariwen, a collection of Malian blues masters who can express our thoughts better than most. Set to the typically lilting rhythms associated with the desert blues genre, they ask in a song from their album, *Tassili*, for us all to reflect on these painful times we are living through.

This book contains our thoughts on 'this painful time', a period brought about by a series of environmental and social crises impacting the world.

Some years back, Ian McCallum and I undertook the Tracks of Giants expedition, a necessary path of discovery and learning that took us on a journey through the natural worlds of southern Africa, including some of the region's most iconic national parks and wilderness areas.

We undertook that trip because we were concerned about the ongoing environmental damage from human activities worldwide; the looming impacts of climate change; the state of many protected areas and ecosystems across Africa; the increasing levels of poaching and wildlife trade; and the loss of biodiversity on this continent and elsewhere. We were concerned, too, about the rising inequality and the social challenges that these disparities were bringing, and of course, about human attitudes and behaviour – the ultimate drivers of everything.

In essence, we – that's you and me – are threatening Earth's life-support systems. Without them, it is impossible for us to live. The Tracks journey was about finding out more. It was about going to the coalface of the natural world, and it's a journey that continues today.

Central to any understanding is acknowledging that our relationship with the natural world is complex. This reality is reflected in the multitude ways we describe and interpret our own evolutionary, biological, spiritual, and economic interaction with it, as well as how we understand our individual place in the natural world.

Many of us believe Nature to be priceless – intrinsically and ecologically precious and independent of our anthropocentric conferrals. Conversely, there are uncompromising 'utilitarians' who regard the development or use of Earth's natural elements as a human right, no matter the damage inflicted. And there are many ideologies in between. Some follow a simple Biblical view of our world – one that grants humanity dominion over all creatures and ecological processes, which they incorrectly believe also absolves them of any further culpability, while others go about progressing our societies with varying degrees of consciousness and reflection. As hard as it is to fathom, nonsensical concepts still exist – the flat-Earth theory being just one that appeals to a handful of folks.

In the end, the truth is that the debate is steeped in dogma – it's as much about our belief systems and philosophy as it is about evidence and science. However, the crux is that no matter these persuasions, we cannot escape another reality, one that exposes our relationships as way more layered than we think. We have to extend our understanding beyond a simple justification. This includes accounting for our behaviour, current living patterns and conservation paradigms, as well as the way we go about our work.

Our very existence springs from a nourishing planet; our health and the medicines we require; the foods we eat; the homes we build, and our careers and economic activity which sustains our living and development. Let's not forget recreational time in the great outdoors – activities that are vital to our emotional and psychological well-being. Everything about our individual lives and societies is provided by the natural world – at a price, of course. For this reason alone, we confer upon it, at the very least, a subjective value of sorts.

Once we recognise this, we get to understand that instrumental value thinking, in which things are selfishly valued as a means to an end, dominates our collective goals and objectives. These are all directed and monitored through national and international institutions and other agencies, as well as law, predominantly for human benefit. This is reflected in our economic and political systems, and then framed and focused through global development initiatives, such as the Sustainable Development Goals (SDGs). Our conservation and recreational models, defined by nearly every major agency in existence, are all similarly based on this instrumental value thinking.

To this end, there have been attempts to place a set of financial values on the environment. At its annual meeting in 2020, the World Economic Forum (WEF) referred to nature as 'an entrepreneurial system' that provides ecosystem services valued at more than US$100 trillion a year. 'The cost equivalent of humanity replicating nature's systems is incomparable,' they went on to say.

The World Wide Fund for Nature (WWF) Living Planet Report 2018 refers to US$125 trillion of economic activity being provided to humanity by Earth on an annual basis.

The most recent attempt at 'natural capital accounting', the Dasgupta Review 2021 was commissioned by the British government – the first attempt by a government to do so. Authored by Prof Sir Partha Dasgupta, the review is harsh in its judgment of humanity's record towards the Earth. One particular claim stands out: Between 1992 and 2014, produced capital per person globally doubled, yet the 'stock of natural capital per person declined by nearly 40%'. In other words, we continue to produce and consume more, but with a significant impact on the natural world.

Indeed, acknowledging and accounting for the natural world is immensely complex. My dilemma is one in which many of us find ourselves when it comes to understanding and interacting with the natural world. It's an ongoing grapple with the grey areas between a compassionate version of instrumental thinking and objective assessments of intrinsic value. Currently, most of us have a general acceptance that working within current global conservation and environmental management, law, policy, and thinking is the best way to engineer fundamental change.

But is that so? Perhaps a complete paradigm shift is more appropriate.

I have an ecological and evolutionary grasp of my place in what I know to be a web of life. By definition, that understanding requires me to respect and protect Earth beyond my own horizon and needs. This flows into the recognition that biodiversity and our environment have value beyond its utility to humanity.

Besides what I do for a living, I am also a user of the natural world through ecotourism and other recreational and spiritual activities. While I understand that conservation is currently practised through mostly Eurocentric utilitarian principles that seek to secure a healthy environment, as much for our own good and benefit as for any other reason, I don't always accept this narrative. These anthropocentric ideals and values seem to miss the point that the natural world will thrive without us.

Also, given current population levels and the global reach of humanity, preservationist thinking is compromised by our existing paradigms. Sociopolitical ambitions dictate our development path. They are unrelentingly based on maximising utilisation of every component of Earth – and more recently, even beyond our heavenly horizons.

We face an immense challenge in fathoming the best way forward for the environment, ourselves, and our societies. And, as noted, it's clear that cultural, philosophical, and experiential indicators that are every bit as significant as the scientific, economic and political ones. This is exacerbated by current levels of polarisation and disagreement between and within cultures and societies, which means it is not unrealistic to think that humanity is unlikely to ever reach a consensus on how we know and treat the natural world – let alone each other.

Whatever your worldview, I believe one aspect remains certain: Under current circumstances, we are not taking responsibility or accounting for the costs incurred, or the destruction we are causing to our greatest asset. Since the rise of statehood, and certainly since the advent of the Industrial Revolution, conventional economic principles place zero value on the environment. As a result, we are massively indebted to it. This is nothing short of a calamity.

For some of us, it is patently clear: The current instrumentalist approach is central to the problem rather than the panacea for all ills. The natural world becomes destabilised, less productive, and in some instances, lost forever.

The following chapters explore our relationship with the natural world by focusing on several principal factors: Climate change, habitat loss, ecosystems and biodiversity loss, as well as human behaviour and leadership.

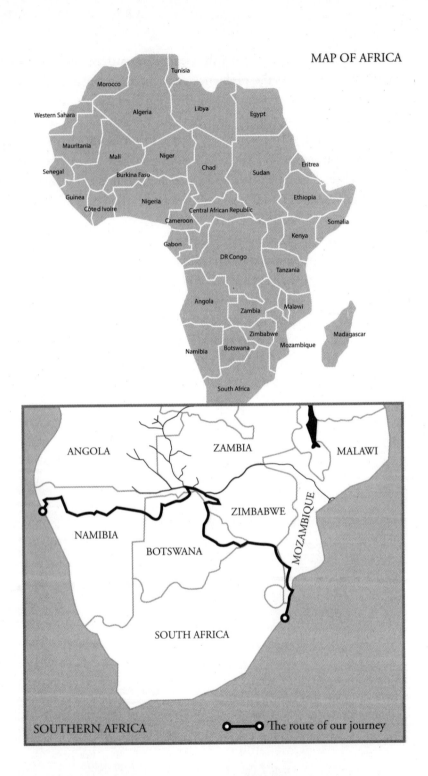

MAP OF AFRICA

Tunisia
Morocco
Western Sahara
Algeria
Libya
Egypt
Mauritania
Mali
Niger
Senegal
Burkina Faso
Chad
Sudan
Eritrea
Guinea
Côte d Ivoire
Nigeria
Ethiopia
Cameroon
Central African Republic
Somalia
Gabon
Kenya
DR Congo
Tanzania
Angola
Zambia
Malawi
Zimbabwe
Madagascar
Namibia
Botswana
Mozambique
South Africa

ANGOLA
ZAMBIA
MALAWI
NAMIBIA
ZIMBABWE
MOZAMBIQUE
BOTSWANA
SOUTH AFRICA

SOUTHERN AFRICA   ○━━○ The route of our journey

The team during the walk across the Namib Desert.

Ian McCallum (second left) with Chris Bakkes and Mandla Buthelezi (right)
in the Namib Desert.

The Namib offers some spectacular scenery.

From left, Ian Michler, Garth Owen-Smith and Ian McCallum cycling up the
Hoarusib in northern Namibia.

A relaxing mekero ride in the Okavango Delta, Botswana.

Wild camping was a highlight of the journey. This site is in the
Okavango Delta, Botswana.

We were extremely fortunate to hit perfect
flood levels when kayaking the Selinda
Spillway and Savute Channel in Botswana.

Cycling across Hwange National Park was another highlight.

The role of fencing and its impact on wildlife remains a contentious issue within conservation circles. This fence extends into the Makgadikgadi Pans, Botswana.

Approaching Mashatu in Botswana, we passed the 4 000-kilometre mark.

Meeting traditional leaders throughout the journey added valuable insight
to conservation and socio-economic challenges. In Tsumkwe, we met with
Johannes Koolbooi and his mother.

The final leg of our journey included a beach walk from Maputo, Mozambique to Cape Vidal in South Africa.

Dr Ian Player, Founder of Wilderness Foundation Africa, was in Cape Vidal to greet us at the end of the 5 164-kilometre journey across six countries.

{ PART B }

1 /

I CAN'T BREATHE

{ *Ian McCallum* }

The following chapter has been adapted from an article I wrote in July 2020 for the Huffington Post Journal, *Thriving in the New Normal. It was titled: 'An Ecological and Psychological Perspective On the Year 2020: A reflection on the year in which our basic assumptions about our future would be challenged'.*

> '*The truth is that "I can't breathe" ... hints at the apocalypse of human values.*'
>
> **– Ben Okri**

Who would have thought that the human species would one day be held to ransom by a microbe? And yet it happened. The first two years of the COVID-19 pandemic did just that. It was a time and event in which the human world not only stood still, but in which any convictions of human superiority over all living things would be seriously questioned. It remains a time when our basic assumptions about our future continue to be challenged. For those most severely affected by the COVID-19 viral infection, the presenting symptom was one of increasing respiratory distress. Their plea was one that haunts every human being – the suffocating cry: 'I can't breathe.'

How ironic that 2020, the year the pandemic started, is the symbol of perfect vision. If we had such vision, then we must have seen it coming. And we did. Deep down we knew that something like this had to happen. The so-called 'black swan' – the creature that no one believed existed – a metaphor for events that not only catch us by surprise but have a major impact on our lives – suddenly pitched up? No. It did not arrive unannounced. The 'black swan' dynamics of rising human populations; high-density urbanisation; habitat fragmentation; plastic and biochemical pollution; the burning of forests and fossil fuels; climate instability, and with it the zoonotic consequences of the way we treat, eat, farm, corral, transport and trade domestic and wild animals – legally and illegally – have come home to roost. The swan was staring us in the face. Its call was the warning cry of the Earth itself: 'I can't breathe.' Watch out!

Lockdown

Of course, this is all hindsight. As I write, the pandemic, with all of the anxiety and uncertainty that comes with it, is still upon us. It is real. We have no choice but to deal with it, each in our own way. As challenging as it has already been, for some more than others – particularly the poor and those living in countries where medical services are scarce – it may be of small comfort to know that we are in the midst of a process that, for better or worse, will pass. Perhaps we will be better prepared for the next one? The fact remains: It has been a wake-up call for us all.

For those of us privileged enough to know where our next meal is coming from, it has been a time to gather ourselves, to be still, and to open ourselves to some honest self-examination. After all, crises shape us, and they shape history. They reveal us for who we truly are; for who is advantaged or worse off than us; for who or what holds our power, and for who and what we value in life. They ask searching questions of us, such as: How important, really, are those things that we want to rush back to doing? Crises teach us to look and to listen differently. For example, it did not take long to see the world's reactions to the phenomenon in a different light, and to realise and to be reminded just how wide the gap is between the 'haves' and the 'have-nots' in the world today. Something unfair and unacceptable was being unmasked.

On the other hand, it did not take long to notice that the animals were coming closer. Bird song was louder. In some cities, after years of smog cover, the stars were once again visible. In northern India, the Himalayas, for the first time in many decades, could be seen from more than 200 kilometres away. It was as if the Earth was saying: 'I can breathe again.' It makes logical sense. Or is there something deeper, something ethical in us that knows there has to be a way of preserving and protecting these visible benefits to the natural environment?

I looked up the root meaning of the word 'crisis' and was surprised. Originally used as a medical term to denote a turning point of a disease, its roots are in the Greek word '*krisis*', from '*krinein*', meaning 'decision'. As we begin to face up to the social and human-induced ecological injustices of our time, could it be that this crisis is a time and turning point in our history for the makings of some of the most important political, economic, ecological and personal decisions of our lives?

After more than two years and the official end to the state of disaster in South Africa, the general mood of the public has shifted. For many – particularly those who have lost their livelihoods without a financial cushion – the situation has become desperate. Fuelled by uncertainty, we have found ourselves increasingly irritable, frustrated, restless and impatient, which are all natural signs and symptoms of grieving. We are not necessarily grieving the loss of a loved one, but a certain loss of freedom and a way of life. For some, it's the loss of a sense of a future. The feeling has been of an increasing sense of suffocation. A breath of fresh air – the easing of the worst pressures of restrictions – has been badly needed. Even in countries where a considerable portion of the population has been vaccinated, the uncertainty around further waves of infection and the mutating virus remains.

Returning to the early days of the pandemic, more specifically, 25 May 2020, the world at large watched footage of a man suspected of trading a counterfeit $20 bill being pinned to the ground in a fatal throat-hold by a police officer in Minneapolis in the United States of

America. The officer, his knee firmly pressed into the extended neck of the handcuffed victim, ignored the repeated plea of the dying man: 'I can't breathe ...'

That man's death will not only be remembered for the brutal manner in which he died, but for the depth, significance and timing of his dying words: 'I can't breathe'. His name was George Floyd and he was a black man. The police officers involved were white. It was an all-too-familiar script, but at that time, assisted by unprecedented social media visibility and outreach, the reaction was swift, fearless, focused and united. The suffocating dynamics of longstanding systemic racial, ethnic and cultural discrimination, not only in the USA but globally, had been unmasked. Watch out! No one can say that they did not see or hear it coming. Like the COVID-19 outbreak, it was not a black swan phenomenon.

Quick to grasp the relevance of the event and the words: 'I can't breathe', Nigerian novelist and poet Ben Okri wrote:

These few words should become the mantra of oppression and spark the real change our world so desperately needs.' He added: *'Never in my lifetime has the case for such visible injustice moved white and black people, moved them as human beings.'*

I value Ben Okri's recognition and inclusion of both whites and blacks in his analysis of the emotional impact of this historical event. I don't believe there is a single human being who does not understand the personal significance of the words: 'I can't breathe'. Like Martin Luther King's 1963 'I have a dream' speech, these very human expressions belong to us all. We are all in this together. What an opportunity, and what a responsibility.

As a psychiatrist and analyst, the psychological and ecological relevance of these three words: 'I can't breathe', is inescapable. It is happening to the Earth, too. Let me put this into context.

With the easing of the COVID-19 lockdown restrictions, I have slowly begun moving from Skype and Zoom consultations to once more seeing my patients face-to-face. In keeping with the regulations, each patient enters my consulting room, hand-sanitised and fully masked. Once seated and appropriately distanced, I invite them to take off their mask. For a start, it makes it easier to breathe. 'You may take off your mask' is a powerful metaphor for the meaning of analytical therapy ... that in this room, in this hour, in this space and time together, no words, utterances, declarations and dreams are forbidden. You can remove your social masks. You can be yourself ... and when you leave, you can put them on again, not only for your sake, but for the sake of others.

Seated face to face, the first question I ask any new patient is simple: 'How can I help?' My task then is to listen deeply. There are many reasons for seeking professional help, such as the need for career or relationship guidance; identity issues; the sense of having lost one's way in life, and issues of loss, betrayal, abandonment and grief. Sometimes quickly and directly, sometimes slowly and circumventing, the response from almost every individual has somewhere within it the mantra: 'I can't breathe.' Individuals are suffocating in bullying relationships; stifled in their careers; strangled by political correctness and bureaucratic inertia; claustrophobic in their marriages, and choked by commitments, deadlines and the expectations of others. Sometimes, people are simply 'out of breath' and burning out ... desperate for a place to gather themselves, to catch their breath and to be inspired.

What follows is a process intrinsic to many therapeutic approaches: The task of assisting my patients toward a renewed perspective of themselves and of their relationships; helping them to recognise and own up to their personal contributions to their suffering. Perhaps most challenging (and rewarding) of all, my role is to help them find their voice – an authority that is natural to them. That takes time, trust and patience, as well as the patient's willingness to be disturbed. Owning up to one's personal contribution to one's suffering is not easy. It is far easier to identify the source of one's problems as a phenomenon external to oneself ... to the 'system' or to any individual (husband, wife, parent, boss, etc.) than it is to admit to the possibility that one's own assumptions, pretences, neediness, entitlement, manipulations and demands have been suffocating for others.

Finally: The task of finding one's own voice – of learning how to take the 'knee' of fear, conformity and self-doubt off the throat of that which you have silenced within yourself; to hear the plea of an often-forgotten voice within you, and to let it breathe. Finding one's voice, of course, is not without challenges, consequences and responsibilities. It can sometimes come at a considerable cost to one's family or to one's place and status within society, and to those who could not see beyond your masks. However, it can also bring a measurable renewing of relationships within those same families and societies. Sometimes, to find your voice is to inspire others to find theirs, to be a voice for the voiceless, and most urgently of all, to be a voice for the Earth.

To me, ecology is far more than an academic study of environmental sciences ecosystems. It is a state of mind, an attitude; a way of listening and of seeing. It makes sense to me that the chemical and biological patterns of relationships between the atmosphere, the forests, rivers, mountains, oceans, landscapes, as well as the micro- and visible animals in our lives, are inseparable from our existence as human beings. Our identity and sanity are dependent on them. These patterns of relationships are in our psyche and in our blood. Who and what would we be without them? And yet, on our watch, the Earth is suffocating.

Look! The human knee is on the throat of the biosphere. We are polluting the air we breathe; choking the rivers; deforesting the lungs of the Earth, and poisoning the seas and soils that sustain every living thing.

Listen! The biosphere is crying: 'I can't breathe'. Watch out! In response to human activities and human-induced ecological injustices, the biosphere will protest. It is already doing so, and with increasing vigour. With rising global temperatures – undeniably linked to fossil-fuel burning – the climate is becoming less stable. As a result, climate extremes in the form of floods, droughts, wildfires and hurricanes are the order of the day. No one can say that we didn't see it coming.

The Earth is not out to 'get' us. By all means, take our environmental crises personally, but the biosphere won't. It will simply continue doing what it has been doing for billions of years. The evolution of life on Earth is a two-way process. It is not enough to marvel at the way organisms have improvised and adapted to changing environments over millions of years. The biosphere, in turn, adapts to the way that organisms behave. It is an ongoing, bilateral process of give and take ... a formula for all relationships. The timing of the biosphere's response to human consumptive behaviour should not come as a surprise. Adding to this problem, of course, is that multiple other species on Earth are suffering and suffocating because of us. A human-induced 'sixth extinction' is staring us in the face.

Is there anything we can do about our deteriorating relationship with the biosphere? The answer is: 'Yes.' We need to get the suffocating human knee off the throat of the ecosystems of our planet, and we need to do it quickly. This will not happen until we effectively address the deeply engrained human traits of denial, entitlement, indifference and defeatism.

Denial

Denial and ignorance are not the same thing. Denial is best described by Bob Dylan in the line of his 1962 classic song, *Blowin in the Wind*: '*How many times can a man turn his head, pretending he just doesn't see?*' And it's not because we don't care. We know what is happening; we know that our current lifestyle is damaging to the biosphere, but for reasons of timing, inconvenience, commitments, conformity, the economy and other personal aspirations, we don't want to know. We rationalise and minimise what could be described as a contract with ignorance. 'Things are not that bad,' we say, or: 'If others are not changing their behaviour, then why should I?' The question is: Are you willing to be disturbed? Are you willing to say: 'No,' to that contract?

Entitlement

Human entitlement: A pervasive sense of self-importance in which our denial becomes justifiable. Assumptions become systematic, ritualised and, ultimately, systemic. Our habits become addictions. When challenged, no one warms to being advised that we may be wrong, that our personal philosophies, assumptions, expectations and lifestyles are inappropriate, anachronistic or worse ... that we are suffocating the lives of others. There's a difference between a sense of self-importance and a sense of self-worth. In children, the former is natural, necessary, and when appropriately guided by parents and teachers, it enhances a sense of resilience, agency and self-worth. In adults, and particularly in times of crisis, self-importance is regressive, narcissistic and pathetic. For self-proclaimed 'stable geniuses' and others in positions of power, it is dangerous.

The question remains: Are we willing to be disturbed? Are we willing to remove the knee of human self-importance from the throat of our planet? Are we willing to re-examine our priorities, assumptions, values and conveniences – what could also be described as our addictions: Food, work, adrenaline, lifestyle – and so on? Are we willing to question the possibility that we may be wrong about our understanding of our human position in a web of life and consider that we are not at the apex of creation where all else is secondary, for our benefit? Or are we going to resort once more to our contract with ignorance? If it is the latter, then we will be faced with the third, most toxic challenge of all: Human indifference.

What makes this behavioural phenomenon so toxic is that we know exactly what is going on, but simply don't care. Part of my work includes helping people sort through relationship issues. Often, in answer to the question: 'What is the opposite of love?' I hear the word 'hate'. To me, it is anything but hate. Hate has energy, chemistry and substance. You can work with the emotion of hate. The opposite of love is indifference. You don't give a damn; you don't care. In a marital relationship, it is toxic. Instead of energy, there's apathy. Instead of chemistry, there's emptiness. Instead of substance, there's frivolousness. The relationship is all but dead. The same goes for our relationship with the Earth and the biosphere.

Are you willing to be disturbed, and to test your own sense of self-importance and indifference? Are you willing to ask yourself: 'How much consciousness, awareness, sensitivity, memory, intelligence, resilience and expertise am I willing to grant to a tree, a bird, an animal, or anyone that I believe to be less important than me?'

The answer to this question hinges on the word 'willing'. How willing are you to grant these assumed human-defining qualities – at whatever level or intensity – to all living things? Remember, this is not a test of whether butterflies, birds and whales are more important than us. It is a measure of the degree to which we value and validate the rights of other species to exist. How willing are you to look at the Earth through a different lens and to listen with a different ear? If unwilling, could the hardening of your thinking be anything to do with the final phenomenon and challenge.

Defeatism

Defeatism is the saddest of the challenges. It addresses the part of us that believes it is too late to turn the tide of what we have done to the environment … that we might as well give up. Hamstrung by a pervasive sense of hopelessness, we might as well eat, drink and be merry. Yes, we have good reasons to be cynical and to see all of our endeavours to make a difference as no different to the futile task of the legendary Sisyphus. The mythical Greek hero, who scorned the gods of the underworld, was condemned to push a heavy boulder up an ever-increasing gradient until, inches short of the summit, it would become too heavy and overpower him, only to roll back to where he had started. Then he would have to start all over again, and again.

Instead of giving up, as the gods had expected of him, Sisyphus turned once more to that rock. Embracing it, he recommenced his impossible task. In that act, he scorned once more the punishing gods. In that act, he showed that he was bigger than that rock and bigger than his fate. Within the rock itself lay hidden possibilities. That is the challenge of human defeatism. Don't fall for the trap of hopelessness.

Here then, is the challenge: Are you willing to make a stand, to say: 'No,' to the voices of entitlement, indifference and defeatism within ourselves and others? Are you willing to be an advocate of hope; to refuse to be overwhelmed by the weight of the environmental tasks that we all have to face? Since we are not a keystone species on Earth and ecosystems will be better off without us, do you have it within you to be a keystone individual? To be someone who gives a damn and who makes a difference, however small – someone who knows the difference between optimism and hope?

Hope is not the same as optimism. It is not the conviction that everything is going to turn out well. We don't know how things will turn out.

'*Hope,*' said writer, poet and first president of the Czech Republic Vaclav Havel, '*… resides in the faith that things have meaning … in the certainty that something makes sense regardless of how it turns out.*'

Do the right thing, have faith in your values and be surprised at how things turn out. It is an individual task, but you are not alone. There are thousands of others who are, each in their own way, already making a difference. In our diversity, there is strength, but in unity, there is power.

Finally, let us not forget that justice is an ethical concept … a deep sense of what is fair, respectful, unbiased and validating for all living things. And so, as a way of coming to terms with the impersonal manner in which something as miniscule as a virus has forced us to re-examine not only ourselves, but the injustices it has unveiled, let's become hunter-gatherers again – not with bows, arrows and loin cloths – but hunter-gatherers of values, hunter-gatherers of the wild roots of fairness, humility, unpretentiousness, beauty, fertility, generosity, patience, play, freedom and compassion. Let's value fiercely the social, personal and ecological significance of these three words … 'I CAN BREATHE'.

2 /

THE SMOKE, THE SCORPION, THE SPARKS AND THE STARS

{ *Ian McCallum* }

'*There is a place on Earth where all things come together ...*'

In early 1981, I was invited to speak in Johannesburg at a meeting that, in those days, would have been regarded as typically 'new age' or 'fringe'. It was a gathering of individuals with an interest in finding common ground between conventional and alternative medical practices, like acupuncture, homoeopathy, naturopathy and the healing significance of Nature. While finding my way as a young general medical practitioner in Cape Town, I was curious about these alternative approaches.

One of my reasons for accepting the invitation was because one of the presenters was Ian Player, a game ranger who was well known at that time for his personal contribution to saving the wide-lipped rhinoceros (white rhino), *Cearatotherium simum* from almost certain extinction. He was also the founder of the Wilderness Leadership School in South Africa. Sensitive to the scientific scepticism of 'new age' thinking, I figured that if a game ranger was on the programme, then it was okay for a rugby-playing doctor to be there, too. Besides, I wanted to hear what he had to say on the subject of healing. I subsequently learned from him that he was attending because of me ... He wanted to hear what a former rugby player had to say!

Borrowing from a quote by the 15th century renaissance physician, Paracelsus, the title of my talk was: 'As above, so below'. I remember showing a series of 36-mm slides that compared and linked images of stars and galaxies to the micro-world of cells and chemical crystals in the human body. I spoke of the inner, microbiological world as a mirror of the outer, macro- and tangible world of human existence. It made sense to me. Ian Player, on the other hand, spoke passionately about the wilderness, more especially how the experience of it can change people's lives … that there was a wilderness without, and a wilderness within.

The connection between us was immediate, and it would be the beginning of a long and meaningful relationship with one of the global giants of conservation. At dinner together that night, he invited me to join him and Magqubu Ntombela, his friend and mentor, on a five-day wilderness trail in the Imfolozi Game Reserve in Zululand, in what was then known as the province of Natal in South Africa.

* * *

One month later, carrying a backpack with a single change of clothing, as well as an allocation of food and cooking utensils, a thin mattress and sleeping bag, I set off on my very first walking trail into the wild. It was July, so winter in the southern hemisphere. The days were expected to be clear and still, and the nights cloudless and cold.

The trail began with a briefing – a combination of safety rules and a handful of challenging instructions: No watches and, if they had been around in 1981, certainly no cellphones. For the next five days, the movement of the sun, stars and the diurnal songs and calls of the birds and animals would be our timekeepers. Finally, with Magqubu nodding his head in quiet approval, Ian asked us to regard ourselves as guests entering a home where every animal and bird and tree was to be treated, at the very least, as an equal. Magqubu led the way, Ian behind him. There were two journalists and a filmmaker in the group, and I brought up the rear.

My task, I was told, was to keep an eye and ear on what was happening behind us. It is one of the laws of survival in the wild: Watch your back.

It was on that trail, on foot, and not behind the windscreens of motor vehicles, or the guaranteed safety of animals in cages, that I experienced and understood for the first time the richness … the apprehension and thrill of wild animal encounters. I also learned how far removed I was from being able to live and survive in the wild. It was a reminder of how modern humans may know *about* wild places, but with rare exception, we no longer *know* them. It is one thing to marvel at photographs and documentaries of wild places, it is another to *experience* them; not just the fierce beauty of these places, but to know what it means to be vulnerable.

The five-day event would dramatically shift my understanding of wildness and more. It would challenge any attitude I may have held that anything wild was to be kept at a distance and, if not, to be tamed for human needs and pleasure.

In the unfolding days, sparked by an ancient response to that wild territory, my senses sharpened. I began to see differently; to listen with another ear. The gap between taste and smell narrowed. What followed was a realisation that has never left me. If I were to drop dead, they wouldn't give a damn. Life would go on. I liked that, but did it mean that I could justify an attitude of indifference to them? To me, the answer was a resounding: 'No'. Instead, I felt a deepened sense of debt and gratitude for their presence. It also left me with a keener sense of responsibility for them and for their future. With an increasing sense of reciprocity, I found myself reaching out to the land, the animals and the slow-flowing river. I began to discover that, given time and attention, they reached back. It was a profound resonance. Although I was unable to articulate it at that time, today I call it a homecoming. At last, I had found my church … a church with no dogma and no judgment … sacred but untamed. Spanish poet Juan Ramon Jimenez describes this realisation beautifully:

Deep down
My boat has struck a great thing.
And nothing happens! Nothing … silence … waves.
Nothing happens? Or has everything happened
And I am standing in a new country.

On the third evening of the trail, we enjoyed a wholesome supper, and with the temperature dropping, we huddled around a glowing log fire. It was a scene and ceremony probably no different to that repeated over hundreds of thousands of years by our hominin ancestors. Prior to turning in, Ian pulled out a well-thumbed book he had brought with him. It was a collection of selected insights and interviews with Swiss psychiatrist and analytical psychologist C.G. Jung. He read from a chapter titled: *The two-million-year-old man in all of us*. In a fascinating group discussion, I warmed to his suggestion of 'an age-old forgotten wisdom stored up in us'. With that in mind, I began my preparations for the night.

Unrolling my sleeping bag just a little beyond the flickering rim of the fire, Magqubu approached me. Extending his arm, he held out a small branch he had cut from a nearby tree (*Zizyphus mucranata*). 'I have a gift for you,' he said. Pointing to a double row of thorns on the branch, he told me that in Zulu tradition it was the branch of an important tree. 'The way the thorns are pointing tell you how to live your life,' he said.

Not quite sure what Magqubu was trying to convey, I looked closer. Sure enough, the paired thorns along the length of the branch were each differently shaped. 'Do you see these thorns here?' he asked, indicating a row of robust, outward-pointing thorns. 'These thorns tell you to face the future,' he said, adding: 'You must think of the future generations.'

Pointing to the other row, all of them hooked and backward pointing, he said: 'These ones say: "You must never forget where you have come from."' Magqubu turned away, and with his gift cradled in my hands, I watched him amble toward his bed roll.

I lay awake for a long time, watching the stars and listening to the night sounds of the fiery-necked night jar's onomatopoeic call … 'May the Lord deliver us …', the chorus of bell frogs from the river's edge, and in the distance, the roar of a territorial lion. Magqubu's words kept coming back: 'Think of the future generations … Never forget where you have come from.' To this day, I have never heard a simpler yet more profound life philosophy. What a gift.

I eventually fell asleep, only to be awakened in the early, dark hours of the morning by Ian. 'It's your turn,' he whispered, gently prodding my shoulder to ensure I was awake. As it was in our hunter-gatherer past, I re-enacted one of the most important requirements for group safety and security: Staying awake during the night while others slept. It was my turn for the night watch, a duty and ritual requiring each of us in turn to sit alone, alert for possible nocturnal visitors and not, in this instance, the human kind. It was a time to listen and watch for the animals that come alive in the night: Lions, hippo, hyaenas and sometimes, elephant and rhino. For me, the night watch is always one of the most precious experiences of a wilderness trail. The fire and the solitude of the night belong to you. It is a time when thoughts, dreams and reflections – those other animating forces of our imagination – come alive. I welcomed them.

It was bitterly cold at that early hour of the morning, but the fire was strong and inviting. I made a cup of tea and, before sipping it, I scanned the full circumference of the night with my flashlight. I heard the call of a spotted hyaena. Somewhere among the cliffs a baboon barked and was then quiet. The night sky was a brilliant, star-filled quilt. With one-and-a-half hours to myself before the next person's turn to take watch, I positioned myself in the warm glow of the fire and sipped my tea and my thoughts.

On a flat stone close by was the book Ian had been sharing with us before we had turned in. I picked it up and turned to the section from which he had read. I had hardly begun the first sentence when a thin plume of smoke from the fire found its way into my eyes. 'How strange,' I thought, questioning the direction of the smoke. There was no wind to guide it. I moved my position to the opposite side of the fire and opened the book again. Once again, the fire, as if adjusting its own compass, sent a snake-like plume of smoke toward me. I put down the book and did something I had never done before. I spoke to the fire: 'I'm going to move once more and if you follow me again, I will put the book away,' I said. With that, I repositioned myself and re-opened the book. Like a moth drawn to lamp light, a solitary tentacle of smoke sought me out. Waving the smoke away, I put the book down and stared into the fire.

The smoke settled and was followed by the faint movement of something in the shadows in front of me. I looked hard into the flickering light and there, perched on the non-burning end of a log was a huge, black-bodied *Parabathus* scorpion. With its curved tail and its pincers held high, it began scrambling up the log toward the burning end and to what would be a fiery death. I thought: 'What on Earth is it trying to do?' Suddenly, the burning end of the log collapsed into the red-hot bed of coals. The result was an explosive shower of sparks scattering upwards into the night. My first thought was for the scorpion, but with nothing to confirm its escape or fate, my eyes were drawn to the upward curving shower of sparks. And then I saw it. Brilliantly outlined in the sky directly above me was the imposing winter constellation of the scorpion … Scorpius.

Like an unfolding drama, unpredictable and almost certainly un-repeatable, what appeared as random, disconnected events – the smoke, the scorpion, the sparks and the stars – came together in a continuum of space, time and imagination. And I was a part of it.

Say what you wish, what happened to me that night was synchro-nistic – a deeply meaningful coincidence of mind and matter. Rich in measurement, metaphor and meaning, I have thought long and hard about that magical night. Would making the event a little more measurable, tangible and grounded, spoil the experience? Would it lose its magic? I didn't think so.

Fire, scorpions and stars are easily understood as metaphors of the human imagination. However, they are more than mere representations of human values, dreams and personalities. Let us not forget that they also exist in their own right, for what they are and for what they do. To rob a scorpion, a fire, tree, star, or human being of its individuality, is to rob it of its uniquely tangible presence and magic.

I have learnt a lot about scorpions and stars since that unforgettable night. As for the eight-legged arachnids, scorpions have been around since the Silurian period 430 million years ago. Sharing more than 40% of the human genome, they are part of the common ancestry of all biological life, including you and me. Yes, they are connected to the stars, particularly the big ones, and the one closest to Earth – our sun. If it wasn't for the stars, there would be no scorpions, nor any other living organisms on Earth. We would not be here.

To find out why, let's examine the 'heart' of Scorpius. In the middle of this huge constellation is a reddish star. Sometimes referred to as the heart of the constellation, it has the beautiful name Antares. It was named because of its similarity in colour to Ares, the Greek name for Mars. To the naked eye, it may not appear that large, but approximately 600 light years away from Earth, Antares is so huge that if it were positioned where our sun is, Mercury, Venus, Earth and Mars would be inside of it! The fate of this star, like all other red giants, is sealed. Coming to the end of its life, it will go out not with a whimper, but a bang. It will explode, and like all exploding stars, it will scatter into the surrounding universe the heavy elements of the periodic table, including iron, magnesium, potassium, sodium, calcium and phosphorous. These trace elements are essential to the life and livelihood of scorpions, plants, and trees, as well as to the life of that star-struck observer on a night watch in the Hluhluwe-Imfolosi all of those years ago.

When we die, the elements in our bodies, like those in the burning log, and whose flames, fuelled by the sun, will return once more to the universe. Think about it: we are stardust. We are connected. The wilderness told me so. Paracelsus is right: 'As above, so below.'

3 /

WHY ARE WE SO CONCERNED?

{ *Ian Michler* }

John Legend, the popular American singer-songwriter, wrote a song *If you're out there* in 2008. Written as a call to action when Barack Obama got elected, he refers to the urgent need for change because the "future started yesterday". Keep this thought in mind when pondering the global concerns we all face.

According to *Nature*, more than 77% of the Earth's surface (excluding Antarctica) and 87% of the oceans have been impacted and modified by human behaviour in some way. Of the portion that remains wilderness, most of it is uninhabitable desert and ice.

In a 2021 research report, *Frontiers in Forests and Global Change,* published by 16 global biologists and scientists, it was found that only 2.9% of Earth's land surface can be regarded as 'faunally intact'.

On these facts alone, there is reason enough to be concerned. However, to respond effectively to any such warnings, both the broader scientific community and decision-makers would need sound information based on extensive research detailing the dynamics of each challenge. In this process, the specifics of exactly what's at stake become apparent. We now have a multitude of reports and assessments describing everything we need to know.

The science is clear

The World Economic Forum's (WEF) Global Risks Report (GRR) is an annual in-depth global assessment of the biggest threats facing humanity during the year of publication and beyond. When compiling the data for their rankings, the WEF works closely with a global network of almost 800 experts involved in government and many different scientific, economic, social, security and academic institutions. The risks are listed in terms of likelihood and the level of impact.

According to the 2022 report, the top three most severe risks on a global scale over the next 10 years are environmental, with climate action failure being the biggest concern. The last two that round out the five are issues concerning the erosion of social cohesion and livelihoods.

In 2021, four of the top five listed likelihood risks fell into the environmental category, while the fifth (infectious diseases) came about because of the current global COVID-19 pandemic and is linked to an unstable environment. In the 2021 report, of the top five ranked by impact level, three were environmental risks. Various other risks on both lists, such as global governance failures and super-power confrontations, will also have serious knock-on impacts on the environment.

Almost 90% of the experts involved in compiling the 2022 report saw the future in a negative way. The trends are just as telling. Over the 16 years since the first report was released, environmental factors have grown significantly in terms of both the likelihood of occurrence and the impact they will have. The 2010 report, for example, ranked six financial risks in the top seven, and not a single environmental risk appeared in the top 10. Now, the environment, followed by social concerns, dominate every marker in the report.

These rankings should be of the utmost concern to every citizen worldwide. As the GRR makes clear in its title and content, these are global challenges – every corner of the planet and all spheres are at risk, and every citizen will somehow be impacted. This means that the reasons for being concerned have nothing to do with wealth brackets, social status, intellectual understanding, or geographical location. To a greater or lesser extent, these factors may all play a role in different scenarios, but in the end, we should all be concerned because our own survival is at stake.

To survive, each one of us requires clean air to breathe, fresh drinking water and fertile topsoil to secure food. We also need effective carbon sequestration systems and healthy biodiversity levels to ensure functioning ecosystems and access to wilderness or aspects of the natural world – at the very least for recreational and spiritual purposes. Without these, our families, communities and societies cannot thrive. As the pressures increase, our living is compromised.

Many additional detailed indicators clearly reinforce why we need to act. The Global Footprint Network (GFN) and the indices they publish are particularly compelling. While the GRR warns of threats and the likelihood of them happening, the GFN publishes an Ecological Footprint Index that quantifies the available resource base Earth produces against current global usage and waste production.

The GFN also provides country assessments in which National Footprint and Biocapacity Accounts that measure ecological resource use against national capacity are published. As of 2022, the network has accounts for most of the world's countries and territories going back to 1961. Those using or consuming above the biocapacity level are regarded as being in 'biocapacity deficit', or 'ecological overshoot'. In common literature, terms such as ecological deficit or resource overdraft are also often used. They all refer to living patterns that are simply unsustainable.

In 2022, 136 countries were listed as being in biocapacity deficit. Singapore had the worst, or most unsustainable ranking, with an ecological footprint exceeding biocapacity by a staggering 10 300%. Most of the top 10 nations are either islands or small countries. Other interesting rankings include Saudi Arabia (12th), China (39th), South Africa (50th), and the USA (66th).

At the other end of the scale, 51 countries were listed as having 'reserve biocapacity', or as living within their ecological limits. Most in the top 10 are small or underdeveloped countries and territories with small populations. French Guiana and Suriname have the highest levels of biocapacity reserve. Many African countries appear on the list, as do developed countries like Finland, Canada, and Norway.

The GFN lists numerous other footprint measurements, including a per capita basis that ranks the number of global hectares used. On the 2022 list, Qatar (14.7 hectares), Luxembourg (12.8 hectares) and United Arab Emirates (8.9 hectares) rank as the worst offenders. The USA comes in at 8th (8 hectares) and South Africa at 79th (2.2 hectares). There is another way of looking at these deficits: If everyone on this planet lived as they do in Qatar, we would need more than 10 planets' worth of resources to be sustainable.

Earth Overshoot Day, which annually marks the date when humanity's demand for ecological resources and services outstrips what Earth can regenerate for that given period, is another indicator. Since 1970, and with each passing two-year period, the ecological deficit has occurred earlier. To use a financial analogy, this would be the equivalent of an individual or family spending way more than their annual budget and funding the deficit out of their cash reserves. If they did this annually and reached the deficit point earlier and earlier with each passing year, they would eventually have to face the fact that nothing was left in the kitty.

For 2019, Earth Overshoot Day occurred on 29 July, the earliest date ever. For 2020, it was pushed back three weeks to 22 August – a respite that came about only because of the COVID-19 pandemic, which significantly reduced economic activity. In 2021, Earth Overshoot Day once again fell on 29 July.

In summary, humanity (our combined global footprint) requires 1.7 Earths' worth of resources to survive at current levels of consumption and waste production. If we continue at these levels, by 2050 we will need 2.3 Earths to meet consumption and waste production demands.

We also have the background issue of population growth. As we near eight billion people – a threshold we may well cross before the end of 2022 – every challenge is exacerbated. With a diminishing resource base and depleted planetary functionality, Earth's life-support systems will begin collapsing and it will not be possible to sustain all life on Earth.

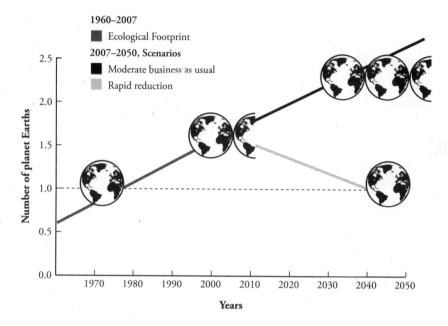

FIGURE I: Global Ecological Footprint Scenarios 1970–2050

Source: Global Footprint Network

The complexity involved

These indicators all provide a big-picture snapshot of collated data on an annual or bi-annual basis. They also highlight the multifaceted nature of our challenges.

Discussions around the definition of complexity (known as complexity science) are vigorous and beyond the scope of this book, but we have to accept that the challenges humanity face involve a multitude of threads and components – including social ones – that are all enhanced or exacerbated by technology and the processes of the environment. These can all play out or impact on each other, often with lengthy time lags, in ways that science cannot immediately measure or precisely predict. In some ways linked to systems theory, understanding the nature and variability of these aspects is crucial to giving ourselves a chance to engineer fundamental change to current living patterns.

On a simpler level, actions in one sphere, while seeming clear and logical, may well have implications for, or even undermine another seemingly unrelated sphere. A good example relates to the move towards electric motor vehicles to mitigate carbon emissions. If the electricity consumed by these vehicles continues to be supplied by a coal-powered grid, the switch may have little to zero impact.

Besides the broad components already outlined, the scientific and conservation communities are concerned about a host of specific indicators that are warning us about collapse if current living patterns continue. These can be summarised as three linked crises, along with a fourth:

1. Climate change
2. Habitat loss and biodiversity
3. Ecosystems loss
4. Human behaviour and leadership patterns cause or exacerbate the first three crises.

Let us explore each of these four crises in more detail.

1. Climate change

Since the advent of sedentary communities, human activity has become the most destructive force on the planet. Over the past few decades, human-induced climate change has become our most pressing concern, with the situation now so critical that many scientists and decision-makers rank this as the defining challenge of our time. (See 'Living in the Anthropocene'). With the release of Making Peace with Nature, yet another report detailing the damage, UN Secretary-General António Guterres was moved to challenge humanity's behaviour as 'senseless and suicidal'.

But what exactly is climate change? The USA's National Aeronautics and Space Administration (NASA), a world leader in climate and Earth science, defines it as the 'long-term change in the average weather patterns that have come to define Earth's local, regional and global climates'. This includes factors such as wind patterns, ocean flows, ice ages, rainfall levels, and flood cycles, as well as global warming – the one indicator that has come to represent the entire process of our changing climate. Because of this link, global warming is often used interchangeably with climate change, but this is incorrect. The former is merely one facet of the far broader phenomenon of climate change.

While changes appear mostly as environmental indicators, there are also severe social and cultural consequences to our way of living. These come with the added component of uncertainty, as erratic, fast-changing weather patterns involve so many variables that many of them are beyond science's current capacity to give precise predictions. This makes current and future planning far more problematic.

We know from various scientific disciplines that climates have been changing naturally ever since Earth was formed more than 4.5 billion years ago. Natural processes, such as volcanic eruptions, the sun's activity, and changes to Earth's orbital path have all been causes for the countless periods when the planet has experienced wide temperature fluctuations. Since the beginning of life on Earth about 3.5 billion years ago, each major change has had hugely disruptive impacts, including mass extinctions of various life forms.

However, the current cycle is different. This time, the changes are being primarily driven by the activities and behaviour of a single species: Us – *Homo sapiens*. We are mostly driving this through the burning of fossil fuels, habitat destruction and other factors relating to our living patterns. Furthermore, the rate of change is happening appreciably faster than any natural cycle. The consequences will be similar: Significant and even catastrophic impacts on life on Earth.

The build-up of greenhouse gases

With a membership of 195 nations, the UN's Intergovernmental Panel on Climate Change (IPCC) has become the leading voice on the science related to climate change.

The body was established in 1988 as a global authority to centralise climate science and develop a streamlined policy for the benefit of all governments. Assisted by thousands of scientists worldwide and divided into three principle working groups, the IPCC collates and assesses data for its comprehensive summary, including mitigation recommendations.

It is important to stress that the IPCC does not conduct its own research; its remit is to compile and assess the work of scientists from member nations. Its latest release in March 2022 was based on 34 000 reports. This approach has the added advantage of identifying areas of overlap and calling for further research where needed.

The IPCC has released various reports, ranging from global warming's widespread impacts to more detailed analyses on how specific habitats, such as land, oceans, or the cryosphere will be affected. Also important is the work done by United in Science, a group comprising the IPCC, and various United Nations (UN) and non-governmental organisation (NGO) bodies.

It is clear from their work – and that of all other leading climate change agencies – that the build-up of greenhouse gases in the atmosphere is the primary cause of global warming and climate change.

Greenhouse gases occur naturally, with the principal ones being water vapour (H_2O), carbon dioxide (CO_2), methane (CH_4), and nitrous oxide (N_2O). Oxygen (O_2) is not one, as it does not absorb radiation. In the form of visible, ultraviolet and infrared light, the sun's radiation strikes Earth daily, and about 70% is absorbed by the landmasses, the oceans, and our atmosphere. The remaining 30% is reflected back towards space by white surfaces, such as clouds and ice coverings.

The difference between the amounts of incoming and outgoing radiation is what keeps the Earth's temperature at optimal levels for life to thrive. Greenhouse gases play a vital role in this process, as heat radiated back into the atmosphere gets absorbed and trapped. Now acting as a thermal layer of warmth, this is known as the greenhouse effect. Without this insulating blanket of gases, temperatures would simply be too cold. Scientists estimate that the average temperature would be -18°C, which is not fit for life as we know it.

Scientists have established a clear and direct correlation between human activities and the increase in greenhouse gas emissions, principally carbon, into the atmosphere. This comes primarily from the burning of fossil fuels (coal, oil, and natural gas) associated with industrial, agricultural and transport activity, as well as deforestation.

CO_2 is the primary culprit, owing to its abundance. It comprises more than 80% of human-related emissions and can remain in the atmosphere for thousands of years. CO_2 concentration is measured by the number of CO_2 molecules found in a million molecules of dry air. This is expressed in the abbreviated form 'ppm' – one of the key indicators for global warming.

According to NASA, the build-up of greenhouse gases has reached its highest level in 800 000 years, with carbon levels having risen 40% since preindustrial times. The average atmospheric CO_2 level over the past 12 000 years has been between 200 and 280 ppm, but in 2013, the 400 ppm level was breached. At the time of writing in early 2022, the measurement was already close to 420 ppm.

Methane is produced from fossil fuels, livestock production and municipal waste, and is now 2.5 times higher than pre-Industrial Revolution levels, with the most dramatic rises occurring during the last 50 years.

Nitrous oxide comes from fossil fuels, agricultural activities and the treatment of wastewater, while a range of synthetic fluorinated gases are entering the atmosphere due to industrial processes.

To understand the extent and rate of current emissions, NASA claims that if trends continue, extrapolation models indicate that CO_2 levels could reach over 1 500 ppm within the next few centuries. This highlights how important it is for the global community to reach a consensus in climate negotiations in order to reduce emissions. According to the IPCC, nations would have to cut their emissions to zero by 2050 to ensure the 1.5°C average rise is not breached. Despite the evidence and the predicted consequences, the IPCC research shows that emissions continue to rise.

Leading emitters

Unsurprisingly, the leading emitters are the current industrial powerhouses. As of 2021, China was responsible for approximately 28%; followed by the USA (15%); the 28 countries comprising the EU (9%);

India (7%); Russia (5%); and Japan (3%). Together, they account for almost 70% of all emissions.

On a cumulative ranking that lists emissions over time, the USA (25%) leads the EU (22%), followed by China (13%), Russia (7%) and Japan (4%). The combined total of emissions for the rest of the world is 26%.

On a per-capita basis, the order changes somewhat. At 16.6 tons per person, the USA is the worst offender, according to the GCP, followed by Russia (11.7); Japan (9.1); China (7.0); the EU (6.7) and India (2.0). By comparison, the rest of the world produces 4.8 tons per person.

In 2017, the Carbon Disclosure Project (CDP) released a study that looked more closely at the actual source of emissions. It found that 71% of emissions since 1988 were linked to just 100 global fossil-fuel companies. Furthermore, those companies were found to have released more emissions in the past 28 years than the total released in the 237 years before 1988. For the complete lists and a breakdown of economic sectors and other data, see the Global Carbon Project annual carbon budget reports.

Global Carbon Dioxide Emissions (Gigatons of Carbon per Year)

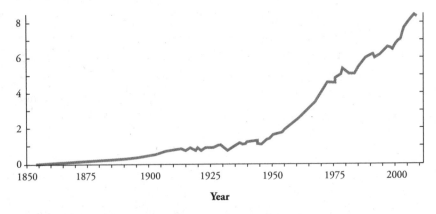

Year

FIGURE 2: Global carbon dioxide emissions since 1850

Source: NASA Earth Observatory

The science is clear: Increased human activity is causing a greater build-up of CO_2 and other greenhouse gases in the atmosphere, which in turn causes temperatures to rise.

Turning up the heat

NASA describes global warming as: 'The long-term heating of Earth's climate system, observed since the preindustrial period (between 1850 and 1900), due to human activities, primarily fossil fuel burning, which increases heat-trapping greenhouse gas levels in Earth's atmosphere.'

As mentioned, one of the primary reasons our planet carries such an incredible diversity of life is the result of optimal land temperatures that enable species to flourish. Placing exact parameters on the average temperature range is problematic, as this measurement differs according to species type. In this regard, the Proceedings of the National Academy of Sciences of the United States of America (PNAS) suggest the climatic envelope, 11–15°C being optimal for human development. However, we do know that once temperatures rise 1.5°C above the long-term average, most species are likely to be pushed closer to extinction.

NASA has been keeping temperature records since 1880, and 19 of the warmest 20 years on record have occurred since 2001. The exception was 1998, while 2016 and 2019/2020 tie as the warmest on record. Scientists believe the planet is now the hottest it's ever been in the past 12 000 years. The very latest reports from the IPCC and United in Science indicate that temperatures continue to rise at 0.2°C per decade towards the crucial 1.5°C above preindustrial average levels. The period 2015–2020 evidenced the warmest average global temperature range of any equivalent timespan since keeping records: 1.1°C above the preindustrial era average.

As the heat gets turned up, various agencies have warned that if temperatures warm beyond the optimum niche for humans, between one billion and 3.5 billion people will be at risk over the next 50 years, resulting in widespread displacement, migration and remapping of population densities. The worst affected regions are likely to be central and eastern North America, central and southern Europe, the Mediterranean (including North Africa and the near-East), western and central Asia, and southern Africa.

Climate science agencies have all warned that immediate and far-reaching changes to our living patterns, particularly our fossil fuel consumption, are required to avoid breaking the 1.5°C threshold. If temperatures climb, then the worst-case weather scenarios and eco-system tipping points start kicking in. If we move towards a 2°C rise above averages, the situation becomes catastrophic.

The consequences

Like natural climate change cycles, this current cycle of human-induced warming will also have highly disruptive, even catastrophic, consequences in unprecedented ways. The financial costs of reparations due to climate-related disasters are already at record levels.

The GRR makes this clear, as the top-ranked risks are mostly environmental ones, with climate action failure the most significant and pressing of these. In its 2022 assessment, the IPCC scientists discuss humanity's window to act as being 'brief and rapidly closing'.

Some of the most concerning specific impacts from global warming and climate change include:

- **Extreme and shifting weather patterns**: Broadly defined as events not typical to a region, or that bring significant consequences to economies and life, extreme weather patterns are being increasingly recorded across the world.
- **Melting polar regions and rising sea levels**: If current global warming and ice melting trends continue, the Arctic could lose its summer ice entirely, by as soon as 2035, but certainly by 2050. In a worst-case scenario, weather agencies predict that by 2100, sea levels could rise by as much as 2.5 metres above 2000 levels.
- **Warming oceans**: Ocean warming is now at its highest level since records began over 100 years ago. Because more CO_2 is dissolving into the oceans, seawater is becoming increasingly acidic.
- **Increased fire risks**: The regions prone to wildfires are seeing longer fire seasons. Hot and dry conditions, often fanned by high winds,

mean that fires have become more intense and deadly. Fires over the past 20 years in California, USA, the Amazon Basin in Brazil, and parts of Australia, southern Europe, Siberia and South Africa have proved to be the worst on record.

- **Disruption to food security**: Flooding, drought, fires and rising sea levels will increase the likelihood of global food supply disruptions and price shocks.
- **Health risks**: The World Health Organization (WHO) claims that nine out of 10 people on the planet now breathe polluted air. In those parts set to receive higher rainfall, insect-borne diseases such as malaria, dengue fever, and Lyme disease will increase.

As a result of these consequences, a new field in climate science research has opened up. Known as 'extreme event attribution', it involves researchers studying the human influence on global warming and the links to long-term trends in extreme weather events worldwide. In this way, scientists are learning the extent to which these events are influenced by humankind rather than being natural weather patterns.

Climate agreements and policy

The first attempts at mitigating climate change took place under the UN's auspices, as the Framework Convention on Climate Change. Adopted at the Earth Summit in Rio de Janeiro, Brazil, in 1992, the climate convention sought to recognise the impact of emissions on global climate systems, and to moderate their use.

The convention came into force with 50 ratifications in 1994. It underwent its first significant revisions as the Kyoto Protocol in 1997 when parties agreed on commitments to reduce emissions. After years of debate and bargaining, the protocol eventually came into effect in 2005. Since then, the UN, climate authorities and the scientific community have met annually to upgrade and strengthen conventions and protocols. This has taken on an increasing sense of urgency as the threats from climate change have become better understood.

In 2016, the Paris Agreement was signed, making it the most ambitious and far-reaching attempt to date. All 197 member nations of the UN signed up to a deal offering a long-term path to significant emissions cuts, complete with targets, a regulatory framework and monitoring platforms.

The agreement and subsequent sessions not only brought home the urgency of the actions needed, but also revealed how vulnerable these efforts are to political whims. In 2017, the Trump administration announced its decision to withdraw the US from the Paris Agreement, putting the entire policy in jeopardy. However, sanity prevailed in 2021 when the current Biden-led administration re-joined the agreement.

For climate policy to be effective, it must have the co-operation and involvement of all nations, especially the USA, as the world's biggest per-capita emitter of greenhouse gases. According to the IPCC, the bottom line is simple: Collectively, global governments need to find ways to reduce emissions by 45% from 2010 levels by 2030, and then reach a net-zero position by 2050, to avoid exceeding the 1.5°C threshold and worst-case scenarios that would ensue. While some view climate negotiations and policies as flawed, they remain vital in the absence of any global agency to enforce frameworks or legislation.

Denialism and alarmism

Despite the overwhelming evidence showing the links between human activity, increased emissions and global warming, dissident individuals and corporate climate change deniers continue to voice contrarian messages. Because they are likely to be most affected by climate legis-lation, this lobby is a powerful political and economic bloc primed to support those industries and companies identified as the principal emitters. Given the significance of climate change and its consequences, the degree of obfuscation is concerning.

According to the Smithsonian, the five largest oil and gas companies are spending approximately US$200 million annually to delay or block attempts to secure new climate legislation to limit emissions. In a similar vein, the *Independent* reported in 2018 that since 2000, lobby groups representing the largest emitting industries – primarily the electrical utility, fossil fuel and transportation sectors – had spent more than US$2 billion to hinder or stop climate change legislation.

Understanding denial, notably strategic denial, is fundamental to understanding why, despite the overwhelming evidence, societies and countries remain slow, or even hostile, to change. Denial plays a critical role in humanity's current predicament.

On the flip side, it is also true that we need to be aware of 'climate alarmism', in which the rate and impacts of climate change are exaggerated. With significant advances in technology, and increased focus on the issues, it is true that recording and measuring capabilities have improved. This can account for unfavourable data that was un-attainable for earlier generations. In addition, the use of language in reporting or recording is important, as inappropriate words, comments and exaggerations can have emotive and psychological impacts on the well-being of communities.

The poor use of data ultimately undermines the true nature of our challenges. But in being critical of alarmism, let us not lose sight of the fact that given the consequences of worst-case scenarios, referencing extravagant claims as a reason to deny climate change is exceptionally short-sighted.

2. Habitat loss

There is an inextricable and complex relationship between habitat, ecosystems and biodiversity (including the genetic variation of all species). One way to understand this is to view ecosystems and bio-diversity as two peas in the pod that is habitat.

Loss or destruction of habitat is regarded as the primary threat to all biodiversity – the variety of life found on the planet. Ecosystems, in turn, relate to a collection of species living within an interconnected community. The health, or otherwise, of biodiversity and their eco-systems are prime indicators of Earth's vitality.

These three pillars of all life on Earth appear as the basis of the Convention on Biological Diversity (CBD), which is arguably conservation's most important framework.

The words 'habitat' and 'ecosystem' are sometimes used interchangeably, which is incorrect. At other times, they are used so broadly that they become meaningless. The CBD refers to habitat as: 'The place or type of site where an organism, or population naturally occurs.'

The International Union for the Conservation of Nature (IUCN) simply says habitat is 'the locality or environment in which an animal lives'. Based on these definitions, every niche of a continental landmass, island, ocean and expanse of freshwater is a potential habitat for some form of life.

Earth has a total surface area of 510 064 472 square kilometres, and of this, 70.8% consists of water, with the remaining 29.2% comprising islands of land. Of the water, 97.5% is salty, and 90% of it is made up of three of the five major oceans: The Atlantic, Indian, and Pacific. These metrics indicate how important the oceans are: They provide 99% of habitable space on the planet and are vital to climate regulation, oxygen provision and carbon absorption.

Landmasses cover approximately 148 million square kilometres. Of this area, more than 99% comprises the seven continents: Asia; Africa; North America; South America; Antarctica; Europe; Australia, and all of their associated islands.

Broadly speaking, four principal habitat types exist: marine, estuarine, terrestrial, and freshwater. Depending on the institution one is referencing, and the depth of analysis provided, these types can, in turn, be subdivided into more specialised habitats. For example, terrestrial habitats can be sub-classified into tundra, forests, grasslands and desert. The IUCN Habitats Classification Scheme recognises the following terrestrial habitat types: forest, savanna, shrubland, grassland, inland wetland, rocky zones, such as inland cliffs and mountain peaks; caves and subterranean areas, and desert.

Threats to terrestrial habitats

Terrestrial habitats for wild species face many threats, almost all from unsustainable human activity. This is driven by a growing global population and increasing levels of consumption and waste production, which also feed into the broader threats of global warming and climate change.

Every environmental agency will have a list of threats, often highlighting those relating to their specific area of expertise. For a general summary, the IUCN has compiled a comprehensive Threats Classification Scheme that lists all the factors impacting habitats and species they have assessed.

One of the more comprehensive habitat assessments is given by WWF in their bi-annual Living Planet Report. The most recent edition (2020) claims that only some 25% of Earth is free from the impacts of human activities, and that under current trends, this will decline to 10% by 2050. The report lists wetlands as the worst affected habitat type, with over 85% already lost or severely degraded.

The GRR makes a similar claim. Owing to agricultural and industrial activity, 75% of all land surfaces has already been altered, 85% of wetlands has been lost, and 66% of oceans has been impacted.

The primary drivers or causes of terrestrial habitat loss are:
- **Global warming and climate change**: Extreme weather patterns play out with melting polar regions, warming oceans, rising sea levels, increased drought or rainfall, and the growing number of large-scale fires. In turn, these significantly impact habitats as they become temporarily or even permanently altered.
- **Deforestation**: According to the WWF, the planet has already lost approximately 40% of forest cover, and we continue to lose about 10 million hectares every year. South America remains the worst affected region, but Africa has the highest increase in deforestation.
- **Infrastructure development**: Given current population and urbanisation trends, an Oxford Economics study of only 50 countries forecasts that for infrastructure development to keep pace with living

requirements, a combined investment of US$3.7 trillion is needed every year until 2040. This will further add significant impacts to habitats across the natural world.

- **Agricultural practices**: By most accounts, agriculture, especially in industrialised forms such as monocultures, is already responsible for almost 80% of global deforestation and about 26% of global greenhouse gas emissions. This is set to increase as the WEF forecasts that farmers will need to produce more food in the next 40 years than they have in the last 10 000 to meet demands from a growing population as well as increasingly affluent tastes.

- **Pollution and waste disposal**: According to the United Nations Environment Programme (UNEP), over 80% of the world's waste-water is returned to the environment without any treatment. In some of the least developed nations of the world this can be as high as 95%. With regard to plastic, UNEP estimates that over 8.3 billion tons of plastic have been produced since the early 1950s, and approximately 80% remains in landfills or in the natural environment.

- **Alien and invasive species**: Typically, alien invasives can cause extensive damage to habitats because they enter new environments with no co-evolutionary history with competing species or predators. With these advantages, they out-compete native species. According to *National Geographic*, alien and invasive species cost the global economy approximately US$1.4 trillion annually.

Once habitats are changed, biodiversity losses set in, and tipping points and regime changes can occur. In this regard, scientists from the Stockholm Resilience Centre released research in October 2020 indicating that because of inconsistent rainfall patterns, about 40% of the Amazon rainforest is at serious risk of reaching a tipping point that could see it become a vast savanna region. While that process will likely take decades, the switch will result in significant biodiversity losses and have severe implications for carbon cycles.

Threats to marine habitats

Covering just over 70% of Earth's surface, marine habitats are as crucial to humans living as terrestrial ones. They are vital for the life-support systems of oxygen generation, climate regulation, and their role as carbon sinks. Besides, they hold an immense array of biodiversity, providing food and economic activity.

In addition, there are about 620 000 kilometres of coastline around the world. Approximately 32% of the global population lives within 100 kilometres. The WWF claims that over three billion people rely on marine life and farmed seafood as their primary source of protein.

Also, the oceans are the world's primary transport routes. Over 70% of all goods are moved across waters that also provide us with a range of recreational activities. Furthermore, various ecosystems: Mangrove swamps and estuaries and islands, for example, act as a buffer zone for mainland systems and people living close to the sea.

The IUCN habitat classification scheme recognises four different types of marine habitat: Oceanic, deep ocean floor, intertidal, and coastal/supratidal. All face threats similar in nature to those impacting terrestrial habitats. In other words, global warming and climate change, together with human development and expansion as well as overexploitation, are as threatening to the oceans as they are to the land.

Among the specific threats:

- **Ocean acidification:** This is significant, and according to the IPCC, since the 1970s, oceans have absorbed 93% of excess heat generated from greenhouse gas build-up. As the waters warm, they undergo physical changes, which result in increased acidity levels – a situation marine specialists believe has become as severe as the warming process itself. In addition, deoxygenation sets in, and all of these aspects lead to the significant alteration of all ocean habitats and ecosystems.

  Coral reef systems have also been severely impacted by these processes. According to the World Resources Institute (WRI), almost

40% of coral reefs are already threatened with extinction. Under current trends, about 90% of reef systems will be threatened by 2030.

- **Pollution**: In various guises, pollutants are another principal destroyer of marine habitats. More than 80% of marine pollution comes from land activities. Chemical and fertiliser run-offs from mining and agricultural projects, for example, end up in the oceans, killing estuarine and mangrove swamp habitats.

  Plastic and discarded fishing gear have become increasingly severe threats to pelagic habitats and the species that inhabit them. The Great Pacific Garbage Patch (GPGP), which extends over approximately 1.6 million square kilometres of the Pacific – a region three times the size of France – is the most well-known example. According to UNEP, if current trends of plastic use and disposal continue, the oceans may well end up containing more units of plastic than fish.

  Of additional concern to marine biologists is that collapsing marine stocks from overfishing, particularly of sharks and other apex species, such as tuna, can result in an ecological cascade. Such events end up altering entire habitats – to such an extent that they may not recover to their original natural state.

3. Biodiversity and ecosystem loss

Every comprehensive global assessment and scientific study confirms that biodiversity and ecosystems, often referred to the barometers of life, are being lost or degraded at unprecedented rates.

In May 2019, the Intergovernmental Science-Policy Platform on Biodiversity and Ecosystem Services (IPBES) released the findings of its comprehensive global assessment:

- Approximately 1 million species are now threatened with extinction.
- All ecosystems are deteriorating at unprecedented rates due to unsustainable human activity.
- Transformative change is needed to restore and protect the natural world, as the destruction is a direct threat to human well-being.

- It is to be expected that vested interests will attempt to disrupt efforts to change our living paradigms.

In summary, the authors refer to 'a global and generational threat' and warns: '*We are eroding the very foundations of our economies, livelihoods, food security, health and quality of life worldwide.*' Furthermore, they call for 'transformative change', which they describe as '*fundamental, system-wide reorganisation across technological, economic and social factors, including paradigms, goals and values*'.

Mirroring these findings, the WWF's latest Living Planet Report assesses data from 20 811 populations across 4 382 species. It reveals that since 1970, the '*population size of mammals, birds, fish, amphibians, and reptiles has seen an alarming average drop of 68%*'.

The report highlights that species population declines are especially pronounced in the tropics, with South and Central America suffering the most dramatic decline of 94% since 1970. African populations have dropped on average 65%, and the Asia-Pacific region, 45%. Freshwater species numbers have also declined dramatically, with the Freshwater Index showing an 83% decline since 1970.

Other important references are the IUCN Red Lists, a global source of information for scientists and researchers tracking the conservation status of species. As of 2020, they contain conservation assessments for more than 128 000 threatened species. According to the most recent lists, 35 765 of the assessed species (27%) are threatened with extinction. This includes 41% of amphibians, 26% of mammals, 14% of birds, 33% of reef corals, 34% of conifers, and 27% of crustaceans.

In an update for late 2020, the IUCN announced that 31 species, mostly amphibians and fish, had moved into the extinct category and that all five freshwater dolphin species are now on the threatened list. The one positive note was the recovery of European bison populations.

The Millennium Ecosystem Assessment (MA), the precursor to the IPBES assessment, was the first ever extensive report on ecosystems. The MA found that over the previous 50 years, humans had altered ecosystems more extensively and rapidly than at any other time in human history. More specifically, of 24 separate ecosystems identified (all vital for life on Earth to thrive), 60% of them had been irreversibly damaged or degraded. In turn, this degradation had resulted in significant biodiversity losses.

The report concluded that access to ecosystem services for future generations had already been compromised, and to halt and reverse the degradation, current 'policies, institutions and practices' would have to be changed immediately.

Threats to biodiversity and ecosystems

Humans represent only 0.01% of Earth's biomass. However, according to the PNAS, since the dawn of humanity, we have caused the loss of 83% of terrestrial mammals, 80% of marine mammals, and 50% of all plants.

The same study found that of all the mammalian biomass on Earth, including domesticated livestock (cattle and pigs being the majority) comprised 60%, and humans made up 36%. Wild mammals made up a paltry 4%. Of bird biomass on the planet, farmed poultry comprises 70%, while wild birds comprise a mere 30%.

These startling statistics indicate in the starkest terms how *Homo sapiens* and our domesticated beasts have come to dominate Earth. In this process, the same human-induced factors that have destroyed habitats are also the primary factors for the loss of biodiversity and their ecosystems. Simply put, species are not capable of escaping or adapting to the pace at which humanity is altering environments, exploiting resources and fragmenting habitats. With the impacts of climate change, some mobile species will be able to migrate to higher or cooler altitudes or latitudes, while inland ones may escape sea-level rise, but many more sedentary species won't be able to do this.

Trees and plants, for example, can only migrate through reproduction and seed dispersal. The polar bears of the Arctic are another sobering example. If current greenhouse gas build-up persists and Arctic ice continues to melt, researchers predict that by 2040, this iconic species will begin to experience reproductive failure. By 2100, the great white bears will likely have disappeared from their range, other than for the far, northern-most islands of Canada.

Overexploitation

The overexploitation of natural resources is particularly impactful on biodiversity and ecosystems, and because the practices are so prevalent worldwide, they warrant further discussion.

The IUCN defines natural resources as those produced by Nature – and they distinguish two categories: Non-renewable and renewable. Non-renewable resources include fossil fuels (those that will regenerate, but only within a geological timescale) and minerals. On the other hand, renewable resources include naturally renewable plant and animal life and life-sustaining resources, such as water and solar radiation.

Overexploitation is defined by the IUCN as the 'use or extraction of a resource to the point of exhaustion or extinction' that arises from unsustainable harvesting – processes in which consumption rates exceed natural regeneration. Ironically, there are no legal consequences attached to unsustainable use.

Overexploitation is widespread in every economic sector and covers activities such as the demand for raw timber or marine foods; the extraction of mineral resources; our desires for vanity and comfort products, as well as the excessive development occurring in certain tourism hotspots. In essence, overexploitation relates to humanity's rapacious consumptive-driven lifestyles, the services we demand and, our ignorance or wilful disregard for the consequences.

The IPBES report notes several indicators that point to over-exploitation, including the observation that the extraction of renewable and non-renewable resources has increased by 100% since 1980. WWF's Living Planet Report 2020 corroborates this. Using the Ecological Footprint Index as an average indicator, it calculates that over the past 50 years, the global footprint has increased by 190%.

As already mentioned, humanity already requires 1.7 Earth's worth of resources to meet our current demands, and if unchecked, this will rise to 2.3 Earth's by 2050. On a per capita basis, the UN states that global domestic material consumption, the goods and services used by an economy to meet consumption and living needs, rose more than 40%, or from 8,7 to 12,2 metric tons, from 2000 to 2017.

Clearly, we cannot escape personal responsibility for this situation. We are all consumers, and as such, every single one of us is involved. This means that we have to ask uncomfortable questions about the choices we make:

- Are our lifestyles and levels of consumption necessary?
- Should we be eating seafood, for example, and if so, what species and to what extent?
- What about red meat consumption?
- Have we used rare hardwoods in our home, and was this necessary?
- What forms of transport do we use and at what frequency? What sustainable alternatives, if any, are available?

We have to question every aspect of our consumption and living, as reducing overexploitation – our individual ecological footprint – is all about purchasing and consuming less while also reducing waste loads.

Poaching

Poaching poses a significant threat and is a menacing form of overexploitation, as it generally refers to the illegal killing and/or removal of wild species from any protected and non-protected area.

The International Fund for Animal Welfare (IFAW) points out that poaching is not only about killing or removing the species involved, it also entails the loss of offspring. Over time, ongoing poaching impacts the general health of a targeted species' population and the ecosystem of which it is a part. Furthermore, poaching endangers the lives of park rangers and others who manage wildlife and protected areas.

Poaching happens at one of three different levels, and it is essential to distinguish between them, as each is driven by different factors and should be dealt with accordingly.

- **Subsistence poaching:** This refers to localised incidents and its occurrence can be linked to the colonial processes of conquest and dispossession of ancestral lands. These are usually perpetrated by people living in or close to poverty who trap/collect and hunt animals/plants to feed themselves or an extended family. Typically, they use snares or dogs to seek out small species, such as warthog, smaller primates, and small to medium-sized antelope. Subsistence poachers are also actively involved in illegal fishing, using gill nets on freshwater bodies around Africa. They collect firewood, building materials and plant-based foods.

- **Commercial bushmeat poaching and logging**: This involves commercial activity, primarily by people from the region, and often working in extended family networks. These poachers seek out species, like buffalo, zebra, wildebeest and other large antelope, as well as larger primates, such as gorillas and chimpanzees, to sell in local bushmeat markets and butcheries. They will also collect hardwoods and other trees/plants for collectors or syndicates.
- **Syndicate poaching**: This form of poaching involves large, well-funded criminal networks who operate on a more widespread or international scale. Typically armed with powerful weapons and aided by technology, the focus is on high-value species for the international markets, where prices are significantly higher than at source. Examples include species such as rhinoceros for their horns, elephant for their ivory, pangolin for their scales, and lion for their bones and other body parts. Expensive timber and sought-after plants, such as cycads, are also traded. Syndicates are also involved in bribery and corruption, as well as other forms of crime, such as arms trafficking, money laundering, and the drug trade.

Wildlife poaching can, over time, have devastating impacts on a species' population levels. South Africa has lost more than 9 000 rhinos to poaching syndicates since 2008 – numbers that significantly increase the extinction risks to the species.

Elephants serve as another example in this regard. IFAW estimates that almost 100 elephants are poached every 24 hours across Africa. Furthermore, National Geographic research suggests that the continent lost over 100 000 elephants between 2014 and 2017, with Central and East Africa being most affected.

Rampant syndicate poaching also occurs in the oceans. In a 2018 report released by NGO TRAFFIC, the estimated annual value of the illegal abalone market in South Africa was US$60 million. The same report claimed that approximately 96 million abalone had been poached in the prior 18-year period – a rate that places the species in line for extinction in South Africa's waters.

Plunder of the Commons

The *Plunder of the Commons* is a book by British economist Guy Standing that details why shared or communal natural wealth – which is every aspect of the environment – is so important to human health, and how it has been plundered by self-interest over the centuries.

Standing's book is founded on a concept known as the 'tragedy of the commons'. The phrase came into being way back in 1833 in the writings of economist William Forster Lloyd, who defined the commons as 'common property' – the natural resources, such as rivers, oceans, and open land shared by all, for the benefit of all.

The tragedy arises when people or communities, without the constraints of private property or exclusivity clauses, and acting in their own self-interest, overuse or overexploit these resources to the extent of depletion, placing the common interest at risk. American ecologist Garrett Hardin argued that the short-term interests of individuals, corporates and countries would result in overexploitation of unprotected common resources, with significant negative consequences for society at large, if limits or restrictions were not in place.

The exploitation of global marine fish species serves as an interesting example. During the 1980s and 1990s, with little to no restrictions, overexploitation of marine stocks was at its most rampant with harvest rates at times being well above the abundance of fish. Consequently, certain fisheries started collapsing, and alarm bells rang throughout the environmental community. Then, in the late 1990s and early 2000s, nations from North America and Europe got together and implemented long-term, science-based fishing management policies – including an enforcement capacity.

This approach has paid dividends, as the Food and Agriculture Organisation of the United Nations (FAO) assessments within the last decade indicate that stocks are stabilising, or even increasing, but only where sound management policies are in place.

The plunder continues in regions with no protection. In 2015, the IPBES reported that 33% of global 'marine fish stocks were being harvested at unsustainable levels'. They also noted that a mere 7% were 'harvested at levels lower than what can be sustainably fished'. In 2021, the Global Seafood Alliance found that almost 50% of global fish stocks have been depleted to less than 40% of pre-fishing population levels.

Most areas within the oceans remain unprotected or unpoliced, and are used as a 'commons', especially in regions such as Africa, Asia and the southern oceans. In these regions, stocks are being overexploited, or in some cases, are on the verge of collapse. Unregulated fishing by various Asian nations has played a significant role in reducing fish stocks in both West African and East African waters. According to *Science Daily*, a recent study sample of coral systems and reef species across 239 sites reported plummeting fish stocks and that 70% were 'below levels that will produce the maximum fisheries yields'.

Certain groups of marine species – sharks and rays, for example – remain under serious threat of overexploitation. According to the latest IUCN assessments of these groups, the oceanic whitetip shark, once regarded as abundant, has lost 98% of its global population and is now considered critically endangered. Other shark species, such as the great white and hammerhead, as well as the rhino ray, are all facing widespread declines from overexploitation.

While marine species are an obvious example, global pollution levels and carbon build-up in the atmosphere are other examples of this prophecy of tragedy.

Genetic pollution

Under its Threats Classification Scheme, the IUCN Red Lists include genetic pollution as a primary threat to biodiversity. Genetic pollution arises via genetic engineering techniques and refers to the introduction of altered or contaminated genes into wild populations. These include hybridisation methods commonly used to improve yields in food products – known as genetically modified organisms (GMOs) – and a host of animal husbandry procedures for domestic and wild species.

There may be examples of genetic intervention having positive impacts, but without strict controls and the scientific community's guidance, these contaminated genes can enter the wild gene pool and destroy what has taken evolution millions of years to produce. In most cases, the wild gene is compromised, and sometimes the gene can collapse, putting species at risk of extinction.

These concerns are particularly pertinent to South Africa's flourishing wildlife ranching industry, where a host of wild species are being commercially exploited, at times through the manipulation of the gene pool. Some operators interbreed recognised subspecies and populations, such as sable antelope, wildebeest, and lion. The emphasis on specific morphological traits holds worthwhile commercial incentives for the trophy hunting and wildlife trade industries. For example, such breeding practices produce longer horns or larger manes, while in extreme cases, entirely new variations or mutants, such as 'golden wildebeest' and 'white springbok', are created.

Because of the obvious risks to wild populations, these practices are contrary to every aspect of the CBD. Besides, breeding these wild species occurs on heavily fenced and managed farms where the principal objective is to maximise commercial gain. In essence, these crude methods are simply agricultural and have nothing to do with conservation.

In October 2019, the South African government went a significant step further down the path of genetic pollution. A brief amendment to the Animal Improvement Act (AIA) declared lions, cheetah, rhino and zebra among 33 wild species to be farm animals.

In early 2020, a group of biologists and ecologists from various South African universities declared the move 'fundamentally flawed' when measuring the risks to wild species. 'The genetic consequences of intensive or semi-intensive breeding (farming) of wildlife species are negative, and considerable,' said the authors.

In addition, the risks will be significantly increased if the private sector is allowed to self-regulate. They are currently lobbying to get this approved, claiming that the industry should be entitled to reach its full potential. In effect, they are asking for approval to do whatever they wish with the gene pool of wild species to make farming them as profitable as possible.

The extinction crisis

Extinction is a natural and inevitable biological event. It's as integral to the evolutionary process as the advent of new species. In fact, the scientific community believes that 99% of all species that have ever lived on Earth are already extinct.

The IUCN describes extinction as 'an irreversible process whereby a species or distinct biological population forever ceases to exist'. This happens when the last member of a species dies, taking with it its entire genetic heritage. Although extinction is a natural process, it is important to understand the difference between background extinction and mass extinction.

Background extinction (sometimes referred to as normal extinction) relates to the ongoing rate of species extinction over extended periods and without cataclysmic or other naturally disruptive episodes to habitats and biodiversity. Typically, background rates are slow and occur owing to genetic, competition and environmental reasons. Fossil records suggest that these rates are between 0.1 and 1 species per 10 000 species per 100 years. Depending on how many species exist on the planet, this translates into somewhere between 10 and 100 species per million years.

In contrast, mass extinctions occur over much shorter periods and are associated with cataclysmic natural events, such as volcanic eruptions, meteor strikes and rapid temperature changes. During these events, large numbers of species die out. Typically, this equates to at least 75% of a group of species, but in some instances, up to 90% of all species have been lost. Mass extinctions have always resulted in a new wave of speciation after the die-off, as other life forms take opportunities to flourish under novel conditions.

The fossil record shows that Earth has experienced five mass extinctions in the past 500 million years:

- Ordovician-Silurian Extinction: About 445 million years ago.
- Late Devonian Extinction: About 383–359 million years ago.
- Permian-Triassic Extinction: About 252 million years ago.
- Triassic-Jurassic Extinction: About 200 million years ago.
- Cretaceous-Paleogene Extinction: About 66 million years ago.

According to the scientific community contributing to the IPBES report, the world is heading towards another major extinction event. Widely referred to as the 'Sixth Mass Extinction', this one is entirely different because the cause is not natural – it rests on human activities.

More than a million species are currently threatened with extinction and, depending on the number of species taken as the baseline, species loss is occurring at between 100 and 10 000 times higher than the background rate. The most comprehensive extinction list is kept by the IUCN, and in their 2019 Red List assessment, 873 species have gone extinct since 1500 – a figure significantly above the average background rate.

Ecologists are also concerned about the phenomenon known as an extinction cascade, in which the loss of one species can cause a domino effect of further losses to many more species. In such cases, entire ecosystems can become vulnerable. Avoiding such catastrophic cascades is of huge consequence for life on Earth.

We also have the notion of extinction debt. The IPBES refers to this as the future extinction of species due to events in the past, and owing to a time lag between an effect such as habitat destruction or climate change, and the subsequent disappearance of species.

As we have established, habitat loss is one of the biggest threats to species extinction, but the actual disappearance may only occur long after the destruction occurs. This process provides significantly greater conservation challenges as it relates to a compounded situation.

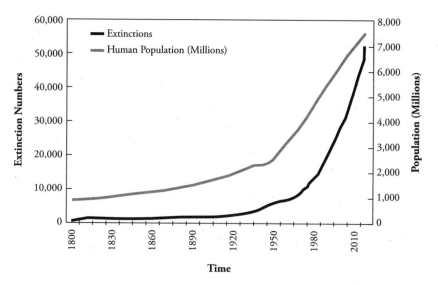

FIGURE 3: The link between rising human population and the extinction rates of other vertebrates.

Source: Center for Biological Diversity

Trophy hunters going after the gene pool

With so many scientists talking about a mounting mass extinction crisis, the role of trophy hunting from both an ethical and conservation perspective needs to be reviewed (see 'Trophy Hunting will End Up Killing Itself', for a more detailed discussion).

Ethics and conservation are inextricably linked in this thorny subject as the entire premise of trophy hunting is based on killing animals so that the hunter can claim and display a trophy. Take a little time to review the marketing websites and magazines within the industry: Almost every operator sells their services based on the size of horns, manes, tusks, and whatever other body part is desired by prospective hunting clients. Then there are the record books in which the prize kills are proudly listed, and the hunting fairs where the stories are recounted.

To support the marketing claims offering the biggest trophies, hunters are unavoidably targeting the fittest and healthiest animals within populations, as these carry the prize body parts. In the words of one particular hunting operator: 'The excitement of the hunt, thrill of the chase, the final result of a spectacular trophy, this is why we hunt ...'

Hunters also go after rare species, at times in locations with low and vulnerable population densities. By targeting prize trophies, the hunters follow the unnatural process of human selection over natural selection. Once the quarry is killed, its genes are lost forever.

These same targeted animals are often prime breeding specimens – a genetic core vital to the survival of endangered and threatened species. For any species in decline, every breeding animal is critically important – not only for the survival of its population, but also for the species as a whole. Furthermore, if the chosen animal is either an apex or keystone species, is not the overall health of the entire ecosystem at risk?

In Africa, such impacts play out with lion and elephant. By way of example, trophy-hunting offtake and dispersal reduced the average size of male elephant tusks in Botswana's Tuli Block, while in various parks and reserves in Tanzania, a decline in the number of prime breeding male lions has been documented by researchers. We also know that when pride males are removed, the entire cub group is at risk of being killed by new males taking over the territory. Trophy hunting has had similar impacts on lions in West and Central Africa.

Given this, we have to ask the ethical question: Is the recreational killing of species that everyone else is trying so desperately to conserve an appropriate way to attempt conservation? Besides, if we know the ecological costs, is the continued sanctioning of trophy hunting not an act of recklessness?

Developing without ecological considerations

Since the onset of the Industrial Revolution, human societies have grown and expanded their reach significantly. In the process, vast amounts of habitat (along with the biodiversity found there) have been lost, degraded, or fragmented because of indiscriminate development.

The establishment of settlements, many burgeoning into the massive metropolitan cities of today, and the network of infrastructure that goes with them, as well as decisions on mining, ports, industrial zones and agricultural projects, continue to be made on economic and convenience grounds for human benefit. Ecological considerations, which may include being mindful of migration routes, feeding grounds and territorial ranges of animals, or pollution levels, the seasonal flows of wetland systems and tidal activity along coastlines, have seldom been accounted for.

Typically, the environmental destruction and loss of natural habitat resulting from development has merely been seen as an 'externality'. We have assumed that the damage or loss is perfectly acceptable, in the same way that civilian deaths in military actions are casually accepted as 'collateral damage'.

It is imperative that decision-makers, both at government and private sector level, accept that we can no longer afford to simply pursue development agendas in this manner. Development of all types must avoid the ecological damage wrought over the last 300 years. It's not an argument about being against development; rather, it should be about why we develop, where we develop and how we develop.

Here in Africa, have we learnt anything from the historical destruction of the natural world on other continents? Or do we continue to base our development agendas purely on economic and political terms? The good news for the continent is that we still have significant tracts of wilderness and biomass to protect. However, according to the African Development Bank, the continent also needs to spend between US$150 billion and US$175 billion on infrastructure development per annum to meet the demands of population and economic growth.

To avoid the losses that occurred across much of the northern hemisphere, the continents development agendas are going to have to include extensive environmental research and science into their policy-making processes. These ecological considerations must become the basis for policy decisions, otherwise we are doomed to repeat what has gone on elsewhere.

The development of tourism facilities is not exempt from this concern. For example, large hotels and apartment blocks catering to mass-market tourism have degraded vast swathes of coastline around the world. In Africa, the safari, or so-called ecotourism sector, must deal with the ever-increasing number of camps and lodges situated within or alongside national parks and protected areas. Few would argue that well-known destinations, such as the Masai Mara in Kenya, parts of Chobe National Park in Botswana, the slopes of Mount Kilimanjaro in Tanzania, and the southern regions of Kruger National Park in South Africa, are already overutilised and crowded, to the extent that both the environment and the experience suffers.

All of these camps and lodges require extensive road networks for game drives, as wells as additional facilities, such as airstrips and staff housing. Further impacts include waste disposal, a demand for fresh water, and the population pressure that comes with employment opportunities.

Given this, it is greatly concerning that governments and regional authorities continue to promote tourism growth in protected areas that are already overtraded. The Serengeti in Tanzania is well on its way to matching the madness of the Masai Mara in Kenya. The Okavango Delta in Botswana remains the poster example of low-volume tourism. But, 20 years from now, I would not be surprised if the government opts for short-term revenue streams over long-term environmental integrity by allowing a multitude new concessions and camps. Botswana could well end up just another over-traded destination crammed with too many safari camps and game-drive vehicles.

4. The role of human behaviour and leadership

When describing climate change and the broader environmental crisis, the damaging role played by humans is the common stand-out factor listed by researchers and scientists the world over. Despite the knowing, as well as explanations warning of the consequences of inaction, it is of equal concern that humanity is seemingly unable to respond with the same level of urgency it does to immediate threats – ones that are often less consequential.

Beyond doubt, our behaviour and the role of leadership is central to any critical analysis of change. To understand the full spectrum of how we and our leaders are failing, we also need to understand denialism and wilful neglect. Both are common approaches to defeating or obstructing change, and as we seek to transition our societies, they may end up being just as damaging.

Behaviour and leadership are complex and overlapping, interlaced with links to cultural development, biology, psychology, and sociology, among other fields. And while this is not the place to delve deeply into these subjects, some points are worth noting because they are critical when dealing with our challenges.

Possibly the best way to envisage the critical role behaviour and leadership will play is to outline the nature of the challenges, and so get to understand the enormity of the task. At its core, we face what Al Gore called 'an inconvenient truth' – one that says our current living patterns are simply not sustainable. Almost every concern we have raised has emerged as a primary result of human behaviour. If current practices continue, our existence becomes very uncertain. Logically, this means that all societies, including every far-flung community, needs to consider and champion ways to change our living patterns.

It also means that each one of us will have to make fundamental and, in many instances, 'inconvenient' changes to our own and our families' lifestyles. The scientific community is also telling us that the changes required are urgent. Short-terminism won't do – the changes required must incorporate long-term thinking and actions. These decisions are likely to have profound implications for the environment as well as for future generations. They need to be extremely well considered.

Our solutions will also need to be collective, based on consensus and a single vision built on partnerships and shared thinking across many regions, sectors and disciplines. We are starting out on our transformational challenge in a world that already carries high polarisation and mistrust within societies, cultures and across nations and regional blocs. This erosion of unity and trust permeates the political structures of individual states, their electoral systems, courts, parliaments, and the media. It extends into global institutions, such as the UN and the range of conventions and protocols that exist to keep our global fabric intact.

When we match the average leadership profile currently in positions of power with what we need, it does not bode well. The fact-denying populism favoured by the likes of Bolsonaro in Brazil, Trump in the USA and Masisi in Botswana, for example, competes with the misery brought upon nations led by authoritarian and dictatorial leaders who cling to power in countries such as North Korea, Russia, and Egypt. And let's not forget the failed states of Zimbabwe, Libya, and Haiti, where most citizens are battling to survive.

None of these leaders, and many others, have grasped the extent of our inconvenient truth. And it's unlikely they have the inclination or intuition to unravel what German design theorist Horst Rittel referred to as a 'wicked problem' – one that carries untold complexities, contradictions and dilemmas.

The dreadful irony is that as we face our greatest set of challenges, we arguably have the poorest global leadership in recent history. Central to this is what I believe to be a truism: we the electorates of the world have failed to grasp that political life no longer has anything to do with leadership. There are far too many people without leadership skills entering the political space as a career move, while very few true leaders volunteer or survive in the cauldron of politics.

Our best hopes are likely to come from social entrepreneurs, agents of change, people and leaders who can empower our societies through a bottom-up approach. Innovative and bold by nature, they can disrupt the status quo through honest, inclusive and consistent leadership at community and regional levels of society. These actions will hopefully translate into a common vision and message; a shared purpose that inspires effort towards greater collective behavioural change.

No doubt, it's an extremely tall order, and I believe humanity is now faced with our greatest challenge ever.

Another warning: The COVID-19 pandemic

It hardly seems possible that we needed another warning about the implications of our living patterns, but maybe we did. Despite so many telling events over the past decades, fundamental change has not taken place.

According to *Live Science*, the first case of COVID-19 was traced back to November 2019, when a 55-year-old from Hubei Province in China contracted the virus. It started spreading, but by the end of the year, it was still regarded as a localised outbreak centred in the province of Wuhan.

That all changed on 11 March 2020, when the WHO declared a pandemic. Now, by mid-2022, the global tally of cases has passed 600 million, and over six million have died across 223 countries and territories worldwide. What started as a health crisis defined by its contagious nature, and death rates above most other viral diseases, soon became a series of interlocking crises. Fanned by severe economic slowdowns, the pandemic spread anxiety and confusion around the world. Most countries went into lockdown, some stricter than others; international travel and trade ground to a halt, and most regions of the world ended up dealing with a range of serious social consequences, too.

In such times, nations typically experience rising anger and distrust towards institutions and the politicians or authorities that manage them. This pandemic has proved no exception. As the infection and death rates soared, so, too, did the debate around its origins, who was most to blame, how best to deal with it, and the implications for global societies.

Covid literature has already spawned a mountain of thought and debate, not least being whether this was an unforeseen crisis, or an entirely predictable eventuality. Looking back, we would have to admit the signs were there, with localised outbreaks of other zoonotic diseases, such as severe acute respiratory syndrome (SARS), Middle East respiratory syndrome (MERS), and various occurrences of Ebola over the last two decades.

As the global community continues to pick itself up off the floor, this warning unmasks a number of gaping holes that exist in our societies and living patterns. It has shattered our health systems, exposed the true nature of environmental policies, and highlighted vulnerabilities in our political and leadership regimes. With the poor and various ethnic groups suffering the brunt and significantly higher death rates, it has also magnified many economic and social inequalities. As UN Secretary-General António Guterres rightly observes, Covid has exposed 'the lie that free markets can deliver healthcare for all; the fiction that unpaid care work is not work, the delusion that we live in a post-racist world, and the myth that we are all in the same boat.'

In an African context, the pandemic also revealed frailties within our ecotourism and conservation models. With no visitors, the funding for most protected areas and the biodiversity they hold almost dried up, leaving the environment exposed to the underworld of poachers, illegal loggers and wildlife traders. This should serve as an incentive to the conservation community and governments to review all existing funding models.

An ironic twist on all of this has reaffirmed the links between human activity and the environmental crisis, a reality Ian McCallum has highlighted in an earlier chapter. Unfortunately, relief for the wilderness only lasted until global economies began recovering, but that window was enough to highlight the destructive role we play.

One of the pandemic's more intriguing sideshows has been a tussle that has continued through the entire period: The peculiar anti-collective stance taken, initially by anti-mask groups, who were then joined by anti-vaxxers. Given the scientific clarity on the contagious nature of COVID-19, as well as near unanimity among the medical community that mask-wearing and vaccines (including historical successes dealing with polio, chickenpox and tetanus, among others) clearly assist with preventing the spread and further deaths, why would people use an anti-approach as a tool to make a political or social stand when it could kill others?

Researchers and sociologists have come up with various insights into the justifications, often not expressed by the protagonists, but underpinning the behaviour. These range from a host of related and unrelated anti-government grievances, from religious reasons to stands against poor or muddled communication and policy directives from medical and government officials. Other misguided revolts include perceptions of threats to personal freedoms, and support for fringe or even conspiracy theories.

Such stands during a deadly pandemic seem foolish and utterly inappropriate. In the words of the CNN campaign that ran during much of the pandemic: 'A mask can say a lot about the person who wears it; even more about the person who doesn't.' Paul Ash, writing in South Africa's *Financial Mail*, recounted how a psychologist had referred to not wearing a mask as 'a lazy, sloppy way to be a psychopath'.

In addition to the needless threat to so many lives, the anti-mask and anti-vax stand also speaks to society's deep-rooted disunity and polarisation, as well as to levels of general disgruntlement. They serve to highlight the nature of a 'wicked' problem, and how problematic the engineering of a shared vision on any transformative change is going to be.

Ultimately, this pandemic has also been unlike other in recent memory. It spread with lightning speed, caused havoc globally, and killed millions of people. Covid is likely to prove a defining period for an entire generation, as its features have exposed how vulnerable our living and personal freedoms are. Despite our smartness, it has also peeled back the notion that we have complete control over our destiny. While we seemingly understand a fair amount about our own human world, we clearly still have much to learn about the natural world and how to co-ordinate a unified global campaign. This begs the question: Will we have the vision to learn anything from this and take the transformative actions needed at the scale that will prevent similar and possibly far worse events?

4 /

SCIENCE, POETRY AND NATURE

{ *Ian McCallum* }

This chapter is derived from a presentation I made at a conference in San Francisco October 2016. Titled 'Science, Poetry and Nature', it addressed the need to find new ways to convey the environmental message.

'There was a time when science and poetry were one … and its name was magic,' wrote Irish-born poet Cecil Day-Lewis. It is time to bring science and poetry together again, to rekindle that magic, to reawaken our forgotten sense of kinship with all living things. It is time to find our voices and to raise them, so that others may raise theirs for the Earth.

Central to my work as an analytical therapist is the task of self-examination: Helping my patients to come to know themselves a little better; to recognise their personal contributions to their suffering and, most challenging of all, to assist them in the discovery of a voice. It is an authority that is natural to them. Honest self-examination, however, is not confined to a consulting room.

I have had the privilege of travelling and working in some of Africa's most beautiful and remote wild areas. It has been a learning journey. I have learnt a lot about myself from my patients, but I have learned even more from the wild. I have come to understand that the identity we seek for ourselves as individuals is impossible to define outside of our relationships – not only human to human, but to animals, the landscapes, oceans, forests and rivers in our lives. Who and what would we be without them?

I have come to realise with a deepening sense of awe and excitement that you and I are living museums of the entire history of life on Earth and more ... the history of the universe itself. William Blake was right: We are indeed 'stardust'. It makes sense to me that there is no such thing as human nature, that there is only Nature and the very human expression of it – that we are in it and of it. Somehow, we have forgotten this. We speak of Nature as something 'out there', to be utilised, visited or tamed. Our disconnection has come at a significant cost to the natural environment.

Spanish poet Antonio Machado in his poem *The Wind One Brilliant Day* puts it this way:

> The wind, one brilliant day,
> called to my soul with an odour of jasmine.
> In return for the odour of my jasmine,
> I'd like all the odour of your roses.
>
> 'I have no roses; all the flowers
> in my garden are dead.'
>
> 'Well then, I'll take the withered petals
> and the yellow leaves and the waters of the fountain.'
>
> The wind left. And I wept. And my soul said to me:
> 'What have you done with the garden that was entrusted to you?'

What have *we* done to the garden? Let's put this question into perspective.

One of the most iconic photographs of the 20th century must surely be that taken by the American astronaut William Anders on 24 December 1968: The picture of the Earth rising above the surface of our moon. The image and memory of the event deeply influenced the lives of Anders and his fellow *Apollo 8* astronauts, James Lovell and flight commander Frank Borman. Anders had this to say: 'We came all the way to the moon to discover the Earth.'

James Lovell's response was equally poetic: 'From this distance ... you can hide the Earth behind your thumb. Everything that you've ever known of the Earth is all behind your thumb.'

In the nearly 50 years since that picture was taken, half of the world's wetlands, peat beds and rain forests have vanished. In the wake of accelerated global warming, 400 000 square kilometres of Arctic Sea ice – the size of Germany and Switzerland combined – have melted. The human population has doubled, while that of the world's wild mammals, reptiles, amphibians and fish has halved. Africa's iconic elephants are being killed by poachers for their ivory at a rate of roughly five animals every hour. As for the critically endangered rhinoceros, one animal is killed every eight hours for its horn.

We are in the grips of an ecological amnesia. Simply put: We have forgotten where we have come from. Psychologically disconnected from our wild origins and from the elements, a predictable human behavioural pattern follows: What we cannot understand or embrace, we either demean or fear. That which we fear and belittle, we inevitably destroy. What we have here is not an animal tragedy, but a human-animal tragedy. It is a condition in which there are no winners.

Deep down, we all know that we have to live differently, but could it be we don't want to know? The scientific message, and with it human accountability, is too depressing for many, and for some too late. I refuse to accept these excuses. If we can't hear the ecological warning calls of science, then the only voice left that can awaken us belongs to the poets. In his poem from *A Passage to India,* Walt Whitman writes:

> After the seas are all cross'd (as they already seem cross'd)
> After the great captains and engineers have accomplish'd their work,
> After the noble inventors ... the scientists, the chemist, the geologist, ethnologist,
> Finally shall come the Poet ...

Finally shall come the poet? Finally, there shall come the songwriters; sculptors; artists; photographers; musicians and writers who 'speak' for science and soul – who narrow the gap between subject and object. They are individuals whose work and words speak with anger, beauty, outrage, care and compassion, all in the same breath. Poetry is, in essence, self-examining. It tells the truth. As Emily Dickenson insists, it tells it 'slant'. It comes from the depth of oneself, sometimes silencing you as it speaks. It is a language of protest, but also a language of hope. It shows the way.

I wrote this poem in 1998:

Have we forgotten
that wilderness is not a place,
but a pattern of soul
where every tree, every bird and beast
is a soul maker?

Have we forgotten
that wilderness is not a place
but a moving feast of stars,
footprints, scales and beginnings?

Since when
did we become afraid of the night
and that only the bright stars count?
or that our moon is not a moon
unless it is full?

By whose command were the animals
through groping fingers,
one for each hand,
reduced to the big and little five?

Have we forgotten
that every creature is within us
carried by tides of earthly blood
and that we named them.

Have we forgotten
that wilderness is not a place
but a season
and we are in its
final hour?

I believe that there is a poet in every human being. By this, I do not mean a talent restricted to the composition of written rhyme and verse. Rather, it is a force, a creative instinct that once awakened, naturally rhymes with the elements. It is the untamable voice of the soul ... that part of you that knows without having been taught or advised that behind yours and my thumb is the entire history of life on this planet ... that we are connected, that we belong.

It is the poet in you, who when looking into the eye of an animal, a child, a flower or a tree, asks: 'Who is looking at who?'

Look! Listen! Genetically bound to all living things, there is so much of us in them, and of them in us. Every mammal has more than 90% of the human genome. Birds and reptiles share more than 80% ... insects more than 40% ... trees and plants between 10–24%. We are the human animal. What a privilege, and what a responsibility. This is the science. Here is the poetry: Written in 1918, long before the unravelling of the human genome, American poet Carl Sandburg put these words together. Listen for the magic.

There is a wolf in me ... fangs pointed for tearing gashes ... a red tongue for raw meat ... and the hot lapping of blood – I keep the wolf because the wilderness gave it to me and the wilderness will not let it go.

There is a fox in me ... a silvery-grey ... I guess and I sniff things out of the wind and air ... I circle and loop and double cross.

There is a hog in me ... a snout and a belly ... a machinery for eating and grunting ... a machinery for sleeping satisfied in the sun – I got this too from the wilderness ...

There is a fish in me ... I know I come from salt-blue-water-gates ... I scurried with shoals of herrings ... I blew water spouts with porpoises ... long before land ... long before Noah ... long before that first chapter of Genesis

There is a baboon in me ... hairy under the arm pits ... ready to sing and give milk ... waiting – I keep the baboon because the wilderness says so.

There's an eagle and an owl and a mockingbird ... O, I got a zoo, I got a menagerie, inside my ribs, under my bony head, under my red-valve heart – And I got something else: it is a man-child heart, a woman-child heart: it is a father and mother and lover: it comes from God-knows-where: it is going to God-knows-where – for I am the keeper of the zoo: I say yes and no: I sing and kill and work: I am a pal of the world: I come from the wilderness.

* * *

In search of a renewed sense of sanity, I turned to the animals. On our 5 000 km journey through six southern African countries in 2012, we followed traditional elephant migration routes and clusters. Although we had various objectives for that initiative, but the underlying message was this: If we can't take care of an animal this big, how on Earth are we going to look after the little things?

Finally, 125 days later, physically exhausted and with much to digest, I wondered what I had learnt most from the journey. It eventually came to me.

If the *Apollo* astronauts went all the way to the moon to discover the Earth, I went into the heart of southern Africa to discover a different perspective on the future of human co-existence with the wild. It centred on the concept of keystone species: Creatures that play an essential role in maintaining the integrity of ecosystems. The word 'keystone' refers to the wedge-shaped stone at the top of an arch. If you remove that stone, the arch will collapse. It is a powerful metaphor. Elephants, termites and bees are perfect examples of keystone species.

A different perspective

To appreciate the bigger picture, it helps to be able to look at elephant dung a little differently. Apart from its value as a fertiliser, the retained moisture in elephant dung is, in the dry season, often the sole source of water for countless species of butterflies, moths, and insects. The undigested seeds and grasses provide food for baboons, birds and beetles. Despite their impact on trees, elephants are historically, via the recycling of the undigested seeds, Africa's greatest tree planters.

Human beings are not a keystone species. The Earth's ecosystems will be better off without us. Herein lies a personal challenge. Although we are not a keystone species, we can each choose to be a keystone individual: Someone who is prepared to be disturbed, and to reject assumptions about what we are told we need and should want, despite the cost to the Earth and our fellow species. We can make a difference to the lives of others, to the animals and to the Earth. Are you willing to be disturbed, to stand firm in the knowledge that there are some things worth fighting for, and some things that are simply not for sale?

There are many keystone individuals out in the world – poets of the Earth who, in their own way, say: 'Yes,' and 'No.' These are individuals who, through their work, courage, commitment and conversations, bring a message of hope – not the cavalier belief that everything will turn out well, but a consciousness that redefines our sense of history, our sense of Nature and our sense of stewardship.

Imagine once more that image of the Earth rising up above the moon. Stretch your imagination ... see that Earth as a miracle, a gift and a garden. See it as a home that has something to do with you and me. After all, our thumbprints are on that Earth. It has given us a voice and more ... a sense of soul.

The Rising

One day
your soul will call to you
with a holy rage.
'Rise up!' it will say …
'Stand up inside your own skin.'
Unmask your unlived life …
feast on your animal heart.
Unfasten your fist …
let loose the medicine
in your own hand.
Show me the lines …
I will show you the spoor
of the ancestors.
Show me the creases …
I will show you
the way to water.
Show me the folds …
I will show you the furrows
for your healing.
'Look!' it will say …
the line of life has four paths –
one with a mirror
one with a mask,
one with a fist,
one with a heart.
One day,
your soul will call to you
with a holy rage.

5 /

TROPHY HUNTING WILL END UP KILLING ITSELF

{ *Ian Michler* }

> '*If a person spends that time really watching, listening, and getting close ... it becomes harder to look at animals as a "resource", or merely meat to harvest, or a certain number of points in a record book. They become endowed with qualities that must be respected. Eventually, it becomes impossible to take their lives for shallow reasons.*'
>
> **– Ted Kerasote**
>
> (As quoted by Brian Luke, *Brutal – Manhood and the Exploitation of Animals*)

As an environmental journalist and activist, I have spent much of my time writing about and lobbying against trophy hunting and its more shameful relatives, predator breeding and canned hunting – also tagged as captive, ranch, or high-fence hunting.

These latter travesties include several other associated but no less exploitative activities. The lion bone markets in Asia and the trade in live animals are obvious ones, but the range of tourism activities that rely on a steady churn of lion cubs is, in many ways, more insidious. These commercial offerings range from cub petting to volunteer tourism and walking with lion options, to bogus sanctuaries, and some venues offering photographic and film-making opportunities. Mainly appealing to ignorant or selfish tourists, each of these revenue streams is part of an industry of horrors that relies on the continued breeding of predators in captivity.

I was first drawn to the hunting debate during the early 1990s, while living and working in Botswana's Okavango Delta. Hunting operators were everywhere, claiming that going after the gene pool of threatened species was one of the best ways to secure survival in the wild. It seemed incongruous – a contradiction of the most perverse kind. Yet, it was a cornerstone of conservation policy in most parts of Africa.

Soon after that, I got to see and understand the extent of the industry after visiting a Safari Club International (SCI) hunting convention in Las Vegas in the USA. I came away bewildered and utterly shocked at the range of animals that hunters kill; the weapons and paraphernalia involved; the people and their language, as well as their marketing claims. They did not look or sound like a crowd of concerned conservationists to me. No doubt, though, there were some in the hall.

I was also intrigued by their dress: A form of battle gear, it seemed. It looked like they were preparing for confrontation and combat against the natural world – a way to deal with their own demons, perhaps? The visit certainly widened my eyes and spurred my interest in covering every aspect of the industry.

During the following years, I was fortunate to do so, but not without the assistance of three resolute and principled people: Peter Borchert, the founder of *Africa Geographic*, and two of the magazine's editors, Eve Gracie and Sarah Borchert. Our scrutiny resulted in much pushback and resistance from many quarters. Academic intimidation, legal and death threats, and a barrage of verbal abuse were all part of their arsenal. However, we refused to be cowed and continued to publish. I owe Peter, Eve and Sarah sincere thanks for trusting my journalism, and for their firm commitment to the debate.

After decades of research and exposure to hunting operations across Africa, both in the wild and behind high fences, I remain convinced that there is only one logical conclusion: Whether viewed from the perspective of intention or consequence, there are profound operational and conservation concerns, along with moral and ethical ones, attached to trophy hunting on this continent. It results in far more harm than its supposed benefits.

Why all the killing?

The killing of animals has always bothered me, but nothing more so than trophy hunting, where it is done as a 'sport' – a leisurely pursuit. Brought up on a farm, I still carry those earliest recollections of being confronted with the bloodied and lifeless forms of dead animals. Whether domestic or wild, the memories remain vivid. It has always engendered a strong sense of unease, a mood bordering on distress. We fished and shot the occasional bird, and while the sentiments in that regard were not as intense, there was always a feeling of regret, a question of: 'Why?'

And then, like many kids in their early teens with a curiosity for the outdoors, I read books and stories on wildlife, history, and colonial Africa. The adventures were mostly thrilling, but I was always curious why the colonials had to do all that shooting. I understood the need to be secure and have food, and there was a good case for collecting specimens as part of the fledgling scientific endeavours of the day, but for the rest, killing vast numbers of animals seemed senseless.

At the time, I never really understood my anxiety or apprehension. Now, I can only imagine it to have been an innate response. As youngsters, we have no way of telling how we, as individuals, process our learning and socialisation. Each of us has our own path and pattern. This process of discovery, including our experiences and the impact they have, are crucial in shaping our principles and priorities later in life.

Only when I started to recognise my own philosophical framework did I begin to understand those early fears, and to grasp the meaning and power that encompasses death. I started to reflect on what it means to be so exploitative of non-human animals: From animal welfare and rights to recreational fishing, our food-processing systems, dietary choices, denial strategies, and how crucial an understanding of web-of-life thinking is. The act of killing and the reasons for doing it remain one of humanity's most complex and controversial dilemmas.

Anachronistic and inappropriate claims

Trophy hunting in Africa arrived in earnest with the colonists – the time of Europe's New Imperialism and the Scramble for Africa (1884–1914). It has generally been accepted as a pastime, a 'sport' for a wealthy few, and a lifestyle for some that continues today. It has also become integrated into our wildlife management and conservation policies in many regions across the continent.

At the outset, and during the decades that followed, there were few dissenting voices. Today, the scrutiny has begun to increase. However, the scope tends to be dictated by vested interests, including those of some of the largest conservation agencies, with the debate around trophy hunting typically still confined to the practical benefits, and legal parameters centred on its implementation and effectiveness.

If trophy hunters had their way, they would require the status quo to remain in perpetuity. However, given the significant scientific, ecological, philosophical, and ethical advances that society has made over the last century, there is no compelling reason to keep the discussion so narrowly confined.

Progress should be measured by our ability to adapt to new information, intellectual and scientific breakthroughs, and revealing insights. It is not about clinging to dogma and anachronistic practices. In modern progressive societies, ethical reckonings are a fundamental component that underpins much of our development and enlightenment.

Today, fewer and fewer countries allow wild animals to be cruelly caged or trained as circus props. Breeding programmes of captive orcas are being stopped, and laboratory experiments with all animals are in the process of being banned in the European Union. Regarding blood sports, bullfighting is now banned in many Spanish cities and in most countries, and dogfighting became a felony in all states of the USA in 2008.

In May 2021, the United Kingdom (UK) struck a significant victory for animal welfare campaigners and scientists when it announced that non-human animals would be recognised as sentient beings. In so doing,

141

the UK joined the ranks of 30 other nations, including New Zealand, Sweden, Switzerland and Denmark. In South Africa, local courts have handed down several significant judgments over the last few years that indicate a shift towards recognising animal welfare as a major factor in how authorities treat wild animals.

Now we have a far greater understanding of other species and their genetic links to us, and to each other. We also understand far more about their cognitive abilities, social structures and behaviours. We are also far more aware of our shared environment and our role in its rapidly advancing destruction. It adds urgency to the voices calling ever more loudly for an enlightened approach to non-human animals and our broader relationship with the environment.

To date, the trophy-hunting industry has been unwilling or unable to respond to these developments in any meaningful way. Participants remain mired in self-serving and tribal thinking. Their age-old justifications include links to conservation and anti-poaching benefits, a raft of economic arguments, and pitting skills in a so-called fair chase. Most bizarrely, there are those who reference religion and some sort of higher sanctity that allows them to kill because they 'love' Nature and the animals.

They also attempt to soften the description of their activities through the smart use of language. For instance, they replace the word 'animals' with 'game', as if to lessen their culpability. More cunningly, instead of 'killing', words such as 'harvest', 'take', and 'bag' are used to sanitise the act. Targeted animals are often referred to as 'vermin', 'problem animals', or 'beyond their breeding age', as if these terms bestow hunters with a right to intervene. In their eyes, they get to claim a moral victory that goes with the trophy.

Trophy hunters also continue to aggressively defend their 'right' to kill animals and, in some quarters, to denigrate opponents in a bullying manner that speaks of ethical bankruptcy. And with practices allowing the baiting of predators, hunting with dog packs, and the use of high-powered rifles and technological aids, such as telescopic sights and drones, amongst other aids, notions of 'sport' and 'fair chase' cannot be taken seriously.

For some foolish reason, there is still a belief among many within the hunting fraternity that political leverage is gained by tagging opponents of trophy hunting as animal rightists, and often extremist or ignorant ones at that. It's a scare tactic from a bygone era. Are these people suggesting that they have the right to treat animals and the natural world as they wish, and to do so without moral consideration? If so, it's a shameful defence of what they do. It's also worth noting there are numerous animal rights and welfare organizations that are increasingly well regarded in general conservation circles.

More recently, an argument has emerged that implies the majority of people opposing trophy hunting are celebrities or wealthy foreigners, and because of this, their voices should not be heard. This is a duplicitous defence, often put forward by wealthy foreigners who support trophy hunting. Let's be very clear on this: There is a growing list of African conservationists, scientists, academics and community leaders that oppose trophy hunting. And trophy hunting is a non-African construct, introduced by Europeans during the colonial era. The majority of Africa's trophy hunting clients are not Africans – they come from out-side the continent, and most are wealthy, while some are celebrities. In addition, since the 1980s at least, the most significant contributions to conservation funding in Africa has come from the countless foreign NGOs who continue to do incredible work across the continent. Without outside assistance, Africa's conservation record would be significantly worse off.

Integrating all of these claims, the hunting community will often purposefully present the debate as an all-or-nothing outcome. In the protagonist's world, ending trophy hunting results in the loss of protected areas and wildlife – plain and simple. Any alternative or more effective and sustainable land-use options to preserve the natural world are ignored or simply rejected as non-viable. Their favourite marketing tagline: 'If it pays, it stays' – a narrow financial interpretation of 'sustainable use' – is a simplistic approach that misleads and distorts the narrative. This premise suggests that if endangered species cannot be killed by hunters, they have less value, or even no value, to anyone else or the environment.

These are all profoundly flawed arguments, and such responses are no longer acceptable.

It just doesn't add up.

Over the past 120 years or so, we have seen tens of millions of wild animals killed for their skins and trophies, but with a conservation dividend that is not commensurate with the loss. We continue to face a species population and biodiversity extinction crisis that worsens by the year. We are desperately trying to staunch a runaway poaching crisis and an illegal trade in wild animals. This is irrefutable. It is within this context that trophy hunters try to justify their activities that add to the loss of Africa's animals and its gene pool.

Can we afford to sanction a sport – at times even a claimed cultural activity – in the face of overwhelming evidence that most wild animal populations are in such sharp decline? The question is especially pertinent when we *do* have sustainable alternatives that can work.

All scientists will tell you of their concerns about the loss of genetic diversity, and how disruptive the loss of individuals or groups are to the dynamics of social structure within populations. This is well explained by the authors of *Rarity Value and Species Extinction: The Anthropogenic Allee Effect*. They argue: '*Human predisposition to place exaggerated value on rarity fuels disproportionate exploitation of rare species, rendering them even rarer and thus more desirable, ultimately leading them into an extinction vortex.*'

In essence, hunters that go after rare and endangered species contribute to pushing them into a feedback loop towards extinction.

It is important to add that trophy hunting is not the only activity highlighted in the paper. Others include wildlife collecting, the demand for luxury goods, the exotic pet trade, traditional medicine, and poorly managed ecotourism.

Similarly, the Zoological Society of London published *Rarity, trophy hunting and ungulates* in 2011. The authors state that '*high hunting prices may promote a disproportionate harvest of species that are the least abundant, therefore escalating their threat of extirpation or extinction.'*

Indeed, in one particular study, over-hunting and poaching are recognised by the IUCN as the 'primary cause of decline in 30 out of the 39 threatened species. While stating that if well-managed, hunting can have benefits, they also warn about the rarity effect encouraging exploitation "with potentially profound consequences for populations'.

Lion, a species that tops many hunting wish lists, serve as an excellent example of these impacts. Various studies on the species, including those published under the IUCN, have shown how trophy hunting can be the 'main or sole driver of decline' through the disruption of social structures, particularly the 'vacuum effect' and infanticide that results due to rapid turnover of pride males.

In one particular IUCN report, *Guidelines for the conservation of lions in Africa*, Version 1.0, December 2018, a leading lion scientist claims that trophy hunting 'was the single largest cause of mortality for male lions' in Hwange National Park, Zimbabwe.

Fortunately, we don't need trophy hunting to protect parks and wildlife. We now have good comparative studies showing the merits of non-consumptive options: Ecotourism and other models embracing conservation without the unnecessary killing. Botswana and Rwanda are two countries leading the way with well-managed national legislation in photographic tourism. Over the past 30 years, the substantial economic growth experienced across northern Botswana is attributed primarily to the expansion of ecotourism, as the country moved away from trophy hunting.

Many private-sector and NGO projects in South Africa, Botswana, Zimbabwe, Tanzania and Kenya also serve as excellent examples of land use that is converting buffer zones, degraded agricultural land or hunting concessions into viable ecotourism projects. Notable projects include the efforts of Singita in Tanzania, where over 150 000 hectares of hunting concessions have been turned into prized photographic destinations. In Botswana's Okavango Delta, Wilderness Safaris paved the way for land-use switches in the 1990s by successfully turning numerous hunting concessions into thriving photographic areas. In South Africa,

& Beyond and Mantis Collection have established prominent private protected areas without trophy hunting.

We also have highly regarded conservation agencies, such as African Parks, Peace Parks and Wilderness Foundation Africa, that are securing and reviving vast tracts of wilderness across Africa without trophy hunting as a management option. In Zimbabwe, IFAW has taken over hunting concessions to run successful hybrid projects that combine wildlife sanctuaries with tourism and scientific research.

More specifically, ecotourism offers a variety of substantial advantages over trophy hunting:

- In most cases, safari camps and lodges offer year-round job opportunities with long-term career prospects for many more people, while hunting operators employ only a handful of people on a six-month seasonal basis.

- By nature of its extent, ecotourism generates significantly greater benefits in every sphere for local and regional economies. A recent IUCN study indicates that non-hunting tourism generates over 80% of revenues in protected areas across eastern and southern Africa against the 2% from trophy hunting. Various other studies also make it apparent that the number of hunters visiting Africa is in decline. This further adds to the argument that this sector cannot be relied upon as a sustainable source of funding or employment.

- The anti-poaching benefits extolled by hunters need unpacking. Some of the worst statistics on the loss of wildlife populations come from areas controlled predominantly by the hunting industry. According to the WWF, Selous Game Reserve lost approximately 80% of its elephants between 2007 and 2014. That's about 55 000 animals lost to the ivory trade and, what's more, partly under the noses of the hunting operators who controlled over 90% of the concessions. Similarly, northern Mozambique and parts of Zambia have recorded high poaching levels – regions where trophy hunting has been, by some margin, the dominant land-use option.

These statistics in no way implicate the involvement of hunting operators, but they clearly illustrate that trophy hunting has no distinctive claim or advantage as an anti-poaching deterrent. In fact, it could be argued that ecotourism activities can be more effective, by the nature of the year-round operations. Where hunting activity is prohibited, there can be many other ways to perform anti-poaching duties.

In this light, it's worth considering if the Selous Game Reserve in Tanzania (in 2020, its northern section was renamed Nyerere National Park) would have suffered its present fate if the authorities had rid themselves of trophy hunting decades ago? Currently, the reserve is beset by logging activities within its boundaries; the construction of a massive dam; a low uptake of hunting concessions due to declining wildlife populations; and the splitting of what was once the largest tract of wilderness in Africa. Given the ecological similarities, it's in no way fanciful to believe that if photographic tourism had replaced hunting as the primary land-use option across the entire region, the Selous might well have rivalled the Okavango Delta as a healthy tract of wilderness and driver of local economies

We also need to be clear – these comparisons do not vindicate everything about the ecotourism industry or conservation models in general. The entire spectrum needs scrutiny and change, but as models currently stand, the ecotourism sector remains by some margin a superior, sustainable management option that has little to do with diluting an already diminishing gene pool.

Another example that feeds the all-or-nothing defence put forward by hunters is the Kenya versus South Africa assessment. When comparing the two, the suggestion is that Kenya's decline in wildlife populations resulted from that country's ban on trophy hunting in the late 1970s. South Africa's growth in wildlife populations over the same period is then highlighted as proof of what happens when hunting is allowed.

While the historical population trends for both countries are correct, the self-serving link is a misconception. I am unaware of any science that supports the argument. We all know Kenya has suffered population declines in many species, but so, too, have a range of countries, like Tanzania, Mozambique, Zambia, and Namibia, which allow trophy hunting. Through countless studies and reports, we also know that human-induced habitat destruction is the primary driver of wildlife loss, and that poaching, both at subsistence and commercial levels, is primarily driven by a range of socio-economic factors, often exacerbated by poor or criminal management practices. All these factors were present in Kenya during the decades when the declines were at their worst. The good news is that some species, including elephants, are in the process of recovering – without trophy hunting being introduced.

South Africa's higher wildlife numbers need to be contextualised. True, the headcount of wild animals has grown over the past few decades, but this has chiefly been on private farms where a few high-value species have been selected for breeding to satisfy commercial activities, such as hunting. For the most part, these breeding units operate under agricultural conditions rather than ecological considerations, and most of the animals are not regarded as part of the conservation stock. Instead, these activities serve to highlight significant concerns: An increase in fencing that prohibits biodiversity and corridor conservation objectives, as well as the inbreeding and crossbreeding within certain species, as well as practices and processes leading to genetic contamination and the domestication of wild species.

Let's also recall that untold species across various continents have been brought back from the brink of extinction (see 'Inch by Inch') without trophy hunting being used as a conservation option. Indeed, it is a complete fallacy to imply that in such circumstances, trophy hunting is a necessity. There is a further irony here, one that has been highlighted by Dan Ashe, a past Director of the United States Fish and Wildlife Service (USFWS). By way of example, he pointed out that if Africa's lions were a US species, they would be deemed threatened, and thus, along with all other species categorised in this manner, hunting them would be prohibited by legislation. He has also stated: 'The argument that we need to hunt endangered animals, to conserve them, is old and tired.'

When all is considered, I believe that trophy hunting is inconsistent with long-term conservation goals. I have stated before: Using trophy hunting as an indicator of conservation success is a mismeasurement of what we are trying to achieve. It's much like using growth domestic product (GDP) as an indicator of human well-being across the planet.

Both are crude and short-sighted tools that tell a fraction of the story while concealing the damage.

In summary, these sentiments are succinctly expressed by Dr Andrew Loveridge, a well-known scientist who researches lions in Zimbabwe's Hwange National Park. In his book, *Lion Hearted*, Dr Loveridge says:

'*In reality, hunting greatly undervalues African wildlife. That is not to say that people do not become rich through hunting. They do. But little of the financial gain filters down to covering costs of conserving wildlife.*'

It just doesn't add up.

The kill and that trophy

Ultimately, I believe the claims supporting trophy hunting serve to deflect the debate away from what has become a moral and ethical issue. In this way, those involved hope to avoid exposing themselves to explaining their baser motives: The seduction of the kill and the status and bragging rights that come with the compulsive need to display that trophy, for example.

By sticking to claim of benefits, an attempt is being made to portray a message of altruism – one that implies being involved in a necessary act, rather than a wilful killing – and that they have been granted consent as a result of those perceived benefits.

In an illuminating interview published in *Psychology Today*, Marc Bekoff, Professor Emeritus of Ecology and Evolutionary Biology at the University of Colorado, expands on this factor in discussion with the authors of a paper titled *Why men trophy hunt*. They conclude that trophy hunting large and dangerous species is 'seemingly irrational behaviour', but when one considers the rewards of a successful hunt, this signals 'underlying qualities to rivals and potential allies'. The authors, Chris T Darimont, Brian F. Codding, and Kristen Hawkes refer to this behaviour as 'costly signalling theory'. They also call for more research in this regard, as they are concerned about the negative conservation impacts of trophy hunting.

And in his excellent work *Brutal – Manhood and the Exploitation of Animals*, Brian Luke explores several illuminating subtexts, including the erotics of predation and hunting. He refers to the power of controlling life and death as being 'central to the seductive, exciting romance of hunting'.

As opposition mounts, the hunting community will find itself mired ever more deeply in this bog, caught between defending an archaic legality and dealing with an emerging ethical reckoning. Trophy hunters are in this situation because of a fundamental misreading of their predicament. They are trying to justify a pursuit, their favourite sport or leisure activity, with mismatched reasoning. As so many have pondered in the past, because something is legal, does that, by extension, make it ethical or morally appropriate?

I believe that in time, and given the impulses involved, trophy hunting, killing mostly for fun, status, and commercial gain, will end up killing itself.

The search for alternatives

However, in the interim, we have reason for concern. Trophy hunting needs to undergo an immediate and thorough review, one that is widened to reflect today's collective environmental and ethical consciousness. Conservation concerns will be a focus, but such a review also needs to tackle the social and behavioural issues around patriarchal control, the myths and ideological screens that sanction the collective abuse of wildlife, and the appropriateness of using dead animals and their body parts as symbols of power and status, and as a marker for conservation objectives.

Tasked with defining options to replace hunting in Africa, a forum or working group must also be broadened beyond the historic stakeholder profiles of the government, conservation, hunting and ecotourism communities. Professionals from animal welfare and rights, criminal and constitutional law, social development, human behaviour, African history and cultural studies, and the environmental sciences must also be included.

Within such a review, we must heed the call of so many non-hunting researchers and conservationists working on the front line. They correctly warn that leaving a vacuum without putting well thought-out alternatives in place could be just as bad as trophy hunting. Related to this, the heated debates around communities, particularly concerning ownership, benefits and socio-economic upliftment, should also be considered.

The entire spectrum of funding models for conservation also requires review. This needs to query how and why governments have abdicated their responsibilities to allocate sufficient budgetary funding to the environment – a portfolio as vital to progress as health and education. Related to this: How and why have hunting organisations been allowed to plan, organise and fund what are ostensibly government conservation forums? This practice clearly speaks to conflicts of interest.

Trophy hunting is already banished from most core protected areas, a situation that in itself is an indicator of its merits or lack thereof. This leaves what are broadly referred to as 'marginal' areas – those that fringe nationally-protected parks and reserves or lie between and link two ecosystems – as the most significant areas of contestation.

Marginal areas are typically considered less productive. With erratic rainfall patterns, and less fertile soils, wildlife can be scarce and vulnerable. Whatever species do occur, most are using these areas as seasonal refuges or migration routes. Because of this, conventional wisdom suggests that they are not good for ecotourism development, but suitable for trophy hunting. However, these regions probably have an even greater need for protection, begging the question of whether animals should face the additional stress of being targeted by hunters.

In many ways, the position of trophy hunting in our conservation agenda is akin to that of fossil fuels in global economies and climate change. It's been known for decades that the use of fossil fuels is unsustainable, owing to the significant long-term risks to the environment. However, because of vested interests and their obstructionism, it took governments and environmental agencies far too long to begin developing renewable alternatives. The world now faces a race against climate change – a challenge that could have been avoided if stakeholders had acted on the initial warnings.

Let us not prevaricate on trophy hunting while lions, leopards, elephants, and so many others, teeter at the brink.

Blood Lions®

If trophy hunting has little merit, breeding predators in cages or captivity, only to be killed in confined areas, has absolutely no merit. My work among those involved in these industries has been an emotional rollercoaster, accompanied by physical threats and legal actions.

It started while researching the sustainability of hunting wild lions in the mid-1990s. I received a tip-off from a charter pilot that I should follow certain hunters as they headed south after unsuccessful lion hunts in Botswana. That I did, and ended up in South Africa's Free State province, then the heartland of a fledgling predator breeding and canned hunting industry.

Soon after, canned hunting was revealed to the world through the Cooke Report, which was flighted on British television. It was shocking, but I had already discovered that one shooting of a lioness in a cage-like enclosure at close range was not an isolated event. There were other ghastly practices, too, all seemingly perfectly acceptable to this community into which I had ventured.

To write with conviction, you need to become immersed in your subject matter, so I decided to delve deeper into that disturbing world in several different parts of South Africa. Over many visits across years, I posed alternatively as a buyer of wildlife or marketer of hunts, occasionally as a dumb but inquisitive journalist, and sometimes simply as a naïve tourist or lost trespasser.

Those initial sorties to try to make sense of farmers and operators' attitudes and behaviour were challenging to say the least. I simply had no idea that such brutality and brazen cruelty to wild species existed. What I saw and heard was often beyond my comprehension.

My time on those properties was harrowing, depressing even. They are utterly soulless places, festering sores of concrete blocks, barbed wire, and locked gates. They were utterly unlike the natural world and the habitat of wild animals. Many are owned and run by people with little empathy, consideration or care for the animals – sentiments that often also extend to the poor souls who work there.

These experiences have informed my writings on these topics and my contributions to the award-winning documentary *Blood Lions* and its global campaign.

Working on *Blood Lions* was highly satisfying, not least because the visual and cinematic narrative conveys the horrors in a way that the written word seldom can. Many others partnered with us, and together we have advanced the campaign against these horrific practices in so many ways.

I owe special thanks and gratitude to Jason Bell, Christina Pretorius and Neil Greenwood at IFAW for supporting me in the earlier years. And then to Pippa Hankinson, whose idea it was to do the film and to cameraman/co-director Nick Chevallier. Their professionalism, warm friendship, honesty and dedication to the cause was unflagging. They trusted me to take them into the lion's den, but we came out together and in one piece after some awful experiences, but with a compelling story.

Jeremy Nathan; Bruce Young; Dave Cohen; Dr Andrew Venter; Nicola Gerrard and Lauren van Nijkerk joined the team for post-production and the campaign. They all added significant skills and scope to the project. More recently, Dr Louise de Waal, Cath Jakins, Janelle Barnard and Casey Pratt helped us take the campaign to the next level. The entire team should be immensely proud of shining a light on these industries in a way that spoke the truth.

These efforts may well bear fruit. As of March 2022, and after a lengthy consultative process involving a panel of experts and various public participation opportunities, the South African government is in the process of drafting a way forward that seeks to curb, and in some instances, end these practices.

Why has it taken so long?

While there has been progress towards ending predator breeding and canned hunting in South Africa, there has been little change regarding so-called fair-chase hunting on the continent. As we have already noted, the act of trophy hunting has escaped scrutiny and exposure for too long. Delving into why this is so reveals a history that throws up a multitude of reasons.

In the early years of trophy hunting in Africa, when it was still regarded as a desirable and noble pursuit, the killings were sometimes nothing more than gratuitous slaughter. Though often denied today, sad stories and images of excess that drove some species towards the brink are available to all in history books and hunting journals. Very few concerns were raised, and the mostly outright endorsement of hunting at that time granted immunity from criticism. There was widespread ignorance, and among the few who felt unease, silence rather than opposition was the order of the day.

From the 1960s came the dawning of independence for many African nations. Brimming with hope, those newly-elected governments were motivated to tackle the more pressing social and economic development challenges of the day. Deeming environmental matters a secondary portfolio, they tended to follow the colonial mantra on general wildlife management policies and practices. With time, numerous countries even scaled back their mandated roles in securing nationally protected areas and the biodiversity they held. This came with the increasing promotion of a range of public/private sector initiatives and activities in the hope of filling state coffers. There was also a growing reliance on the NGO sector to raise funding and to perform protection tasks.

Since the 1980s, the glue reinforcing this process has been a generation of managers, scientists, researchers and career administrators in conservation who have established their academic and field reputations on constructing or supporting the concept of 'sustainable use', of which trophy hunting remains a key policy.

They have also had a supporting cast: Journalists, conservation NGOs, tourist operators and others within the research and scientific community. Some give tacit support by turning a blind eye, while others condoned the killing because it remained legal. They attempted to escape any feeling of guilt by expressing their personal abhorrence for the practice.

For this latter group, their stance is a recognition that ethical decisions are part of our scientific endeavours. However, by not speaking out clearly about their concerns, they merely cloud the debate, while providing trophy hunting with a screen to continue. Is this muddled thinking, or does it mean they remain muzzled because the means-to-an-end argument has been sufficiently oiled by vested interests? And if some are being funded, this is another ethical or philosophical choice.

In addition, the trophy-hunting lobby has always had a disproportionately influential voice within the corridors of power and conservation – one that continues to ensure their activities remain entrenched. This comes from its historical links and close association with our patriarchal world and its global, political and economic elites and their lobby groups. It includes residing and ex-presidents, a host of wealthy, influential corporates, and some otherwise highly regarded conservation agencies and researchers.

Their power and influence are all the more remarkable, given the flipside – a demonstrable fall in support for hunting in the US. According to a study by *Outdoor Life* magazine, the number of registered hunters in the USA – Africa's largest source of hunting clients – peaked at 17 million or just over 7% of the population in 1982. Since then, registrations have dropped steadily. By 2016, they had fallen to approximately 11 million, below 4% of the total population. In the UK, the results of a 2019 government-sponsored public consultation on the importation of hunting trophies showed that 86% of the 44 000 respondents called for tighter restrictions and bans on importing trophies.

As a footnote, it would seem the traditional hunting narrative is also losing merit among the younger generations in Africa. A fascinating insight into this comes from *Neo-colonialism and greed: Africans' views on trophy hunting in social media,* a paper published in the *Journal for Sustainable Tourism* in 2019. The authors contend that the anti-lobby in Africa has typically represented a Western view without considering local opinions. They found that African people did object to trophy hunting, but not on grounds pertaining to animal rights or conservation. Instead, their objections were based on hunting's connections to colonialism and the exploitation of wildlife because of political greed, as well as 'the way it privileges Western elites in accessing Africa's wildlife resources'.

Bringing awareness

Lately, I have been struck by another consideration, one that has come about as my son has grown beyond toddlerdom towards becoming a young man.

Some sectors of our societies, whether here in Africa or across the world, permit young kids, some not even into their teens, to go out armed with hunting rifles (supposedly in the company of a parent) and to use them to kill wild trophy animals. Again and again, sad images appear in hunting magazines and on the internet of youngsters posing over their lifeless quarry, rifle cocked, and often with beaming parents at the side. Yet, these same kids are not allowed to drink alcohol (in some countries until the age of 21) or drive, smoke, gamble or have signing powers. They can't get married (in some instances, they can with parental consent), and they have to stay at home until 18. Neither can they have sex until the age of 16 or 18, and they can't even vote because they are deemed not yet mature enough to make choices or decisions on such life-changing activities.

Where on Earth then is the sense in encouraging kids to kill animals, when we deem them incapable of making important decisions on a host of other issues, some of which have arguably far lesser consequences? Is there any reasonable explanation for this, and what does it say about our attitude towards the natural world?

Many will, of course, justify the behaviour in cultural or even religious terms, but such arguments simply bring us back full circle to the discussion about enlightenment. Given what we now know, these arguments cannot excuse a reluctance to change, when the failure to do so may add directly to species' extinction risks. And what are the long-term psychological implications of encouraging children to gratuitously kill animals at such a young age?

While examining these questions is important, I believe they are linked to a deep-rooted reason: Our archaic education systems that continue to let both us and the environment down. If we are to have any chance at fundamentally altering our current abusive relationship with the environment, then education must play a central role. From the moment kids enter school, they should be learning about Earth and its life-supporting ecosystems and the services they provide. They need to understand how critical healthy biodiversity levels are for our own survival; about carbon and other cycles, and about the impacts that current living patterns have on the planet. Learning about one's ecological footprint and how to reduce it is both fun and empowering.

Every living human soul needs to understand that we are simply one species of millions, and to appreciate that, we can't impose dominion at our whim. We are all intertwined in complex ecological processes that are fundamental to the health of our planet and ourselves. In the same way that mathematics and languages are non-negotiable subjects throughout most school curricula, environmental and Earth sciences must be given similar prominence.

In the end, I believe that trophy hunting or killing animals for fun is an act of violence and immense selfishness. It is done as a desire, willingly and calculatingly so, rather than as a necessity. Displaying the spoils is proof of having had complete control in the process. If you still suggest it's not about the killing and the trophy, and that you are passionate about conservation, then in the name of logic and securing the gene pool of so many species, please don't betray the causes and animals you claim to represent. Rather donate that money to sustainable, non-hunting conservation causes.

I would also like to pay tribute to many individuals and organisations, both locally and across the world, who fight against predator breeding, canned hunting and other abusive tourism activities in South Africa.

We may never stop all abuse against animals, but I do believe that in time, South Africa's captive lions and other predators may well get the reprieve that circus animals, primates and orcas are getting today.

Recognition must also go to the growing list of journalists, ecotourism operators, conservation agencies, researchers, scientists and politicians, as well as many concerned naturalists who have actively lobbied against trophy hunting. Your work has already begun to tell. Today, the debate is being given widespread coverage, and there is far less intimidation aimed at hunting's critics.

6 /

LIVING IN THE ANTHROPOCENE

{ *Ian Michler* }

'*For millennia, humans have behaved as rebels against a superpower we call "Nature". In the 20th century, however, new technologies, fossil fuels, and a fast-growing population resulted in a "Great Acceleration" of our own powers. Albeit clumsily, we are taking control of Nature's realm, from climate to DNA. We humans are becoming the dominant force for change on Earth. A long-held religious and philosophical idea – humans as the masters of planet Earth – has turned into a stark reality. What we do now already affects the planet of the year 3 000 or even 50 000.*'

– Paul J. Crutzen & Christian Schwägerl

In the above quotation, Crutzen and Schwägerl voice the scientific concerns about our current destructive and wasteful lifestyle, and they do so with the economy and precision we expect and need from the scientific community.

However, no less telling are more whimsical offerings that offer a poetic perspective and a hint of wryness to soften the apprehension and anxiety that comes with the message.

I like the way Bob Dylan encapsulates humanity's journey. With much fanfare and some surprise, Dylan won the 2016 Nobel Prize in

Literature 'for having created new poetic expressions within the great American song tradition'. After winning the award, a journalist asked whether he ever thought about mortality. In his response, he referred to 'the long, strange trip of the naked ape'.

Indeed, it has been a strange trip for humanity. Based on biomass calculations, humans account for approximately 0.01% of life on Earth. Yet, through our living patterns, we have become the most influential species on the planet. This influence and domination by humans comes with serious consequences for Earth's components: The geosphere, atmosphere, hydrosphere, and biosphere. We know that carbon build-up is heading towards catastrophic levels, that the global average temperature is rising at 170 times the background rate, and that habitat and biodiversity loss is happening at rates previously recorded only during mass extinctions.

These critical indicators confirm that the planet and our societies have entered a new period of instability. Given this fact, some within the scientific community increasingly suggest that our current epoch, the Holocene, be replaced by the Anthropocene, a new geological time reflecting the defining role of humans in shaping these changes.

The geological timescale

Terms like 'Jurassic' and 'Carboniferous' are recognisable to most of us, but they originate from the geological timescale – a system of chronological dating used by scholars of the Earth sciences to account for Earth's history going back to its beginnings about 4.5 billion years ago. They do this by examining the layers of information and vital evidence; types of rock; chemical traces, and, mainly, fossil records laid down in the geological strata.

The categories or units in the timescale appear as a set of five hierarchical divisions. Aeons, each spanning hundreds of millions of years, are the largest geological time units. They are followed successively by the shorter sub-divisions of eras, periods, epochs, and ages, the shortest and most recently added category.

The first attempts by geologists to age Earth using rock strata date back to the late 17th century, but it wasn't until 1913 and the publication of *The Age of Earth* by the British physicist and geologist Arthur Holmes, that the first geological timescale appeared. Since then, and to improve accuracy as our scientific understanding broadens, it has undergone numerous changes and advances, often hotly contested owing to differences in opinion between experts. The process continues under the auspices of the International Commission on Stratigraphy (ICS), an international non-government agency and recognised authority.

The Holocene

Within the Quaternary Period there are two epochs: The Pleistocene followed by the current time still officially known as the Holocene, which began about 12 000 to 11 500 years ago, after the last major ice age. The Holocene covers what could be referred to as humankind's modern development – our recorded history. Our age, which is part of the Holocene, is referred to as the Meghalayan Age. It began about 4 200 years ago, when a 200-year drought gripped a broad swathe of the globe, from the eastern Mediterranean, through Mesopotamia and the Indus Valley, and on to the valley of the Yangtze.

The Holocene started when humans began settling in small communities in the region of Mesopotamia. Nestled between the Tigris and Euphrates rivers in south-west Asia (now parts of modern-day Iraq, Turkey and Syria), the fertile valleys offered perfect conditions for sedentary living. The domestication of wild plants and animals and organised agriculture followed, bringing an end to the nomadic lifestyle of these communities. This foreshadowed the beginning of environmental manipulation by humans.

Historians and archaeologists often refer to this region as the 'cradle of civilisation'. These small settlements soon grew to represent more complex living systems. Technological development gathered pace and, along with swelling population levels, cultural and social stratification under urban living conditions became a characteristic feature. This, in turn, brought about the need for political and administrative structures.

Fast forward a good few thousand years, and we have other factors that have significantly defined the Holocene. It has encompassed the beginnings of written language; inventions that led to weapons; the wheel; the printing press; combustion engines; nuclear power, and computer technology. All have profoundly impacted our living patterns. However, for many, the harnessing of coal and oil that drove the energy and transport industries and the start of assembly lines and mass production have been the defining moments of the Industrial Revolution and the Holocene. There have also been breakthroughs in medicine, communications, and agriculture.

On a social level, the rise of religions, Asian and European expansion along with colonialism, slavery, war, and the genocides this brought, as well as mass urbanisation and institutionalised discrimination based on sex, race, and culture, are just some aspects that define life in the Holocene. Overall, however, it is difficult, if not impossible, to pick one element in our development path as definitive. Instead, there have been a series of civilisations and a multitude of technologies and social breakthroughs. What each has brought has resulted in today's complex and inter-connected globalised societies. It is this progression that has ensured the domination of the planet by one species, *Homo sapiens*.

The age of humans: The Anthropocene

As we proceed into the 21st century, technological advances continue to gather momentum. Some futurists and scientists suggest that we are likely to accelerate through more change in the next 30 years than we have in the last 300. This, linked to rapid population growth and high consumption and waste production levels, has become the critical distinction between what we are experiencing today and what occurred a century and more ago.

However, there is a further defining element for those supporting the notion of the Anthropocene. In an ecological sense, all organisms impact their ecosystems, but seldom in ways that the entire community of species and the system itself becomes imperilled. Yet, as we review Dylan's '... long, strange trip of the naked ape' and the current state of our planet, we find a single species doing just this: Humans are influencing and impacting at a global level, across all spheres, and with such destructive consequences.

We know this because of data collection and the advent of the environmental movement. After decades of measurement, we face an ironic twist on our Latinised name, *Homo sapiens,* which translates as 'wise, wise man'. Today, much of our behaviour has proved to be decidedly unwise. The overwhelming conclusion is that the collective momentum of humanity has changed the Earth so dramatically that our current living paradigms are simply unsustainable. We are destroying our own home. These circumstances have led many within the broader scientific community to suggest marking this time in our history with a change of epoch, from the Holocene into the Anthropocene.

Life in the Anthropocene

Over the past few thousand years, the aims and ambitions of successive civilisations and empires have focused on establishing territory, resource bases and power blocs while pursuing increasing levels of economic activity and trade. And the world has fashioned economic, political and military systems to achieve this in the swiftest and most profitable ways.

While this paradigm remains, the focus is shifting. As the 21st century progresses, the consequences of our previous and continuing endeavours have resulted in environmental and social crises on an unprecedented scale. Preventing their continuation, or at least ameliorating their worst effects, has become our most pressing challenge.

The environmental threats and the extreme hardship they visit upon the lives of millions of people are inextricable. This is reason enough to elevate social factors into the discussion – particularly those pertaining to poverty, rising inequality, cultural disintegration, polarisation, a lack of access to services, and deteriorating human well-being. All play into the drivers of the Anthropocene, which disproportionately affects poor and disenfranchised populations.

Close to a billion people are acutely compromised by our current paradigms, and battle to access everything from clean water and air to food and shelter, to health and education services. At the same time, billions verge this state. Unequal and unstable societies and/or aggrieved communities increase division, social unrest, and serious conflict. This, in turn, undermines the legitimacy of governments and their capacity to deal with the initial threats.

Population growth, a defining driver of the conditions that mark the Anthropocene, is ultimately a social factor. As the number of people continues to rise, albeit more slowly than in the past, so, too, will the influence of humans on the environment and our collective future. It's this collective future that concerns us most. Just as COVID-19 started as a health crisis but soon became a political and social fiasco in many countries, climate change, which had been mainly viewed as an environmental crisis, could well end up a social calamity.

There's another significant distinction to be noted from previous eras. In times past, dominant powers used their influence through military might, economic muscle and multilateral alliances to deal with whatever global disturbances or crises occurred. Today, no matter the military or economic power in place, our systems are not structured or inclined to deal with environmental or social challenges in any transformative way. In time, historians may well include our inability to change our lifestyles or deal with their consequences as another key marker of the Anthropocene.

A scientific debate

The concept of the Anthropocene, loosely translated from ancient Greek as 'the age of humans' was first mooted back in 2000. Dutch meteorologist and chemist Paul J Crutzen had also done extensive work on the causes of the ozone hole, and together with his fellow scientists, he won a Nobel Prize for this work in 1995. These findings led him to examine human impacts on all of Earth's physical boundaries. He used the term publicly for the first time when he presented at an International Geosphere-Biosphere Programme Conference in Mexico. Later that same year, Crutzen co-authored a scientific paper on the topic with Eugene F. Stoermer, a limnologist from the University of Michigan.

From their research, they understood human activity to be the primary factor driving changes to our planet. This, they believed, was sufficiently significant to warrant the Holocene's name change.

Despite compelling arguments from many others, along with Crutzen and Stoermer, the debate continues within the broader scientific community. Is there sufficient evidence to change the name of the current epoch? The argument is typically split between naysayers in the geological sciences who maintain that there is insufficient hard data and evidence from the Earth's physical layers, and the environmental and social scientists who claim that the powerful visual impacts and experiences in real-time are clearly measurable and provide the necessary proof.

It is important to note here that no one is arguing against the overwhelming evidence that human activity is now the most significant impact on our planet. Rather, it has to do with scientific confirmation, measurement criteria, and an applicable commencement date for the new epoch.

All other geological time periods have defined markers, and the Anthropocene should be no different say the members of the International Union of Geological Sciences. Some argue that human impacts have yet to appear in the stratigraphical levels, while others debate the specifics of various 'golden spikes' that could be used as the markers of the new epoch. For these reasons, they maintain that we should be cautious when it comes to the concept of the Anthropocene.

Crutzen initially reflected on 1784 as a starting point. This marked the invention of the steam engine and, in all likelihood, when greenhouse gas (GHG) build-up would have resulted as a consequence. Others have suggested it should go further back to when early hominids first started using fire. A case has also been made to mark the advent of agricultural practices. More recently, and after much research, there is a leaning towards the period after World War 2, when the Nuclear Age began. This was followed by the 'Great Acceleration' during the 1950s and 60s.

There are also strong arguments for social elements to be considered. For example, Heather Davis from McGill University has suggested that the Anthropocene cannot only be seen in geological or environmental terms. She avers that the onset of European expansion and colonialism should be seen as a marker. Characterised by violent dispossession and genocide of indigenous peoples and their cultures, this period also heralded humanity's assault on the environment.

However, despite the ongoing debates, there is no doubt that the concept of the Anthropocene and all it represents has already entered everyday use. The media has picked up on the fascination and discussion, and most research institutes have started including the database in their reports and modelling. In trying to explain and define the Anthropocene, it is also important to note that the physical and social sciences deal with multi-layered issues covering many disciplines and cultures that have developed over time. This adds significantly to the complexity involved.

Is there evidence to support the Anthropocene?

Proponents of the Anthropocene point to what they consider to be overwhelming global evidence that includes the fact that almost all of Earth's physical, chemical, and biological systems are being altered by human activities, some at alarming levels.

In addition, several social factors are playing out, adding to the growing instability of the global community. These also impede efforts to mitigate environmental crises.

Then we have the population trends that indicate that global numbers are set to continue growing for decades to come – up from 8 billion to 9 billion by 2050. Quite simply, more people on the planet means even greater pressure on its ecosystems and boundaries.

The principal concerns raised earlier in the book all feed directly into the Anthropocene debate and serve as evidence of our impacts and the Earth in distress. As a reminder, these broad categories include:
- Carbon and other GHG build-ups, global warming, and climate change.
- Extensive habitat and ecosystem destruction.
- Biodiversity loss at levels matching previous mass extinctions.

- High levels of plastic pollution and fertilisers, and toxic chemical waste leakage into the environment.

In each case, a range of human activities is the primary cause. However, additional evidence should be viewed in conjunction with these factors. Together, this provides a compelling narrative to support the argument put forward by Crutzen and many other environmental and social scientists.

The Nuclear Age

Although Albert Einstein began unravelling the intricacies of mass and energy in the early 1900s, for many scientists and researchers, the Nuclear Age, at times referred to as the Atomic Age, began on 16 July 1945, when the USA carried out the first sizable nuclear explosion in the deserts of New Mexico.

Weeks later, the Japanese cities of Hiroshima and Nagasaki were bombed. Those two horror events heralded the atomic era to the world. Those blasts, and the even larger thermonuclear hydrogen detonations that followed a few years on, released fall-out material into the natural world. Later, with the advent of the nuclear power industry, came additional fall-out from the waste produced, along with accidents. Because of those events, radioactive elements (or radionuclides) have been detected in geological structures, including in water, plant material, and even the human body.

More specifically, plutonium 239 has been found. That isotope hardly occurs in the natural world but is a common indicator of nuclear fall-out. Other radioactive isotopes include americium 241 and carbon 14. Some scientists believe that these visible and quantifiable markers in geological layers provide the most compelling direct evidence of our impacts on the planet. For this reason, they should be used as the starting point.

The Great Acceleration

Soon after the advent of the Nuclear Age came the Great Acceleration. This was the post-war boom during the 1950s and 60s, when levels of economic activity and their impact on Earth's ecological systems increased significantly. Inspired by the thinking of Crutzen, the Great Acceleration was depicted by researchers working on the International Geosphere-Biosphere Programme between 1999 and 2003.

In 2004 in the *Anthropocene Review*, the Great Acceleration was explained through the Planetary Dashboard, a platform using 24 global indicators – 12 as socio-economic trends and 12 as Earth system trends. The readings begin at the recognised start of the Industrial Revolution in 1750 and have been updated until 2010. The two graphs used in the dashboard have become a snapshot depiction of changes in the functioning of Earth's systems and their causes.

Subsequently, the Anthropocene Working Group referred to additional factors, such as significant 'increases in erosion and sediment transport associated with urbanisation and agriculture' as well as an 'explosion of domestic animal populations and species invasions' and the global dispersion of concrete and plastics.

Steep population growth, an abundance of cheap oil, innovative technologies, and economic policies promoting growth have all been drivers of the acceleration. All have resulted in higher levels of production and consumption around the world. In turn, these correlate with steep rises in areas such as atmospheric carbon and other GHG build-ups, global warming, deforestation, ocean acidification and biodiversity loss.

The crux is that the indicators on both dashboards correlate to the same time period. The rate of change in the Earth system trends is significantly above the magnitude and rate of variability occurring during the Holocene. In other words, the changes occurring now are happening on time scales significantly more rapid than under natural conditions during the Holocene, and even further back. In addition, researchers are also recording cascading effects from the occurring changes. This acceleration has been a critical factor in calling for the recognition of the Anthropocene and this period as a possible starting point.

Climate change

Because global warming and climate change carry such prominence and weight of concern within the Anthropocene debate, it's worth highlighting them again. Moreover, both are primary causes of increasing environmental, economic and social degradation, which leads to greater instability across the world.

Although climate does change naturally, the current rate and extent of change are beyond what can be attributed to natural events. The evidence is clear that human activities involving fossil-fuel burning and a range of industrial and agricultural processes highlighted in the Great Acceleration are the primary causes. This is resulting in a carbon build-up in the atmosphere which, in turn, leads to global warming and a series of knock-on changes and cascading effects, such as melting polar caps, ocean acidification, extreme weather patterns and rising sea levels. Research clearly highlights that the rate of environmental alteration exceeds natural levels.

This was again highlighted in the 2018 IPPC comprehensive assessment on global warming, climate change and its impacts when the authors concluded governments had to introduce 'rapid, far-reaching and unprecedented changes in all aspects of society' to avoid current trends.

This was followed by an updated Summary for Policymakers in 2021. The report made it clear that 'widespread and rapid changes in the atmosphere, ocean, cryosphere and biosphere have occurred'. It went on to note that the evidence of human influence in these changes is clear and has strengthened since the last assessment.

In March 2021, the International Renewable Energy Association (IRENA) released its World Energy Transitions Outlook. This framework provides options for the world to achieve the Paris Agreement goals by transforming global energy policies. The good news suggests that the world already has the technology in renewables to achieve the carbon reduction targets and avoid temperatures rising through limits set by the IPCC. However, there is a downside: Global spending and investment will have to increase from current levels by at least 30% a year to reach these transformative targets. As a result, a total expenditure exceeding US$131 trillion between now and 2050 will be required. Nations will also have to elect leaders of vision to support changing long-term policy strategies, legislation and budgetary allocations, not to mention seeing off vested interests working against change.

If we fail in this challenge and temperatures rise through the 1.5°C level, then humanity and our technological ingenuity are in unchartered territory. Some scientists predict catastrophic consequences. For the record, if we cannot alter course, the estimates for 2100 are global temperature rises between 3.7°C and 4.8°C.

In a recent report, WEF's Expert Network added further menace to the challenge. It pointed out that 'significant gaps remain between the scientific and political communities when it comes to understanding how climate change risks cascade through environmental, social and economic system'.

Unlimited resource extraction

One of UNEP's markers is to measure annual resource extraction, which relates to all materials, at the primary and secondary levels taken from the natural environment. This includes all forms of biomass, minerals mined, fossil fuels, and less obvious activities, such as the industrialisation of agricultural and fishing production systems and the globalisation of food supply chains. Data reveals that this increased from 22 billion tons in 1970 to 92 billion tons in 2018. At current levels, extraction is forecast to reach 190 billion tons by 2060.

All of these materials are turned into manufactured goods of some sort. The scale of this process was revealed by *Nature* in a study carried out in 2020. The combined mass of human-made stuff, referred to as 'anthropogenic mass', weighs about 1.1 trillion metric tons and has just surpassed the combined biomass of all living material. The acceleration in manufacturing has been astonishing. In 1900, for example, man-made objects represented a mere 3% of total biomass.

These extraction forecasts are all the more alarming, considering that habitat and biodiversity loss is already at critical levels. Every global research assessment – the IPBES, WWF, IUCN and PNAS, for instance – picks up on this and details the impacts of human activity on the planet. During the Holocene, extinction rates have proved to be significantly higher than the background rate, even approaching those equivalent to previous mass extinctions.

Of course, there will be mitigating factors as we move into the future. For example, as economies switch to renewables, fossil fuel extraction will decrease, and increasing technological efficiencies will make a difference. But their impact could well be cancelled out by an increased population and the higher consumption levels demanded by a relentless search for ever-higher GDP growth, and by lifting communities out of poverty. There is another critical point here. The UN notes that until the 1990s, increasing extraction rates added a net positive to the global economy, but since then, the increasing costs of extraction and the impacts on the environment have resulted in a diminishing return. And bear in mind, this relentless search and use of resources continues in spite of us knowing that Earth has a finite amount of them.

Planetary boundaries

The planetary boundaries concept, developed by Johan Rockström, the former Director of the Stockholm Resilience Centre, along with a team of 28 international scientists, has become a leading broad indicator of humanity's unsustainable living patterns and the damage already inflicted on the biosphere.

The team identified nine vital natural processes that regulate the stability and resilience of Earth. These include stratospheric ozone depletion, loss of biodiversity; land system changes and natural habitat loss; biogeochemical pollution levels; climate change; ocean acidification; hydrological cycles and freshwater consumption; nitrogen and phosphorus flows, and atmospheric aerosol loading. For humanity to develop sustainably and thrive into the future, these nine boundaries need to be intact. Conversely, when any are breached, the risks of large-scale and irreversible environmental damage increase significantly.

Two boundaries have already been exceeded, thereby exposing humanity to great risks. These are biosphere integrity, which measures biodiversity and ecosystems loss, and biogeochemical flows, measuring pollution and toxic waste levels. Another two – climate change and land-system change – are in zones of uncertainty, as the risk levels increase at dangerous rates.

Only one boundary, stratospheric ozone depletion, remains intact, but this hasn't always been the case. The ozone layer filters out harmful ultraviolet radiation from the sun that causes skin cancers, cataracts, and other damaging health and environmental issues. In 1985, however, scientists discovered a massive hole in the ozone over Antarctica. A swift global response, through the Montreal Protocol, restored this boundary.

These damaged boundaries are a composite result of the factors discussed upfront in the book: excessive fossil fuel use; agricultural and industrial activities; deforestation; overexploitation of resources, and population growth, among others.

The planetary boundary concept is not without its critics, particularly regarding what constitutes a boundary and its applicability at a local level and within current timeframes. Researchers working on the concept also concede that more research is needed and that risk levels must be updated regularly. Notwithstanding, it is increasingly being taken up within policy-setting institutions as a reliable and helpful big-picture framework. To stay updated on the research into the planetary boundaries, visit the Stockholm Resilience Centre website.

Social influences

The environmental factors used to define the Anthropocene do not occur in isolation. In many cases, social influences are the direct causes of the destruction, and these impacts, in turn, have significant consequences for societies and their living. The Anthropocene is, after all, the age of humans, which means general living patterns, population levels and urbanisation rates, along with social landscapes and other related paradigms, are very much part of the debate.

According to the UN, the broad notion of 'social influences' can be defined as any aspect impacting the way people or communities live, work and interact with each other. Included would be population densities and demographics; education; land tenure structures; religious beliefs and other cultural practices; gender; age and race relations; employment opportunities; poverty levels and income disparities; crime levels, and health standards and conditions.

In addition to the rapid rise in the human population, paradigms that have resulted in mass urbanisation and poverty are vital considerations. All of these aspects will be dealt with later in the book. Rising inequality has undoubtedly become a feature of the Anthropocene, including specific social issues relating to education and consumerism.

For the first time, these social influences have been recognised in the GRR. The 2022 report raises the spectre of 'social cohesion erosion', listing it as a 'critical threat to the world across all time spans – short, medium and long term'. These dynamics are all negative, but because of the visible impacts on our living, and the efficiency of research and communication, this may lead to one positive outcome. Researchers and writers have pointed to this period as potentially the one that might realign humanity's inextricable link to the natural world.

Three principal factors at play

In broad terms, and as an exercise in synthesising what seems to be an overwhelming topic, we can highlight three factors playing out on the macro level:

1. *Population growth and urbanisation.*

People and where they live, as well as age, migration, and urbanisation patterns, are fundamental to sustainability discussions, dictating policy for almost all facets of development. As populations grow or are lifted out of poverty, they place increasing demand on all resources. The implications can be more profound in less developed nations, which often lack the economic and administrative capacity to respond to these challenges.

It took 200 000 years to reach a global population of one billion people in about 1804. It then took about 126 years to double, in around 1930. Our numbers started to accelerate in earnest after 1900, and data from the WEF shows peak growth rates of 2.2% a year during the mid-1960s, when three billion was reached. This also correlates with the planetary dashboards of the Great Acceleration. Then things got a little scary, when the population doubled to six billion by 1999 and, merely a decade later, reached seven billion in 2011. Now, in 2022, the global population is nudging eight billion.

Based on a continental analysis, Asia has over 4.6 billion people (China 1.5 billion and India, 1.35 billion), making it the most populated continent. Africa comes next, with more than 1.3 billion (Nigeria, 200 million). However, WEF data shows Africa to have the highest growth rates and, by 2050, the continent will have more than 3.3 billion people. By then, of every five people born, two will be African.

It's not only birth rates that concern demographers. Population movement patterns are just as important, and none more so than the lure of employment and a better life, which pulls people from rural areas into the towns and cities, and from poor countries to wealthier ones. This process is happening at rates never before seen in human history. In turn, the high rate of immigration and urbanisation places significant burdens on infrastructure. As a result, housing; sanitation; health; education; food security; transport; waste disposal and employment opportunities, for example, have become development issues of increasing concern.

According to the UN, in 1950 some 751 million people – less than one-third of the global population – lived in urban areas. By 2020, about 3.9 billion people (55% of the worldwide population) were living in urban areas and set to reach 68% by 2050. This will add another 2.5 billion people to the cities of the world. Alarmingly, in this environment of rapid urban growth, infrastructural development isn't keeping pace. The UN Slum Almanac provides a stark picture. Of the current urbanised population, approximately one billion people live in slum conditions without any infrastructure or support. Clearly, for those responsible for the sustainability of global metropolitan areas, urbanisation is a formidable challenge.

Peak population

Various population studies over the past few decades indicate that the planet can only support between two and three billion people while living under current paradigms. Some have also postulated that limits on freshwater and fertile land may well become defining factors in this regard. Given current levels, these are sobering assessments.

However, the world population is forecast to peak at almost 11 billion by 2100. Moreover, more than 50% of the projected increase by 2050 will be concentrated in just nine countries: The Democratic Republic of the Congo; Egypt; Ethiopia; India; Indonesia; Nigeria; Pakistan; the United Republic of Tanzania, and the United States of America. Also, by 2027, India will have passed China as the most populous nation in the world.

In contrast, a detailed analysis by *The Lancet* claims that the global population will peak at 9.73 billion people in 2064, and that by 2100, population levels will have dropped back to 8.79 billion people. According to this report, the five most populated countries in 2100 will be India (1.09 billion); Nigeria (791 million); China (732 million); the USA (336 million), and Pakistan (248 million).

The jury is still out on when and at what level peak population will be reached. Still, planners are obliged to always take the high forecasts into account.

2. Economic and political paradigms.

Our current economic and political systems are based on short-term thinking that promotes ever-higher extraction, production, and consumption levels to produce increased growth, wealth and taxes. This contradicts our environmental and social challenges – long-term objectives based on conservation, restoration, and reducing inequality. If ever we faced the ultimate conundrum, this contradiction is it.

Politics and economics are now so intertwined that it is almost impossible to think of one without the other. This pertains irrespective of a system being harsh and authoritarian, state-managed, or at the libertarian edge of the spectrum. In general, the industrial complex and the corporate world support politicians in their election bids. Then, politicians return the favour with economic policies and legislation that benefit growth and profit.

The crux is that both are based on short-term cycles. In the case of the economy, national performance is always focused on achieving annual GDP-based growth targets set by forecasts. For private corporations, it's in the daily share price and annual returns from dividend payouts to shareholders. For politicians, re-election is the objective, with manifestos promising immediate results within terms varying from a year or two at a local level, to four or five years at a national level. Because the aims and objectives of the two spheres are mostly hand-in-glove and dependent on each other, neither plays an effective oversight nor mitigating role. In times of crisis, they look to each other to extricate themselves, thus perpetuating the cycle of dependency and self-interest.

In contrast, ecological cycles, or Earth processes, mostly play themselves out in long-term cycles, with the impacts of human activity seldom seen immediately. At times, these may only become apparent over many decades, even thousands of years, and to generations down the line, long after individual politicians, governments or corporates have played their part and moved on. The difference in the duration of these cycles allows for decisions made today to be carried out with little or no responsibility.

The situation is then exacerbated by frameworks and institutions increasingly less able or inclined to deal with the contradictions or the complexity. At a national level, vested interests seem to hold sway over the vast majority of citizens. Then, at an international level, the increasingly bloated bureaucracies of global agencies and their conventions remain toothless in the face of non-compliance by signatory states.

Sadly, there is an added burden in many countries, as we witness the steady erosion of customs, constitutional rights and democratic institutions – safety and security, for example, and the courts and media. No matter how robust or proud the historical record of a particular country may be, these pillars of society are only as good as the politicians and officials who manage them.

Neoliberalism and promoting a paradox

The policies promoted by political and economic systems are something of a paradox. Our planet has clearly definable ecological boundaries: It can only supply a finite level of resources and absorb only a limited amount of waste. Despite this, our economic models and systems demand from it unlimited resources and growth while producing limitless waste, for which few are held accountable.

Kenneth E. Boulding, an economist by profession and a highly regarded poet and philosopher, was an influential thinker of the mid-1900s. He maintained: 'Anyone who believes that exponential growth can go on forever in a finite world is either a madman or an economist.'

In pursuit of this unlimited growth without accountability, the environment has become critically imperilled. With the vastly different time horizons of the two sides to the paradox, global paradigms can escape scrutiny and responsibility, as well as the necessary reparations. As a result, the consequences of our current irresponsible decision-making are left as a compound challenge for future generations. Not only is this wrong, but it is also utterly unsustainable.

This notion of unrestrained free-market capitalism is the principal characteristic of neoliberalism. It manifests in economic thinking that has dominated since the rise of Margaret Thatcher in the UK and Ronald Reagan in the USA during the late 1970s and early 1980s. It is based on policies that seek to minimise the role of government and oversight through deregulation and privatisation. At the same time, it boosts the influence of corporates through tax deductions, while undermining organised labour and claims of free, globalised trade.

In this way, neoliberalism has become a primary culprit in shaping growing inequality and the poor social conditions of billions of people in the Anthropocene. By way of illustration, Robert Reich, US Secretary of Labour during the Clinton presidency, pointed out in March 2021 that the average hourly income for the CEO of Alphabet, the parent company of Google, was approximately US$140 000, while the federal minimum wage in the USA remains pegged at US$7.25 an hour.

As Alan Greenspan, former Chair of the Federal Reserve in the USA, said at a National Association for Business Economics Conference in 2014: 'I consider income inequality the most dangerous part of what's going on in the United States.'

During this period of uncontrolled investment and development, the assault on the environment gathers momentum. The staunchest adherents of neoliberalism form the backbone of climate denialism and other lobbies against environmental change. George Monbiot encapsulated it best when he said: 'The economy is an environmental pyramid scheme, dumping its liabilities on the young and the unborn. Its current growth depends on intergenerational theft.'

To understand the implications of Monbiot's words, look no further than a series of particular events that occurred through 2022. Due to political uncertainty, war and supply chain disruptions, global oil and gas prices surged in the early months bringing rising inflation and widespread economic and social concerns for billions of people. These disruptions all coincided with extreme weather events and growing climate instability across continents, conditions brought about by the use of these self-same fossil fuel products. These were wretched times for most, but not for the oil and gas multinationals and the corporate world; they celebrated record profit and renumeration levels. Never mind the paradox – absurd, shocking, even criminal are some of the sentiments that come to mind as we ponder how sustainable this menacing convergence can be. Crass profiteering off products that are burning the planet and driving economic inequality and social upheaval exposes the true nature of current economic and political paradigms.

Inappropriate measurement

The paradox is further exacerbated by the political and economic spheres that rate and rank themselves in ways that no longer seem appropriate. Thus, annualised GDP growth, along with various per capita income calculations and stock-market indices, remain the primary way of measuring progress and quality of life in our societies.

While these statistics speak of success through ever-higher growth and performance across recent decades, in no way do they reflect how these benefits or rewards (and declines) are distributed. GDP indices are excellent for portraying specific averages, but they hide human experiences and say nothing about well-being or levels of happiness and security. They are unable to reflect the outcomes of inequality and poverty – the true conditions of living for large sections of the global community.

Furthermore, every input covering labour, financial and overhead costs is factored into economic indicators. We can instantly refer to data reflecting employment status, manufacturing, exports/imports, debt levels and exchange rates amid a host of other factors over time. However, current economic systems typically do not reflect environmental destruction or reparation costs in any way. Such considerations are hugely important, but in today's political and economic paradigm, everything about the environment is valued at zero. The currently favoured indices are also unable to reflect the mismanagement of authorities, corruption, and the failure of politicians to deliver on mandates.

We recently experienced events that lend themselves as an interesting example. In the USA, the Dow Jones Industrial Average, one of the most revered indicators of success and progress, pushed past 30 000 points in November 2020 and went on to reach all-time record highs. Then-president Donald Trump and his government celebrated that as a significant economic achievement. They and many others, particularly those ensconced within neoliberalism, believed that indicated the success of his administration and the route to certain re-election.

However, upon closer scrutiny, it showed those rises to be based on the performance of a handful of companies. Most notably, they were the FAANGs: Facebook, Amazon, Apple, Netflix, and Google. Together, they skewed both the average weighting and performance of the index. So, despite the global ravages of COVID-19 in 2020 and beyond, the shareholders of these stocks benefited, and their founders continued to roll in obscene wealth. At the same time, most Americans battled with unemployment, stagnant wages, falling living standards, little or no access to healthcare, and high debt levels. Thus, 2020 was a year of immense progress for a handful of individuals and, to a lesser extent, those holding the winning stocks and shares. But for the vast majority across the world, it was a time of anxiety, loss and little to no progress at all.

The irony for Trump and the vested interests that had pinned their hopes on his playbook was that without COVID-19, he may very well have been re-elected based on the performance of the US stock market. But because they had no idea how to deal with a crisis that cut across economic, social, and environmental spheres, they lost. The often-heard commentary is that humanity is generally better off today than it was 100 years ago, but could this be based on an awful mismeasurement of our living experiences?

Who do our political systems represent?

Polarisation within political systems and across cultural divides is seemingly on the increase, resulting in less representation for all citizens. Those less fortunate or trapped outside the vested interest groups continue to struggle for a better living.

The Economist Intelligence Unit publishes an annual Global Democracy Index using a matrix of 60 indicators. In the 2021 edition, only 22 countries of the 167 assessed are listed as full democracies. Norway came out as the most democratic and, unsurprisingly, North Korea as the least. The USA, often regarded as a bastion of the democratic system, only ranked 25th, while the average global rating is now at its lowest since the index's inception in 2006. Meanwhile, about 35% of the world's population still lives under authoritarian rule. Given these circumstances, we may well ask who our political systems actually represent.

In South Africa, we have a system in which parliamentarians are appointed by the party and not elected at a constituency level, so they are not beholden to the voters or the constitution, but to the party leadership. Across the Atlantic, voting in the US Senate during the 2020 impeachment trial of President Donald Trump offered up another example. According to *Newsweek*, the 48 senators who voted to impeach Trump represented 18 million more citizens than the 52 who successfully voted to acquit him.

Hilary Clinton lost the 2016 US presidential race despite winning nearly 3 million more votes than Donald Trump. That was the fifth time a president was elected without winning the popular vote. It is situations like these that call into question the system's ability to represent the new demographics of a country.

In Russia, President Vladimir Putin, in power since 1999, won a referendum allowing him to stay in the Kremlin until 2036. While the country ostensibly holds elections, the *Economist* ranks Russia as an authoritarian regime – at 134 in its list of 167.

Fair representation is not limited to the ballot box. In the aftermath of the 2008/9 global financial crisis, who did the systems around the world support? Most governments came to the aid of large banks and other financial institutions, many of which were the very perpetrators of, or participants in, the mess. Corporates, leveraged to the hilt, were also given a helping hand. The rest of society, ravaged by debt and unemployment, was left to their own devices. At most, only a handful of those culpable for the crisis were prosecuted. In time, historians may look back at that meltdown of the global economy and how it was handled and describe it as a defining moment, one heralding the end of something. Perhaps it marks the time when citizens of the world started losing trust in the systems that govern our societies.

So, what does political representation have to do with surviving in the Anthropocene? With democracy in decline and so many people living in societies that are not fully representative, the situation offers a stark reminder of how problematic it is for citizens to enact change through political means. These conditions ensure that our systems are joined in a dangerous alliance that works against true sustainability and transformation. Simply put, change is not in the best interests of those in control. Rather than being the agents of change that the world requires, they have become the enforcers of the status quo. It's worth bearing in mind that when government indifference or neglect of oversight and fairness sets in, systemic failure of the nation is a high probability.

There's no doubt that climate change and other environmental crises impact the vast majority more severely than the vested interests and those in government. Those most affected pay a significantly higher price in terms of death and costs of mitigation or avoidance. That being so, the social calamity scenario looms larger than currently imagined.

3. Denial

Denial, the third macro-level driver, is one of the oldest face-saving tricks in the book of survival or self-preservation.

On a personal level, psychologists will confirm that we all use denial in some form: To get out of trouble with family and friends, to survive in the work environment, when we're sad, and even when affronted by news and information. Even more tellingly, we use denial to avoid taking action, so it can be hugely debilitating. For example, our current political and economic systems sanction strategic denial to maintain paradigms and vested interests, including power, control, and identity. It was probably best summed up by Sigmund Freud, the doyen of psychoanalysis during the early 1900s. Richard S Tedlow, writing in the *Harvard Business Review*, quotes Freud's description of denial as 'knowing-but-not-knowing'. He also quotes Freud's biographer's summary of the great analyst's interpretation of denial as 'a state of rational apprehension that does not result in appropriate action'.

Then in 2007, the *New York Times* ran an article by Benedict Carey titled *Denial Makes the World Go Round*, an immensely insightful piece that reminded readers of another Freudian insight that suggests that denial is a 'defence against external realities that threaten the ego'. The article also commented that, generally, psychologists see denial as 'a protective defence in the face of unbearable news'. The unbearable news in this instance are the grim accounts of climate change and extreme weather events, raging bush fires, habitat and biodiversity loss, as well as the social issues pertaining to poverty levels, financial crises and social unrest across the world.

This news is increasingly presented, sometimes ineffectually, throughout the entire media spectrum by the scientific community and the many environmental agencies to which we donate. Of course, social media platforms and social pressure play an enormous role. In most instances, with the news comes the wicked problem we so dislike hearing: These frightening events are occurring more regularly and often with greater intensity as a direct result of our current, unsustainable living patterns.

Hundreds of millions, if not billions, of us have already been impacted in some way. These experiences range from being caught up in extreme and dangerous weather events to joining the ranks of the unemployed or losing work due to the policies of globalisation, disease or death brought about by pollution, the COVID-19 pandemic, or the consequences of the 2008/9 financial crash. All are linked to the Anthropocene in some way.

If we analyse, understand and absorb this information in its proper context, then there is no escaping the logical conclusion: To avert these catastrophic scenarios, each of us has to make significant, fundamental changes to the way we behave and live. However, if these changes cause anxiety, are deemed too disruptive or costly, or bring about loss of political leverage or social status, and if they require us to give up aspects of current comfortable and affluent lifestyles, particularly in developed nations, denial steps in.

Some argue that humans are hard-wired to gloss over long-term or distant threats and that, as a survival mechanism, we are instead alert to every immediate danger. While this has merit and can, to a degree, explain why we put off action, Carey reminds us that inattention, passive acknowledgement, reframing, and wilful blindness are all varieties of denial that cause people to adopt 'a protective defence'.

Denial may also be associated with confirmation bias – the act of seeking out or only using information that confirms or supports an existing belief. When the two come together, they play themselves out as serious misjudgement and poor leadership. Denial can also serve the strategic aims typically associated with desired political, military, or economic outcomes, as well as direct and selfish personal objectives. History is littered with examples of strategic denial by world leaders and people in positions of authority and influence. Wartime leaders are particularly prone to denial, as are corporate CEOs who run their business empires into the ground.

Currently, the most relevant and dangerous examples of denial involve climate change. These are most evident within the corporate world, especially the fossil fuel, transport, energy, and related industries, and the politicians aligned with them. This cast is, in turn, supported by elements within the media: Insidious platforms that assist the denial and distraction by trashing science and favouring trivia and social gossip as most newsworthy. Typically, these are all agencies we entrust with leadership and giving us the truth, powers that should embrace care for our interests and welfare, our communities and nations. Are we then being let down, misled or even blatantly played as mere voting fools? Their actions cause delay and confusion, and even thwart efforts towards fundamental change.

Climate psychiatry and psychology

If you have ever wondered how serious denial of climate change has become, consider this: Several professional agencies, including the Climate Psychiatry Alliance and the Climate Psychology Alliance, have been established to help people deal with the emotional and behavioural consequences of climate change. These bodies recognise climate change as a defining challenge of our time, one that engenders anxiety, fear, despair, and denial. Moreover, they acknowledge that confronting climate change and its consequences have become serious public health issues.

In this regard, it is interesting that studies have shown people with higher levels of formal education to be more supportive of existing paradigms than those with lower levels of education. This means that the former is less likely to support change. So, our individual propensity for denial on issues regarding the state of our planet may well be based on our own calculation of what we as individuals and families have to gain or lose in the immediate term. Either way, denial plays an instrumental role in obstructing or holding back the change that is so urgently needed.

Why can't we change how we behave?

If we accept that living in the Anthropocene and our efforts to transform our societies are indeed humanity's greatest challenge, then asking about scenario choices and our chances to achieve positive outcomes become crucial questions.

To answer them, and for a more realistic assessment of our future, we first need to understand the factors inhibiting change. We have spoken about the significant role that population, our living paradigms and denial are playing as macro-level drivers, but there are other less obvious factors at play, which reduce or impede our chances of collectively engineering transformative change across the world.

Complexity and consensus

Every socio-economic and environmental challenge facing the world has its own economic, social, cultural, ecological, and political complexities. Understanding this requires interdisciplinary thinking and accounting for uncertainty.

Typically, leadership and problem-solving in the world of multi-lateral global politics and business tends to follow a more linear, one-dimensional, and short-term path. For example, a specific dispute may be dealt with simply as an economic, trade or legal issue, but in reality, it requires decision-makers to understand that the problem and the potential solutions may have an entire range of critical consequences resulting from elements otherwise discounted or ignored. When such multi-disciplinary approaches are called for, it adds immensely to the complexity of the issue and the leadership skills required.

In addition, of course, the world is also hugely polarised, split along cultural, class, religious and political lines. When seeking to transform communities and societies, both socially and economically, these splits need to be overcome. So, at what stage do we accept common ground, or turn to ideological differences as a reason to avoid compromise? If the latter is accepted, then potential outcomes can be rejected, as the required shift in consciousness is seen as counter-productive to one's own interests.

Prof Mark Swilling from the Sustainability Institute points out that for fundamental change to occur, the entire range of societies' structures and institutions need to be simultaneously transformed. Any new reality will need to be based on a consensus that takes this complex nature into account by addressing the interconnectedness of all disciplines. Such undertakings would be extremely onerous and may well be a step too far for most within the current leadership of our nations.

The power of vested interests

Current economic and political systems are macro-level drivers of our situation in the Anthropocene. It's the power of the vested interests that continues to reinforce this status quo and the paradoxical relationship that has been described.

Typically, the term 'vested interest' is a legal one used within the financial or business community. It generally refers to any involvement that an entity or individual may have in a situation or project, and how this relates to any gain or loss occurring because of actions taken.

When it comes to the Anthropocene, the term 'vested interest' can refer to any group with a stake in our current living systems, and how change might bring either gains or losses to their position in our societies. A vested interest (particularly if in the form of a global industry lobby group, or political and social platform) can become a principal and powerful roleplayer, not only in the debate but also in attempting to direct the outcomes.

As an example, the fossil fuel industry is a vested interest in the climate change debate because it will be materially impacted by legislative changes aimed at reducing carbon emissions. Of the 100 companies the CDP claims are responsible for 71% of global GHG emissions since 1998, *The Guardian* reports that five of them (Exxon Mobil, BP, Chevron/Texaco, Royal Dutch Shell, and ConocoPhillips) have spent a combined US$3.6 billion in advertisements and campaigns during the last 30 years to influence the climate change debate in their favour.

This has happened despite ExxonMobil knowing as far back as the 1960s that their business was a significant contributor to the emissions count, global warming and the harmful impacts thereof. Yet, in circumstances not too dissimilar to the infamous tobacco industry's attempts to deny links between smoking and cancer, these vested interests have gone to extreme lengths to protect markets and profit streams, no matter the consequences for humanity or the planet.

How successful has the fossil fuel industry been? Well, in some ways, very much so. For example, in 2019, it resulted in the USA withdrawing from the Paris Agreement, the world's most recent attempt at climate change mitigation. That decision has since been reversed, but in all likelihood, it will stoke further lobbying from that sector.

Another example pertains to the way vested interests are able to manipulate the international community. At the 2021 Climate Change summit (COP26), delegates and the banking community from the developed world made commitments to end funding fossil fuel projects in the developing world. However, they did that without making similar pledges to end such projects in their own countries where carbon emission rates are significantly higher. This type of hypocrisy is found in almost every sphere of current paradigms.

Similarly, global chemical companies will lobby against changes limiting fertiliser and pesticide use in the agriculture sector. Fishing companies will attempt to obstruct changes restricting or banning the use of long lines, while Big Pharma will try to stop the lowering of drug prices despite the billions of profits they already make. And the National Rifle Association will lobby against gun control despite the shocking death tolls in school shootings, while powerful pro-hunting groups will lobby against alternatives to trophy hunting as we search for more effective ways to protect land and species.

On the political front, parties nominate and then assist members in getting elected, typically spending significant sums of money. Very often, these efforts are also instigated or supported by corporates or wealthy individuals. In turn, the elected politicians end up owing their allegiance to their benefactors. Their agendas are then dictated by the power of that machinery rather than by the voters they claim to represent.

All of these interests use practices and language that contrive to dupe voters, workers, investors, consumers and officials into believing that change has occurred or that actions and products are legitimate. Terms such as 'greenwashing', 'brainwashing', 'social washing', and 'pinkwashing' are all used to describe this type of behaviour. References to the green economy or green markets, for example, suggest business practices or products that are ethically or sustainably manufactured. However, carefully crafted language can misleadingly refer to a fair and equitable company policy that does not, in fact, exist.

In early 2021, the EU and a group of consumer watchdog groups released a survey of 344 sustainability and environmental claims made by a range of consumer products that were being sold online. Some 42% of those claims were simply false, while another 37% used vague language that was not substantiated in any way.

Environmental, social and (good corporate) governance investment (ESG) is a new category in which investors can make ethical and socially responsible choices. The idea is to also encourage companies to align with criteria designating them as such. That comes with recognition for their efforts in solving current environmental and social crises. However, according to the Consumer Protection Enforcement Network in the UK, in a survey of 500 websites representing the business community, 40% were posting 'potentially misleading environmental information.'

Our entire economic and political paradigm festers with lobby groups and the influence and corruption they bring in purposefully misleading consumers and investors. This is the power of vested interests and why they have become a major obstacle to change in our societies.

Consumption, consumerism and convenience

In 1958, John Kenneth Galbraith, an American economist and diplomat, wrote an essay, *How Much Should a Country Consume?* When referring to American consumption levels, Galbraith said the following:

'If we are concerned about our great appetite for materials, it is plausible to seek to increase the supply, to decrease waste, to make better use of the stocks that are available, and to develop substitutes. But what of the appetite itself? Surely this is the ultimate source of the problem? Yet in the literature of the resource problem, this is the forbidden question. Over it hangs a nearly total silence. It is as though, in the discussion of the chance for avoiding automobile accidents, we agree not to make any mention of speed!'

The appetite Galbraith refers to relates to global consumption levels and the hunger for consumerism; activities that fire increasing growth and wealth levels under current paradigms. Can you imagine what Galbraith would say today, with consumption levels over five times greater than when he wrote the essay?

Strictly speaking, social scientists distinguish between consumption, the 'buying for need', and consumerism, the 'buying for greed'. Although both require the extraction of raw materials and their subsequent use in manufacturing, the distinction between the two has become increasingly blurred in today's world of marketing and advertising.

Regarded by historians as economic and social trends that developed during the early decades of the last century, consumption and consumerism have been facilitated by technological advances, mass production techniques, global trade, and greater productivity. In turn, there have been significant increases in the choice and availability of goods – a boon to consumers from the rapidly expanding middle classes worldwide. Although initially associated with Western capitalist systems, higher consumption and consumerism levels are now trends within all societies and across all continents.

Based on modern materialistic, social competition and vanity values, this contemporary way of living dictates the high consumption of consumer goods and services. In addition, it's regarded as a desirable leisure activity and lifestyle choice in the pursuit of personal recognition and social standing. Such trends define our development path, so much so that we now refer to 'consumer societies' or a 'consumer culture'.

Consumerism has a twin: Our growing affinity for seeking convenience in every aspect of our living. So, whether we are talking about food and eating habits, transport options or the way we socialise or shop, choices based on convenience have become the focus of decision-making around our lifestyles.

In a 2018 editorial, *The tyranny of convenience*, the *New York Times* said that convenience 'has emerged as perhaps the most powerful force shaping our individual lives and our economies'. An ideal and growing way of life. 'Easy is better, but easiest is best,' claimed the editorial.

The outcome of these twin addictions is the production and consumption of an entire range of products that put significant pressure on the global resource base and the amount of waste to be managed. The product range is endless, and every imaginable service is available. We now even have machines to squeeze our toothpaste, and dentists to tend to our dogs' teeth. Desirability and use levels are fed by marketing, advertising, and planned obsolescence campaigns, all tailored to induce further consumption of the latest models and brands. In addition, there is an endless supply of 'celebrities' who earn a living by endorsing any type of product, no matter how detrimental it may be to the environment or social cohesion.

By way of comparison, I can only imagine that at most, a few tens of thousands of people will end up reading this book. However, in May 2021, Visual Capitalist posted a list: 'The World's Top 50 Influencers Across Social Media Platforms'. All 50 had more than 120 million followers, and 10 of them had access to more than 300 million minds. Of the 50, only one, ex-US President Barack Obama, with 221 million followers, was from the fields of science or politics. The rest were either sports stars or entertainment celebrities.

These factors all have a profound impact on the behaviour and choices of billions of people around the world. The most crucial point to bear in mind is that this is of our own making. We have built professions, entire economies, an internet network, and aspirational societies on these factors. Planners, designers, economists, politicians, marketers and advertising agents, engineers, and even life coaches and psychologists have played their role in conceiving and implementing a way of life that hinges on being part of a chain of events that play out daily.

How are we ever going to reverse this?

Some believe we may never be able to do so. When Daniel Kahneman, an Israeli Noble Prize-winning psychologist and economist, was asked about human decision-making relating to changes we should be making, he offered a rather chilling comment: 'This is not what you might want to hear,' he said, 'but no amount of psychological awareness will overcome people's reluctance to lower their standard of living. So that's my bottom line: There is not much hope. I'm thoroughly pessimistic. I'm sorry.'

Planned obsolescence

Planned obsolescence is a complex issue, as measuring a product's environmental impact can differ depending on whether the measurement is made during the manufacturing cycle or when in use. Plastic bags, for example, have a lower manufacturing impact but a more significant use impact because they could be around for hundreds of years. By contrast, energy-efficient vehicles have a high manufacturing impact, but the benefits of low impact are seen when in use.

Generally, planned obsolescence refers to the principle that goods are designed and built to fail or to be upgraded after a short period of use. Typical examples include electronic goods and appliances, computer hardware and software, clothing and cars. Aided and abetted by an advertising and marketing industry that promotes the companies and their products, this type of manufacturing started with the first cartels way back in the early decades of the 1900s.

The obsolescence is planned by introducing functional concerns or by promoting fashion and style changes. In some cases, the cost of repair is almost the cost of replacement, pushing consumers towards purchasing a new model. In extreme cases, consumers are even prohibited from repairing products.

Today, obsolescence has become a feature of our high consumption and consumerism levels. Cellphone companies provide an excellent example as they now issue new models annually. For instance, since the launch of the iPhone brand in 2007, the company had produced 22 different iterations by 2021. The benefits for corporates and retail outlets are obvious. They consistently generate higher turnover and profit levels, but their success comes at a high cost to the environment.

Your children versus my consumption

When discussing the sustainability of our economic systems, a typical response among the citizens of developed nations is to revert to a distorted version of the Malthusian Theory of Population – pointing to population growth rates in the developing world as the primary culprit. As noted earlier, population growth is a defining concern in the Anthropocene. Still, it cannot be a justification for denying the consequences of high consumption levels and the over-utilisation of resources that characterise the developed world. This poses as much of a challenge as population growth in the developing world, if not a greater one.

According to the UN, the global population is growing at about 1% a year. However, this is substantially outstripped by economic growth. For example, in 2019, the IMF had economic growth rates at 2.9%.

As the saying goes: 'The devil is always in the detail.' When we delve deeper into the Living Planet Report and the Global Footprint Index, and then cross-reference these with the UN's population data, a very different picture emerges. It becomes starkly apparent that the high-consumption and high-footprint nations are mostly not those with high population growth rates.

In 1990, UN data showed that, on average, 8.1 tonnes of natural resources were required to satisfy the needs of an individual each year.

By 2017, this had risen to 12.2 tonnes – an increase of 50%. However, when broken down into national income brackets, high-income countries required approximately 27 tonnes per person, and middle-income countries, 17 tonnes. In comparison, low-income countries made do with two tonnes a year for each citizen.

The USA has about 4.25% of the global population, yet it consumes more than 22% of global fossil fuels. The trends are similar in respect of water and electricity use, per capita vehicle purchases, and carbon emissions. In 2022, the Center for Global Development published a study pinpointing the alarming disparities in carbon footprints between the developed and less-developed world.

The report notes that the 'carbon emissions of the average US citizen is estimated to be over 100 times that of the average Ugandan', and that the average Briton produces 200 times the emissions of the average Congolese. Again, it is the countries with higher population growth rates that have lower environmental impact indices. The point is that both factors are of concern – the one should not be traded off against the other in an attempt to deny the role they play.

Another paradox is encapsulated in what is known as the 'demographic transition'. It is widely accepted that when communities are lifted out of poverty – a process often associated with better education for young women – population growth rates drop. However, the catch is that as people move out of poverty, they enter a category of higher consumption levels and chase aspirational lifestyles. This, of course, brings greater environmental impacts.

Is the answer then to reduce all three: Poverty, population, and consumption levels? This then brings us back to issues of complexity, one of the principal reasons why changing our living paradigms is so problematic.

Leadership concerns

Typically, defining leadership is a subjective exercise because of the range of factors involved in how different communities nominate and elect their leaders. However, when it comes to the qualities that make a good leader, most of us would highlight empathy, honesty, confidence, and boldness. But what about leadership in the context of ideology and culture? How do we define someone with a vociferous and dedicated following, who has the abovementioned traits but stands on a platform contrary to someone else's values, norms, or cultural justifications?

Clearly, we need to be wary of looking for a simplified and standardised version of leadership. It could be argued that recognising good leadership is as much about the positive impacts and results a leader achieves than it is about highlighting specific characteristics.

Some of my best insights on leadership came during my studies at the Sustainability Institute, particularly from author Ronald A. Heifetz. In his book *Leadership Without Easy Answers*, Heifetz argues that leadership is a normative concept. He makes a clear distinction between leaders who use their authority and power to influence (often associated with prominence or dominance) and leaders who are inspirational and adaptive in getting others involved in whatever significant challenge is at hand. This distinction is particularly apt when it comes to the Anthropocene, as the challenges we face clearly require adaptive responses. In a way, that inspires people to be involved in collective change rather than being strong-armed into a set of prescribed behaviours.

When thinking about the crop of global leaders over the past few decades – specifically the likes of Trump in the USA, Bolsonaro in Brazil, Putin in Russia, Jinping in China, Zuma in South Africa, Magafuli in Tanzania, and Mohammed bin Salman in Saudi Arabia – I am reminded of a line attributed to Mark Twain: 'It's easier to fool people than convince them that they have been fooled.'

Unfortunately, those leaders are not the only ones holding back change in favour of maintaining power and control. There are many other powerful autocrats, dictators and oligarchs around the world, and they all understand only too well the words of Mark Twain.

Let's not forget those leaders who base their power on fanning prejudice and fear, both of which increase social unrest and polarisation. Under such regimes, government processes and the ability to effectively implement policies are retarded, even nullified. Significant amounts of time and funding are spent on infighting rather than dealing effectively with the issues of the day. And let's not forget the high number of leaders who are straight-up inadequate and incompetent; leaders who lack the vision, courage, or understanding to tackle what is required of them.

Given these circumstances, what are the chances of the world electing, in the same timeframe, a set of national leaders across the various continents who are visionary, incorruptible, empathetic, and smart? These leaders, representing all political, economic, and cultural blocs, would need to be able to set aside national self-interest and cultural distinctions to work in a transdisciplinary manner in the best interests of tackling the challenges that impact every global citizen. Such a perfect leadership alignment is unlikely, but is that not precisely what is needed to tackle climate change, inequality, and poverty?

There are examples of leaders with successful agendas. Poll numbers reflect this in countries like New Zealand, Iceland, Rwanda and the Scandinavian nations. But generally, we are being failed by a leadership group among the more prominent and influential countries who are seemingly more concerned about national and personal self-interest and cultural hegemony than dealing with the enormity of current global challenges.

I would also make a general call for far greater diversity across leadership structures. Whether at a local or international level, I believe our chances of success and our future as a global community would be better served with far greater representation from women and the youth. This needs to be mixed with perspectives from different cultures. There is not nearly enough intergenerational debate, cultural tolerance or simple compassion. In a world dominated by brutish patriarchal systems, often accompanied by anachronistic thinking and belief systems, the voices of women and the youth are so obviously missing.

Education systems

Among the library of great thoughts from Nelson Mandela, one of the most telling is his belief that 'education is the most powerful weapon which you can use to change the world'.

Zander Sherman is one of many who believe we are not using education in this way, as the process of providing it is fundamentally flawed. In his book, *The Curiosity of School: Education and the Dark Side of Enlightenment*, he says: 'In the twenty-first century, we use a nineteenth-century school model with twentieth-century values. There's clearly something wrong with this picture.'

The challenge then is to overcome what Sherman understands to be wrong to achieve what Mandela believes is possible. In essence, as Sherman points out, we have institutionalised learning into systems that remain focused on a form of social engineering. Rather than inspiring and benefiting individual children, the aim is to churn out like-minded adults who fit into the political and economic paradigms that govern our world.

This pertains as much to the standard government-funded version of school as it does to the expensive private options (bearing in mind the concept of private education was merely to form social and cultural elites). Schools are immensely effective tools to shape human conformity, both here in Africa and abroad.

Educational transformation requires the entire process to be reviewed. A great start would be a discussion around repurposing the role and shape of learning, and then tackling subject matter and how children (and adults) are being taught.

School curricula are generally outdated and continue to prepare students for a time that no longer exists. This happens by aggregating interests and passions using inflexible curricula and methods that emphasise traditional values and discipline in structured institutions. Without appropriate education, we are ill-informed and ill-equipped to deal with the realities of our time, producing graduates with unrealistic expectations.

In addition, children need to be inspired to foster critical thinking. This is especially so now, when the implications of current actions on future generations and the planet have become way more important than focusing on immediate benefits.

My 14-year-old son has already learnt how to destroy the planet with economic models promoting GDP-based growth through commercial mining, agriculture, fishing and logging. He has also been taught the basics of banking, as well as the benefits of increasing profit levels and our global political systems. However, he and his friends have no idea about planetary boundaries, zero-growth economics, or the poverty levels and inequalities wrought by current economic models. They also have little to no exposure at schools to ecosystem thinking or the life-giving services they provide. There is no awareness of carbon cycles, ecological footprints, and cascades, or where they fit into the realm of biodiversity and its richness. They have no idea about intrinsic values relating to the environment, alternative ways of living, or at the very least, global efforts at attaining the SDGs, let alone the collapse scenarios that are possibilities under current paradigms.

At university level, we have similar circumstances worldwide. In economics faculties, for example, curricula still promote GDP growth-based models and per capita calculations as the yardstick for progress and success.

We should also be asking questions about the teacher training colleges and the curricula for education degrees at university level. Have they been transformed to reflect the future, not only at the subject level but also regarding communication, language, cultural context, and how children think and learn? How many kids will actually be in classrooms 20 years from now? Are our teachers sufficiently innovative, skills-literate, and adaptive for these changes? Who or what is a teacher?

Other issues include assessing achievement, granting access to schooling, and the lack of educational funding in many countries. The high debt levels students accumulate to get knowledge and qualifications can be crippling. Furthermore, in some countries, like South Africa and the USA, students have serious concerns regarding personal safety while at school or university locations.

Given the extent and pace of changes in urban living patterns, another significant consideration must be the actual learning spaces. Should schools, as we know them, be the principal way of education? To what extent are we prepared for widespread home-schooling if we see the disintegration of the entire traditional school platform?

This is especially relevant to less-developed nations where school infrastructure falls way behind developed countries. Lack of access to schools or productive learning spaces, which is also brought about by narrow historical interpretations of what this needs to look like, seriously hinders the acquisition of knowledge.

A perennial problem that seems to worsen as urbanisation continues to increase is how to get children and older students out of the classrooms and into the natural world. In urban settings, opportunities to learn from Nature are minimal. But even where they can, educators are not making use of the 'great outdoors', one of the most appropriate and inspirational 'classrooms' imaginable. Outdoor experiences are more effective pathways to understanding everything the natural world represents.

In 2018, WEF ran an article titled *Why schools should teach the curriculum of the future, not the past.* It made a plea for advanced computer sciences reflecting the Fourth Industrial Revolution, with subjects such as robotics, artificial intelligence, data analysis, and cybersecurity to become core components of school curricula. This call is largely valid, but only if you buy into current paradigms. Why is there no mention of topics related to the Anthropocene or transforming societies?

If, for a moment, we accept that the world may well change more in the next 30 years or so than it has over the last 300, why are we not exposing our children to the psychology of this process, and helping them to learn how to cope with a highly uncertain world? The cradle-to-the-grave concept of employment is long over, and the status of being self-employed and working from home is also in the throes of redundancy. After 12 years of school and another four or five at university, how will hundreds of millions of people know how to cope?

Providing reskilling and upskilling conditions are, of course, essential options to keep pace with job destruction. Human ingenuity is a remarkable evolutionary characteristic, but what if the robots have taken all the jobs, and the machines are now thinking for us?

An incongruous environmental ethic

Most of the factors that have already been outlined have contributed to what can only be referred to as an incongruous environmental ethic.

The study of environmental ethics is a relatively recent philosophical discipline – it only came about in the 1970s with the advent of the environmental movement. It concerns the moral and ethical components of our relationship with the environment, including our attitudes, how we articulate them, and the policies and actions taken regarding every sphere of the natural world.

Since the advent of sedentary living and economic systems, societies have viewed and accounted for the environment on an instrumental-value basis. In other words, the natural world around us only has value in terms of bringing benefits to humanity. Under this ethic, a lion or bear, for example, only has worth if we can commodify it with a monetary tag on its head. Land only has value based on its mineral rights, logging wealth or tourism potential. If such land is not used by a particular form of economic activity, it will soon be taken up by another competing form.

These values are asserted or measured through a pricing mechanism traded on 'markets', as one would commodities. These trades or gains for humanity are then accounted for as wealth creation or economic growth. In addition, according to current thinking, the incremental gains reflect our progress. However, there is no mention or attempt to account for habitat and the forests that disappear, water bodies that have been polluted, or the losses to the gene pool of animals. In other words, we neglect to calculate the use and destruction of the things underpinning our living.

Today, this environmental ethic is packaged and marketed through the twin concepts of sustainable development and sustainable use. Both assume that humanity is absolutely entitled to exploit every aspect of the environment to advance our living. By way of justification, the terms come with an apparent softener that suggests this will, or can be, done sustainably or responsibly.

An additional concern regarding the current ethic is that while conservation planning and environmental action should focus on long-term stewardship that seeks to avoid damage, instead (in true corporate fashion), the objective is to maximise extraction and profit in the shortest timeframe possible. Conservation projects and environmental protection initiatives lose out to corporate activity, such as mining, agriculture, or large-scale tourism activities, because jobs, economic activity and quick profit always trump the health of ecosystems and the biodiversity required for survival tomorrow. Comparing and analysing the respective merits on the same basis is simply foolish.

Despite the sustainability fanfare, science attests that the planet is increasingly being impacted, in some instances at critical levels. As long as the explanation and understanding of sustainable development remains broad, vague, and without legislative control, it will be a flawed approach to environmental health. The lack of definitive action to tackle climate issues highlights this approach; it's 30 years since the Rio Summit, and while carbon emissions have risen by about 30%, nine global conferences since Rio have yet to produce a clear strategy.

This reality also begs the question about whether we understand the difference between pricing and truly valuing something. The most descriptive summary of this confusion comes from the Austrian philosopher Ivan Illich who said in 1969: 'The more we viewed nature as a disposable commodity or a convenient resource, the less we would worry about its degradation.'

We also know that the natural world has value way beyond a monetary price; by definition its biological functioning reflects intrinsic value. So, while markets can efficiently direct and distribute financial returns, they pay no attention to the outcomes of this efficiency, distribution or inherent value. In other words, markets are unable to trade in intrinsic values and ethical considerations, or to apportion morality.

By way of example, in 2010, 195 countries delivered the Aichi Targets, which were 10-year goals for reversing habitat destruction and biodiversity loss. By the deadline in 2020, they hadn't met a single goal they'd set themselves. There has been no accounting for this, and not a single country or agency has been held responsible for this failure. Clearly, the political and economic agendas of the day remain the priority.

Are we beginning to understand?

As most of us know, the natural world is the foundation of all life and our activities, making it priceless. Despite this, after thousands of years of instrumental-value thinking, tagging a dollar value on a visit to a protected area, or selling a tourism concession to visit gorillas, is readily imaginable to our planners and decision-makers. But accounting for the life-giving services that functioning ecosystems and earth cycles provide remains improperly understood.

However, the debate may be moving forward, as scientific and social communities continue to tally the damage we inflict. In the recently released Dasgupta Review (2021), the author makes this sentiment clear: 'Our unsustainable engagement with Nature is endangering the prosperity of current and future generations.'

The entire report speaks to our failure at approach, policy, and institutional level as central to our current crises. And the UNEP Making Peace with Nature blueprint makes it clear that the current approach to environmental destruction represents a 'planetary emergency'. But, as Freud has pointed out, knowing is one thing; the response or lack thereof and the ensuing consequences are entirely different matters.

I wrote this two years ago:

'*For well over a century, we have had an abusive relationship with the environment, a reality we can no longer deny or wish away with platitudes of greenwashing. Instead, an entirely new environmental ethic is needed, one that embraces the concept of intrinsic value with an ecological understanding of the planet and our existence within it, not above or outside of it. This ethic must also confront the blatant contradictions of our time. Changing our environmental ethic is not a luxury or even an option to be ridiculed by reactionaries; it is imperative to avoid the collapse of our societies.*'

Today, these sentiments run even deeper.

The two traps

Our current paradigms are characterised by many features. One of these involves poverty, a systemic 'trap' that holds over a billion individuals, often as entire communities, even countries, in conditions that make it almost impossible for them to escape.

The other relates to progress and offers an interesting take on the cycle humanity seems to follow as we search to improve our living.

These two traps appear at opposite ends of the economic and social spectrum. Both are deeply rooted in our societies and occur at such a scale that attempts at transformation become far more complex and problematic. Both play into the social crisis, contributing to the environmental challenges at the levels of cause and impact.

The poverty trap

In 2005, Nelson Mandela said: 'Like slavery and apartheid, poverty is not natural. It is man-made, and it can be overcome and eradicated by the action of human beings.'

Mandela's words reiterate that poverty is the deliberate consequence of a system or paradigm designed and implemented by societies that leave some people with little or no access to elements that could improve their lives. Dealing with poverty is further complicated because there is no consensus when it comes to defining or quantifying the condition. Attempting to do so is based on political and economic persuasions and standing.

Poverty was first recognised in the late 1700s and early 1800s as a social and economic state, but it was not until 1981 that the World Bank began listing poverty statistics to reflect the scale of the problem. It was not until the 2000s that the world turned its attention to addressing poverty through various sustainability agendas.

Poverty is typically measured by a simple monetary tag that embraces a set of characteristics that describe poor people and the conditions in which they live. These levels of deprivation are open to interpretation, depending on the historical context and the regions under scrutiny. Extreme or absolute poverty pertains to the most deprived living at or below what is regarded as the minimum level required for survival. Basically, people living in poverty have very little. How little continues to be defined by institutions such as the World Bank, the International Monetary Fund (IMF) and the leading private-sector banks and organisations that enjoy the support of the status quo.

In 2015, the World Bank increased the poverty limit from $1.25 to $1.90 per person per day. Anyone earning or spending at this level or less is regarded as living in extreme poverty. Of course, for those living slightly above the daily limit, the hardships of poverty don't magically disappear, as they continue to experience deprivation and inconsistent access to the services necessary to human well-being. Women, immigrants and children are disproportionately affected by poverty in the workplace, a lack of education and opportunity, and even cultural discrimination.

Statistics vary, but according to most leading data sources, somewhere between 800 million and one billion people live on or under the monetary poverty line that defines extreme poverty.

Until a few years back, the trend seemed to be improving. In 2018 then-World Bank Group President Jim Yong Kim announced this triumph. 'Over the last 25 years,' he crowed, 'more than a billion people have lifted themselves out of extreme poverty, and the global poverty rate is now lower than it has ever been in recorded history. This is one of the greatest human achievements of our time.' However, he did warn the trend had slowed and that 'rates remain stubbornly high in low-income countries'. His glee was short-lived; as the covid pandemic emerged, and the World Bank reported that over 250 million people have re-entered the poverty brackets. Inequality levels continue to rise.

This approach to defining poverty only has worth in that it is important to know what poverty looks like. As indicated, these statistics only speak to those living in conditions of absolute misery on or below the daily limit. What about the hundreds of millions who 'have lifted themselves out of extreme poverty' and into a category that is only marginally better? There are also hundreds of millions more who, although they might have managed to stay above the line, remain in a constant struggle to survive. They eke out their livings under conditions that are not comfortable, secure, healthy, or conducive to what could be called quality of life.

The world needs to embrace new thinking from scholars like Amartya Sen who won the 1998 Nobel Prize in Economics for his insightful work on welfare economics, including social choice and poverty. Sen, and others of his ilk, believe that the only way out of poverty is to study, understand and act on the institutionalised structures and policies of society that entrench poverty in the way that Mandela describes it.

As Sen points out, using simple monetary tags to define poverty offers little perspective on the problem. 'This dollar-a-day measure,' he says, 'doesn't take into account many variations that influence the conversion of income into good living.' Even if families manage to lift themselves above the simple monetary limit, it says nothing about their ongoing struggle. It doesn't secure reliable work or allow them to escape their marginal status. Neither does it give access to a decent education or health facilities. Nor does it help them to avoid the severe impacts of climate change and other environmental challenges.

Because of this, Sen and other like-minded individuals have long argued for what is known as the Multidimensional Poverty Index (MPI) to become the lead indicator. This index complements traditional monetary metrics by including 1-weighted indicators covering 'acute deprivations in health, education, and living standards that a person faces simultaneously'.

For 2020, the MPI report found that 1.3 billion people from 107 developing countries, with a combined population of 5.9 billion, lived in multidimensional poverty. Most of them (about 84%) lived in sub-Saharan Africa. The fear is that with climate change looming, people within this category will not be able to escape the poverty trap. Furthermore, there will also be rising numbers from communities already living on the edge who fall into the MPI trap.

Are people still being left behind?

In 2015, the UN released A New Global Partnership to eradicate extreme poverty by 2030. This undertaking to 'leave no one behind' is to be realised through transforming economies under the principles of sustainable development.

As already noted, the fundamental transformation of societies' economic and political paradigms requires widespread consensus – a precondition for empowering significant change. By the end of 2020, none of the goals in this partnership had been achieved. And while the world continues to expect current paradigms to solve poverty issues, the words of Warda Rina from the Women's Major Group are a timely reminder: 'Communities are not forgetfully left behind ... It is the neoliberal policies which systematically exclude them.' This exclusion keeps families and communities in the poverty trap, a systemic perpetuation or cycle of poverty reinforced from generation to generation.

Given the recent development histories of so many states across Africa, Central America and parts of the Middle East and Asia, where poverty is at its worst, the words of Mandela and Rina seem to ring true. Poverty, therefore, is not merely a monetary statistic – it has as much to do with moral considerations and leadership challenges for decision-makers as it does with adjusting economic policy.

Poverty versus inequality

While poverty pertains to deprivation, inequality is a relative term that contrasts differences in living across a spectrum. It covers unequal income levels, wealth generation and distribution, and unequal access to opportunity and services. These are all generally associated as worsening under the neoliberal economic policies that have dominated since the 1980s.

According to the Economic Policy Institute, in 2019 the average annual pay of CEOs in the top 350 US companies hit $21.3 million, including 'realised' stock options. This is 321 times greater than the average worker received over the same period.

Since 1978, CEO pay has risen 1 167%, compared to 13.7% for typical American workers. Adding insult to injury, the pay increase for the CEOs far outstripped increases in stock-market indices and corporate profits. Therefore, on a performance basis alone, their gains are not merited.

In Africa, such inequities are just as pronounced. According to Oxfam International, in 2019, three African billionaires had more wealth than the poorest 650 million people – about 50% of the continent's population. Making matters worse, the status of that wealth reveals another aspect of the traps: 75% is held offshore by Africa's mega-rich. This represents approximately $14 billion in annual tax losses to African governments, which partly explains why the conditions of under-development never seem to be alleviated.

Closer to home, in South Africa, the top 1% of the population owns 70.9% of the country's wealth, while the bottom 60% owns a paltry 7%. Further emphasising the gap between those who hold almost all of the wealth and those who have virtually none, the UN's 2020 Inequality in a Rapidly Changing World report revealed that the 'share of income going to the richest 1% of the global population increased in 46 out of 57 countries and areas with data from 1990 to 2015'.

Then, ahead of the 2021 annual gathering of the wealthiest nations in Davos, Oxfam International shared that the combined wealth of the world's 10 richest people had grown by $540 billion during the COVID-19 pandemic, while billions of others battled poverty, unemployment and death.

The Gini Coefficient, or Gini Index, is a commonly used measure to indicate income inequality levels across a given population. Developed by Italian statistician Corrado Gini in 1912, it uses a scale of between zero, representing perfect equality, and one, which is perfect inequality. But, as with poverty, the World Inequality Database and Oxfam International point out that a simple coefficient hides many societal factors playing a significant role in perpetuating inequality. These include, for example, tax laws, investment in public services – particularly in education, social services and technology, access to the workplace, and labour and gender rights.

Although often incorrectly used interchangeably, economists and sociologists make a clear distinction between poverty and inequality. However, there is a relationship between them, as the respective definitions can be related by degrees of earning, government spending and general policy directives. In this regard, the WEF points out that within the EU, the countries that are the least unequal also tend to have the lowest poverty levels. And in Africa, the reverse can be true: The countries with the highest income disparities also tend to have high poverty levels.

Ending inequality is as complex as dealing with poverty. To do so requires leaders to make a mix of economic and social policy choices, terminate specific structural constraints within societies, and overcome the opposition of those benefiting from institutionalised inequalities.

Most economists and decision-makers recognise that current trends in poverty and inequality are not sustainable and that unequal societies also tend to be unstable. In this regard, the SDGs have several goals: To tackle poverty and rising inequality by 2030. However, it's worth bearing in mind that these attempts are being carried out under the same systems that created the twin scourges in the first place.

The trap of progress

Less obvious and understood than the poverty trap, but possibly as consequential, is the 'trap of progress', a concept introduced into everyday use by Canadian writer Ronald Wright.

In essence, the trap refers to humanity being at the mercy of its own technological successes and the so-called progress this brings. For example, each new success, such as the combustion engine; super-tankers; farming techniques; financial derivatives, and medical breakthroughs, opens up significant advances. However, they also bring new challenges that require further advances and innovation in order to manage or improve them. Each advance has a 'chain of successes' that Wright says eventually leads to a scale where the benefits start diminishing, or the path leads to disaster.

Other writers have referred to this situation as a 'progress paradox', where apparent improvements to our lives result in other problems, but very often only further down the line. This results from a failure to understand the full implications of new technology, or simply from irrational behaviour patterns over time. Advances in transport, nuclear technology, and agriculture serve as good examples.

In bygone eras, disasters or collapses were isolated by geography, and with each emerging civilisation, this spurned a new beginning and another attempt. Today, however, we live in a globalised world that links every geographical corner and living aspect of human civilisation. With the environment stretched beyond capacity, today's circumstances are different and unforgiving. The spread of COVID-19 serves as a good example of how a local event can quickly become a global crisis.

Nevertheless, we are seemingly poised to continue with a paradigm that believes that human ingenuity and advancement in technology will always get us out of trouble. Some would suggest that this is a misguided hope that fosters a concomitant belief that it is unnecessary to be concerned, or to act against looming threats like climate change. An unapparent consequence of this thinking plays into the deny-and-delay type of leadership and management discussed earlier.

The frog in the boiling pot

As children, most of us would have heard the parable about the frog in a boiling pot. It was apparently based on actual experiments conducted in the late 1800s. The story (not the science) suggests that if you drop a frog into a pot of boiling water, it will immediately jump out. However, if the frog is placed into a pot of cool water and then slowly heated, the hapless amphibian won't be able to discern the slight but gradual temperature rise until it is too late. The story remains apt – not as a factual account of what does or doesn't happen to frogs in water of variable temperatures – but as a metaphor to describe humanity's response, or lack thereof, to the global challenges defining the Anthropocene.

In our story of the Anthropocene, humanity is the frog, and the heat represents the combined impacts being brought to bear on us and the planet. As the heat is gradually turned up, we seem not to sense any day-to-day difference.

In many ways, this reflects what researchers refer to as the difference in responses to experienced change against anticipated or imagined change. For example, what we read about or see on television is happening to others, not to us. Extreme weather happening in the Caribbean is not happening here, and because I earn a good salary, there is no poverty in my suburb or town.

The delusions are endless. We seem to have little sense of the growing global threat because we deflect it by convincing ourselves that the concerns are not relevant to us. Like the frog, by the time we become convinced of the danger, our fate could be sealed.

7 /

TO BE AN ACTIVIST

{ *Ian McCallum* }

'*Do not lose heart. We were made for these times.*'
– **Clarissa Pinkola Estes**

One of the most powerful press images of political protest I have ever seen, and which continues to haunt me, is that of a Chinese student, widely referred to as 'tank man'. Dressed in a white shirt and long dark pants, his back to the camera, he stands in front of a column of military tanks. The setting is the Avenue of Peace, not far from Beijing's Tiananmen Square. The event: The 1989 student uprising against an oppressive Chinese regime.

The message was clear. In a moment of madness, courage or, as I read it, an ethical imperative, a student said: 'NO!'. Standing his ground, that single human being brought the rolling tanks to a halt.

We can only guess what happened to that brave dissident, but no other image quite captures the quintessence or loneliness of the individual hero as that photograph does. Yes, it speaks of the power of the individual, of never underestimating the influence of individual life, but to me it speaks of something else, something a lot more personal. I see it as a challenge to each one of us to say: 'No,' to that which is oppressive, isolating, indifferent and unacceptable, not only in our societies and nations, but within ourselves, too.

Activism, from the Latin *actus*, 'a driving force or impulse', the human capacity to consciously act, and react to say: 'Yes,' and 'No,' is deeply embedded in the human psyche. We all know the feeling of being unfairly treated, exploited or marginalised … when some kind of action is needed to rectify the situation.

The power of passion

There is always an emotional component to activism. It is born out of frustration, anger, rage, compassion and grief – not only against personal injustice and prejudice, but against the injustices endured by others, such as minorities, the forgotten and the voiceless, our rivers, mountains, and the wild habitats and the animals that belong there. Without feelings, there would be no such thing as morality and ethics. There would be no conscience.

We protest in different ways and for different reasons: Political, economic, religious and environmental. It is mostly recognisable in the form of street marches, vigils, sit-ins, boycotts, strikes, passivism, and sometimes even riots, occupations and take-overs. However, protest is not limited to these activities. Some of the most effective, meaningful and durable expressions of protest have come from writers, artists, photographers, filmmakers, philosophers and from the human story itself: Our myths, legends, folk and fairytales. (See suggested reading).

Then there is poetry – an ancient language of protest; a language that rhymes and resonates with time, place, conscience and calling. It says: 'Yes,' and 'No.' To be moved by it is to know the feeling: 'This has something to do with me.'

Think of Amanda Gorman's *The Hill We Climb*, which was so brilliantly read and performed at the inauguration of the 46th president of the USA on 20 January 2021. Every word, every pause and every movement of her body invited you to be part of her message: '*Somehow we've weathered and witnessed a nation that isn't broken, but simply unfinished ...'* she said. Wherever you were in the world, she could have been speaking to each one of us. This is the secret of activism.

The word 'activist' entered our lexicon in 1915, when Swedish citizens petitioned for the end of that country's neutrality in World War 1 (wwi). On review, that was not only a collective moral issue, but for the individuals involved, a matter of conscience – a choice between 'Yes' and 'No.' Relevant to all activists is the concept of neutrality, and hence, the question: For how long are we as individuals going to remain neutral to the human-induced environmental issues of our time?

'How many times can a man turn his head, pretending he just doesn't see?' asks singer and poet Bob Dylan.

The qualities of an activist

In the process of writing this, I asked my wife: 'How would you define an activist?' Her answer came surprisingly quickly and was not quite what I expected: 'I'll tell you what the opposite of an activist is,' she said. 'It is someone who moans and groans and does *fokkol!' Fokkol* is a colloquial Afrikaans expression that needs no translation into English. Her message was clear, to the point and credible. My wife is an activist or, as she prefers to be called, a catalyst. Self-effacing, yet actively involved in longstanding service to our local community, she makes things happen. She cares. Activists, then, are individuals who are activated, who act with intention, who care, and who give a damn.

Activists are born and nurtured. They blossom at different times and in varied circumstances in the socio-political history of the human species. It is as if they are born for these times. Each has their own particular temperament and personality style, but they are mostly recognised by certain qualities or attributes of character. Whatever their field of endeavour, be they a Martin Luther King Jr, a Nelson Mandela, a Jane Goodall, a David Attenborough, or any of the unsung heroes and heroines in your own neighbourhood, you can be certain that they possess and share more than a handful of the following qualities:

211

- Committed
- Courageous
- Dedicated
- Determined
- Focused
- Articulate
- Humble
- Resilient
- Strong-willed

- Visionary
- Rebellious
- Fierce
- Assertive
- Intelligent
- Adaptable
- Compassionate
- Single-minded.

Which of the listed qualities would you attribute to significant activists in your life? Which ones do you recognise in yourself?

Challenges and pitfalls

One of the many challenges facing an activist is that of competence and credibility. You will be questioned: 'Who do you think you are? What are your qualifications and experience? By whose authority do you speak or act?' Those are important questions. They quickly unveil the difference between the rebels with a cause from those without one, and activists from exhibitionists. Be ready for them. You are going to be scorned, slandered, threatened, condemned and categorised as an animal rightist, bunny- and tree-hugger, a 'greenie' and a communist … the list goes on.

It is well known that slander and scorn usually say more about the ones who voice it than those to whom it is aimed. A good example of this phenomenon is the early (2019) criticism endured by the young climate activist Greta Thunberg, then aged 16. Diagnosed with Asperger syndrome – a term formerly used to describe high-functioning autism – she was scorned for her 'looks', for being 'socially awkward' and 'different'. The implications were clear: She was suffering from some kind of 'disability or disease' and therefore not to be taken seriously. Meanwhile, when the diagnostic features of the condition are properly understood, especially the tendency in these individuals to be direct, to speak their minds, to be unaccepting of human pretence, it becomes clear that it is anything but an illness; it can be a gift. 'It is my power!' said the highly insightful Thunberg, adding: 'When haters go after your looks and differences ... you know you're winning.' I sometimes wish I was a little less tolerant of human pretences.

To be competent, you have to know your subject and to have done your homework. There's an old rule applicable to activists: 'If you want to break the rules, then you first have to know the rules.' This is where an appropriate academic or professional qualification can be important. Provided it is backed by experience, expertise and authenticity, a measurable qualification adds credibility to one's cause. Be streetwise and alert to what is going on both in and around you. This involves a keen awareness of the qualifications, styles, strategies and vested interests of those who oppose your stand. Do not underestimate the intelligence or expertise of the 'other'. However, trust yourself. There's an old saying: 'Don't take a knife to a gunfight.'

Be sensitive to timing and process. Old habits, traditions, economic policies and lifestyles may be anachronistic, but they don't change overnight. Keep the bigger picture in mind. When possible, choose dialogue over debate. The latter assumes that there is a right answer and that you have it. Dialogue assumes the capacity to examine both positions and to find some common ground. Without that, dialogue is almost impossible. Indeed, co-operate where you can, but not at the cost of what you stand for. Stand up against inappropriate, unacceptable and irrational actions and policies. At the same time, be careful of self-righteousness. Examine your own convictions from time to time. They could be incomplete, unrealistic or misinformed.

One of the most disarming approaches – call it a strategy, if you wish – to a creative dialogue is to ask your opponent or challenger for help. For example, 'Can you help me? ... I don't understand your position.' With that approach, the rationality, or irrationality, of convictions soon become clear. Ask questions but keep them short. Let the other person answer. Don't put words in their mouth. Hear their argument and when it is your turn to speak, try to focus on what you are *for,* rather than what you are *against.* A good example of this are the following words of poet and naturalist Henry Thoreau who was asked to announce his 'enterprise': 'My enterprise?' he pondered. 'I am an inspector of snowstorms and sunrises. I sink my capital into hearing the wind ...'

Thoreau's response may seem romantic or sentimental, but his message was clear: He was serious. Saying: 'Yes,' for what he stood for, he was also saying: 'No,' to the increasingly mechanised and (sometimes) stone-hearted world of his time. To me, there is something powerful and paradoxical in the word 'No'. It is another way of saying: 'Yes,' to something else; to something different and meaningful.

An often-overlooked consequence of activism is the impact it may have on the personal lives of the activist: On friends, families, and not least, on their own physical and mental health. Activists are not immune to vulnerability and at times, intense frustration, loneliness, exhaustion, and deep disappointments. Linked to this challenge is the fact that discussions around environmental and wildlife issues can be very depressing. Let's face it – often bewildered by the volume and intensity of information on the state of our planet, there is seldom any humour to be found in this work. If there is, it tends to be cynical. Bombarded by bad news, day after day, people 'switch off'. We become numbed. That is a natural defence against being overwhelmed. Be aware of it and try not to become overwhelmed. Allow yourself some healthy scepticism but avoid the trap of cynicism. It is toxic.

We have to learn to laugh not only at ourselves, but at how dumb, gullible and inflated we, as a species, can be. It sometimes helps to try to see ourselves and our fellow men and women through the eyes of animals or 'extraterrestrial' beings. I often take refuge and relief in the *The Far Side* cartoonist Gary Larson and Australian cartoonist and poet Leunig. To me, their work and craft are comical reminders of our need for a different way of seeing ourselves in the world, especially when we think we are being clever. Self-reflecting humour can be a significant antidote to doom and gloom. For example, in a short poem – Doom and Gloom – Leunig describes a day in the life of a man who cannot escape the 'unmistakable, dog pooh smell of doom'. Later in the day he discovers that the smell belongs to him, that it is 'stuck to the bottom of his shoe'. I ask of myself: Does this poem have something to do with me?

On the other hand, turn your thoughts to the legendary Greek hero, Sisyphus, rolling that heavy boulder up the hill, over and over again. He was vulnerable, but undefeated, and instead of bemoaning his lot, he gave the finger-wagging, cynical gods a wry, audaciously defiant smile. If he had anything to say, I believe it would have been something along the lines of this South African, Nguni proverb: 'If you stand for a reason, be prepared to stand alone. If you fall on the ground, fall as a seed that grows back to fight again.'

Keep faith in your values. Be clear about your task. Why you? And why now? It is that 'why' that will make you get up in the morning. A rich example of this relates to American mountaineer Stacey Allison who, in 1988, became the first woman to summit Mount Everest.

'Why do you wish to climb this mountain?' she was asked.

Instead of a repeat of the famous answer given by the English mountaineer George Mallory in 1923: 'Because it's there …', she answered: 'Because I am here …'

Keep doing what you are doing. Deal with that which is closest to you. Pick up discarded plastic items during your walks. Recycle. Save water. Speak up when you can. Do the little things … little by little.

Be mindful of these words of Jonathan Sacks in his book *Morality*: '*There exists within Nature (including humanity) an astonishing range of powers to heal and to mend that which has been broken … that Nature favours species able to recover, and history favours cultures that can do so.*'

Indeed, we all have a history of being hurt, horrified and even shattered, but we also have within us, a history of resilience and recovery and resurrection. It is this 'risibility' writes Pinkola Estes, that 'supports us to laugh in the face of cynics.'

Finally, returning to the qualities of the activists, and to their example and leadership, I believe that what truly binds them is their capacity to inspire and to give people cause for hope. They are and were, willing to be disturbed.

So, if you believe that you have it within you to be a voice for the voiceless … that you are willing to be disturbed, remember this: You are needed, and you are not alone.

This closing poem is for my friend, colleague, co-author and activist, Ian Michler: Intelligent, insightful, focused, dedicated and honest.

The Roar of the Lion

The roar of the lion
does not come from its throat
or its belly
but from the loins of the earth,
the lungs of rocks and bones
and the hidden spleen of the sea.

The roar of the lion
is the voice of the valleys,
of stars and streams
and human dreams …
it is the song-line
of the wind.

The roar of the lion
is the territorial command
of the sun
saying one thing
which is every thing:
'this is where I stand …'

8 /

INCH BY INCH: MEASURING SUCCESS AND CHANGE

{ *Ian Michler* }

Achieving success in the environmental sphere is based on many factors. While extensive research and sound science are the pillars that direct projects, a range of other influences need to be in place.

All stakeholders, including government and regional authorities, local communities, NGOs, vested commercial interests, and those representing the less obvious disciplines, must be identified and included. In addition, calling on local cultural and experiential knowledge always serves to strengthen the gathered research. These different ways of knowing, which can also include an artistic or aesthetic and spiritual understanding, can make the difference between average or excellent results.

Successful projects combine these aspects in ways that are relevant to the specific work. All of this information needs to be assembled and matched to collaborative partnerships. It also goes without saying that most fruitful projects are typically the ones with lines of secure and sustainable funding.

In the end, though, without bold leadership that embraces gritty determination, a long term vision and the will, from management and team members, to see a project through, the chances of success are significantly limited.

The attitude needed is best summed up by Tom Petty, one of rock's grittiest singer-songwriters, in his hit song, '*I won't back down*'.

Given what we know about the state of our planet and the negative sentiment that accompanies each new story detailing the damage, it is reasonable to ask if we have any positives to glean from the narrative: Do we have any successes worth celebrating?

Not withstanding the increasing level of debate around conservation models, the short answer is 'Yes,' and many more than one may believe. These range from individual species being brought back from the edge, to the resurrection of national parks and entire conservation areas. We also have a constant flow of individuals and organisations, including exciting voices from the youth, bringing fresh ideas and initiatives to stubborn challenges.

However, we hear less about these stories, as they tend to be drowned out by images of destruction, and a sense that pressure on the environment is increasing. If we were to measure the differences, successes would be counted in inches rather than square miles, unlike the number of football fields or country sizes often used as comparisons to highlight the losses.

Nonetheless, and even if one's big-picture prognosis remains negative, we must pay attention to the small victories – those inch-by-inch gains that we do achieve. They must not be overlooked or under-reported, as each one is vital to provide hope, which is an essential ingredient in dealing with present and future challenges.

It is important to remember that hope is not some vague Utopian concept or simply naïve wishful thinking. Neither is it about an exact result or a specific goal and target. Instead, it is bound up in a positive vision, a rational desire that can be a powerful motivator. With hope, we can invest ourselves, both emotionally and physically if one chooses, into a process that brims with promise. It's about having confidence that good people are committed to a programme that is underway, one that is realistic and aims to achieve something meaningful that can bring about a better world for all.

Having hope stimulates belief and commitment, which leads to action. More than ever, this world needs change agents, social and environmental entrepreneurs, people who understand the challenges and have the vision and commitment to make a difference.

Success at habitat level

Back in the 1970s and 80s, conservation was mostly focused on individual species – campaigns that highlighted the plight of whales, elephants, or the giant panda, for example. While the approach of one stand-out or charismatic species as the flagship for an entire ecosystem has merit, the conservation community soon became aware that without secure and flourishing habitats, species-level efforts would be futile.

This understanding forms the basis of most conservation efforts today. It is at the core of the Convention on Biological Diversity (CBD), which recognises that protection must occur at various levels, including the diversity of habitats and ecosystems, and that the basis of habitat and ecosystem protection is achieved through the global network of protected areas. If habitats are secure and functioning, then animals and plants can breed and flourish. But no amount of successful breeding will assist the long-term survival of a species if there is no wild and ecologically functioning space in which they can roam or grow.

Protected areas

America's Yellowstone National Park was established in 1872. Although widely held to be the world's first and oldest national park, Yellowstone was not the first legally protected area. That honour goes to the Tobago Main Ridge Forest Reserve in the Caribbean and the area around the Bogd Khan Uul Mountains in Mongolia. Both were proclaimed as such in the 1770s. In Africa, the Pongola and Imfolozi reserves in what is now South Africa's KwaZulu-Natal Province became Africa's first protected areas in the 1890s. In 1898, the Sabie Game Reserve, the precursor to the Kruger National Park, was formed. However, Kruger was not the continent's first national park. It was pipped to the post in 1925 by

Rwanda's Albert National Park, which was renamed Virunga National Park in 1969.

Fast forward a few decades to 1948, and the International Union for the Conservation of Nature (IUCN) was founded as the 'global authority on the status of the natural world and the measures needed to safeguard it'. The IUCN – still the mainstay of global conservation efforts – defines a protected area as: 'A clearly defined geographical space recognised, dedicated and managed, through legal or other effective means, to achieve the long-term conservation of nature with associated ecosystem services and cultural values.'

The IUCN network

More than 70 years later, and according to the most recent assessment by the IUCN and UNEP's World Conservation Monitoring Centre (2021), there are now 238 563 terrestrial protected areas worldwide. Together, they cover just over 22 million square kilometres, or approximately 16.6% of the planet's land and inland water surface. This figure excludes Antarctica, which has its own agreements under various treaties and protocols on protected area status.

While this global average falls below the 17% targeted, the upward trend is worth celebrating, as protected areas remain a pillar of global efforts to secure biodiversity and keep ecosystems intact. In recognition of how vital protected areas are, African governments held the inaugural IUCN Africa Protected Areas Congress in Kigali, Rwanda, in July 2022.

The overall record remains poor when it comes to marine areas, often referred to as 'blue parks'. According to the Atlas of Marine Protection, only 7.7% of our oceans have some form of protection (targets are for 30% protection by 2030), but only 2.5% enjoy complete protection as no-take zones. Clearly, further efforts need to be focused on the marine environment.

However, there have been some marine developments worth celebrating. In 2016, the USA quadrupled the size of Hawaii's Papahānaumokuākea Marine National Monument to 1.5 million square kilometres, making it the largest protected area on the planet. In 2019,

South Africa took significant steps to improve its network of marine-protected areas by proclaiming 20 new ones, bringing the country's total to 5% of coastal waters. Before that move, South Africa had less than 1% of its marine areas under protection.

African Parks

Protecting remote and isolated national parks and reserves in Africa is one of the biggest challenges facing the conservation community. Because of their locations, these protected areas are nearly always under-resourced, underfunded and poorly managed, making them nothing more than 'paper parks. In other words, they appear on a map, but have little to no management or protection. This puts their ecosystems, biodiversity, and surrounding communities at severe risk.

African Parks (AP), a non-profit NGO, has stepped into this space and built an extremely successful model around managing these protected areas. Established in 2000, AP now controls 20 national parks and protected areas in 11 countries, from Chad and Benin in the north of the continent, to Zambia, Zimbabwe and Mozambique in the south. Together they cover more than 17 million hectares across 10 of Africa's 13 recognised ecological biomes. In addition, they employ more than 1 300 fully trained and operational antipoaching rangers and have reintroduced more than 8 000 animals, representing 24 species. Their work is crucial as, in all likelihood, without their intervention, the areas they now manage would have collapsed.

AP's success is structured around long-term partnerships with governments, local communities and the private sector. Its funding model and excellent management structures make the successful implementation of long-term goals and objectives possible. So, in a relatively short space of time, AP has built an enviable record, which includes the continent's largest antipoaching force, a range of educational and health upliftment programmes, and a fledgling ecotourism sector that is becoming a core component of its success. AP's camps in Zakouma, Akagera and Liuwa Plain national parks for example have already achieved significant popularity.

Anyone who has visited a park under AP management will immediately understand why AP has been one of Africa's biggest success stories over the past few decades. It would be fair to say that they are now regarded as integral to securing the future of many of Africa's protected areas. In this regard, management has set a target of managing 30 parks covering more than 30 million hectares by 2030.

Gorongosa National Park

I first visited Gorongosa, Mozambique's premier national park, in 1997. I was one of the first journalists to enter after decades of civil war across the country. Once a haven for international tourists, the place was barely alive.

Situated in Sofala Province in the central regions, Gorongosa's more than 4 000 square kilometres of savannah and wetland mosaic had been decimated by more than 20 years of war. The armies on all sides in the conflict had used it as a pantry to feed their soldiers. By the mid-1990s, more than 95% of its wildlife populations had been killed, leaving fewer than 100 elephants, a scattering of antelope and primates, a few hippo and zebra, and the odd predator.

With movement curtailed because of land mines, sightings were scarce, but I recall seeing a few baboons, an oribi or two, and some dusty elephant droppings amidst a grove of fever trees. There was no functioning camp, so I took my own food and slept in my vehicle. Sharing stories with Roberto Zolho, the then-warden, was the highlight of the excursion.

In those early years of recovery, Zolho raised the park off its knees, and then in 2004 came a visit by Greg Carr, a successful American entrepreneur. Upon his departure, he left a prophetic note in the park's guest book: 'This is a spectacular park and it could become one of the best in Africa with some assistance.'

A short while later, Carr returned, this time as a philanthropist brimming with ideas and hope. He soon signed an agreement with the Mozambican government that laid out a long-term restoration plan for Gorongosa's turnaround.

Despite a few setbacks, Carr and his team have worked extensively among local communities, and they've successfully completed several species reintroductions and ecological audits. Safari camps and scientific research centres have also been opened. A well-publicised stint in the park by famed ecologist E.O. Wilson confirmed to the outside world that Gorongosa was well on its way to reclaiming its tag as one of Africa's finest.

A more recent initiative involves the region's reforestation through an agroforestry project involving arabica coffee plantations interspersed with plantings of indigenous hardwoods, such as east African mahogany (*Khaya anthoteca*) and flat-crown albizia (*Albizia adianthifolia*).

Gorongosa's rebirth and restoration is regarded as one of Africa's most successful conservation stories. It is also a fine example of how, with long-term vision, restoring and protecting habitats underpins biodiversity conservation.

Rewilding

In 2013, the Wild Foundation and the Wilderness Foundation Africa hosted the WILD 10 conference in Salamanca, Spain. Under the banner of 'Make the World a Wilder Place', the conference's primary focus was the rewilding of Europe. While I had encountered the concept, that was my first familiarisation with the detail of rewilding, and I got to understand its potential as a conservation measure.

Today, it has become an integral part of our lexicon about conservation at scale. While corridor conservation is vital in order to link existing protected areas, rewilding provides the most viable and promising option to rehabilitate those peri-urban or transitional zones that were once thought degraded and lost forever as a result of human impact.

Many will regard rewilding programmes merely as another way to expressing what traditional conservation sees as habitat restoration. To some extent, this is true, but there are some important distinguishing nuances.

According to Rewilding Europe, rewilding is 'a progressive approach to conservation. It's about letting nature take care of itself, enabling natural processes to shape land and sea, repair damaged ecosystems and restore degraded landscapes. Through rewilding, wildlife's natural rhythms create wilder, more biodiverse habitats.'

Rewilding is ultimately about turning land back to the processes of nature, or what some ecologists refer to as self-regulation, with notably less human management and intervention. It includes reintroduction programmes of local or endemic species, including keystone species and apex predators, and removing human structures, particularly fencing. Although rewilders aim to eventually restore the land to something resembling its natural state, with functioning ecosystems, they are less concerned about achieving pristine conditions.

Typically, rewilding occurs on land that has been badly degraded, often under extensive agricultural use or long periods of mining. Included would be land once used for monoculture, left polluted and barren, or overgrazed by livestock and filled with alien and invasive species. In some instances, this has resulted in farmers and their families, even small communities, abandoning the land, thereby allowing rewilding to set in.

Today, Rewilding Europe has programmes running in nine countries, including the Greater Côa Valley in Portugal; Lapland in Sweden; the Danube Delta in Romania and Ukraine, and the Central Apennines in Italy. There are also several projects across England and the Scottish Highlands. To date, efforts have resulted in a re-emergence of various species, including the European bison, grey wolf, brown bear and griffon vulture across the continent. According to the True Nature Foundation, Spain has 'gained over 96 000 hectares of forest every year from 2000'.

In South America, one of the world's most extensive rewilding projects is underway across the valleys and mountain ranges of southern Patagonia in Chile and Argentina. Meanwhile, Rewilding Australia has a network of projects to bring back species and natural vegetation across all states in the country.

Rewilding is also taking place in numerous marine ecosystems. Given how vital the oceans are to capturing carbon and stabilising current climate imbalances, these initiatives may well carry greater significance than terrestrial projects. The UK has eight such rewilding locations, including the restoration of seabeds, kelp forests, saltmarshes, and various estuaries along the coastline. Similar marine rewilding projects are underway in the Caspian Sea, Maldives, and Namibia.

In confirming the crucial role rewilding can play, the journal, *Nature,* published a scientific study in October 2020, calling for extensive ecosystem restoration in degraded lands. This, said the study, is 'central to conserving biodiversity and stabilising Earth's climate'. In a headline finding, the report found that 'restoring 15% of converted land in priority areas could avoid 60% of expected extinctions while sequestering 299 gigatons of CO_2 – 30% of the total CO_2 increase in the atmosphere since the Industrial Revolution'.

Rewilding is an increasingly accepted strategy that could bring significant conservation and environmental benefits.

More African conservation triumphs

Africa has countless examples of successful habitat and ecosystem restoration projects; many of them involving visionary ecotourism operators or private sector philanthropists. And in each of the examples listed, one could make a strong case that they are excellent examples of rewilding that predate the European movement. I sense they were not typically referred to as such simply because the term was not yet in widespread use.

In South Africa, Pilanesberg, Tswalu Kalahari Reserve, Phinda Private Game Reserve, Shamwari and Sanbona Wildlife Reserves, as well as the Samara Private Game Reserve have all achieved significant success in restoring degraded agricultural land to habitats resembling their natural state. In each case, wildlife reintroductions, often involving endangered species, have been central to their success. All are engaged in the ongoing purchase of neighbouring farms for restoration purposes.

The Waterberg Biosphere Reserve, covering over 650 000 hectares, deserves mention for its scope and ambition of including more than 80 000 people living within the boundaries of the biosphere reserves.

The reserve's management refers to the balancing act between people, ecotourism and biodiversity conservation – a process they are managing with some distinction.

Further afield, the poaching crises ravaging communal lands across northern Kenya during the 1970s and 80s were halted through the work of pioneers in the Northern Rangelands Trust. That team then partnered with ecotourism agencies, such as the Lewa Wildlife Conservancy and Ol Pejeta, to forge hugely successful community conservation partnerships.

Across the border in Tanzania, Singita Grumeti has turned lands that were once a haven for poachers and hunters into some of the best game-viewing areas in the greater Serengeti. Further south in Zimbabwe, the Save Valley Conservancy, Malilangwe Trust and Bubye Valley Conservancy all manage large tracts of wilderness through partnerships with national and regional authorities.

In Namibia, conservancies in partnership with local communities have been at the forefront of the country's efforts. The NamibRand Nature Reserve, for example, combines vast regions of the southern Namib Desert, managed under the principles of low impact and responsible ecotourism. In the north, the conservancies of Palmwag, Torra, Marienfluss, and Sesfontein, as well as the Omatendeka and Anabeb Communal Conservancies that are part of the Etendeka Concession, have all established successful conservation and ecotourism initiatives.

For up-to-date information on new, protected areas that are being declared around the world, visit the IUCN's Green List of Protected and Conserved Areas.

Corridor conservation

The natural world faces many threats, mostly stemming from human activities. Among these, centuries of establishing urban settings and supporting infrastructural development, along with industrial, mining, and agricultural activities, have been some of the most severe.

The result has been the complete fragmentation of habitats and ecosystems, leaving tracts of wilderness and protected areas splintered or divided by human structures. In turn, this has ended connectivity, or species' ability to move and migrate. As a result, gene pools have been weakened or lost, and ecosystems have either become compromised or have failed. Now, as climate change sets in, fragmentation will become more telling, with species being unable to migrate. In the longer term, fragmentation also adds significantly to the extent and costs of conservation efforts.

There are various ways to alleviate this, of which better protection measures and declaring more protected areas are the most obvious. Less celebrated but arguably the most realistic, is corridor conservation. The IUCN defines an ecological corridor as:

'A clearly defined geographical space, not recognised as a protected area or other effective area-based conservation measure, that is governed and managed over the long-term to conserve or restore effective ecological connectivity, with associated ecosystem services and cultural and spiritual values.'

These corridors can cover vast expanses, or simply be a narrow migration route connecting seasonal ranges used by a single species. If managed well, ecological corridors will provide additional ranging options for species by linking habitats that would otherwise remain fragmented. They will also strengthen gene pools by allowing different populations to connect, thereby lowering species' extinction risks. In a general sense, corridors will facilitate resilience levels of habitats and protected areas.

While there are some concerns with corridors, for example, the possible introduction of alien species and unsettling resident wildlife populations, the corridor concept is generally one of the most positive developments in the conservation landscape. And even more so when corridors cross international boundaries to create transfrontier conservation areas (TFCAs).

Peace Parks Foundation

The initiator and face of TFCA's and corridor conservation at scale in Africa is undoubtedly Peace Parks Foundation (Peace Parks). Established in 1997, Peace Parks currently has eight established TFCAs under management, with another four emerging, and a further six at the conceptual stage. Together, these projects include over 50% of all declared parks and reserves covering more than a million square kilometres within the 16 countries involved.

The most ambitious and celebrated initiative is undoubtedly the Kavango Zambezi TFCA (KAZA) in southern Africa. It includes more than 30 protected areas, including the Okavango Delta, Hwange National Park and Victoria Falls, and covers over 300 000 square kilometres across five countries.

In undertaking such bold and ambitious initiatives, Peace Parks has committed to embracing the complexities of dealing with many countries, including the diplomatic negotiation of different economic, environmental, and social circumstances. Given the scale and profile of their projects, each requires a long-term vision, with extensive management plans. These are weighty tasks, but organisational and logistical skills are just some of the many strengths Peace Parks bring to African conservation.

Peace Park's story, and the work it has already completed, is another significant success. Besides an excellent fundraising record, it has forged extensive political and environmental networks across the continent. The organisation also provides complementary benefits to those involved in protecting individual parks and reserves on the continent.

Eden to Addo

Eden to Addo (E2A) is an excellent example of how social entrepreneurship at a local scale, driven by the vision and passion of a handful of people, can produce significant results.

Founded in 2006 and now headed by Joan Berning, E2A set about linking three South African mega-reserves: The Garden Route National Park, Baviaanskloof World Heritage Site and Addo Elephant National Park in the Eastern Cape, by introducing natural ecological corridors between the three. The corridors have reopened ancient migration routes that extend across 500 kilometres. They aim to enhance ecosystem functioning and provide improved protection for the biodiversity in each of the linked reserves. The ability for species to migrate both up and down the corridors is particularly relevant, given the looming threats of climate change across the wider region.

In its short history, E2A has already achieved significant results. For instance, an educational show on the corridors has been developed to raise environmental and social awareness among school children. Such awareness programmes inform farmers and communities about the need to embrace ecological thinking and corridor conservation. More than 50 000 hectares of private land has been added to the protected area network, enabling the linkage of vital ecosystems. In addition, extensive alien clearing has been done in numerous catchment areas within the wider region.

E2A has also achieved success in other ways. Its annual 400-kilometre-plus Great Corridor Hike has become a sell-out attraction among the hiking fraternity. The trail is an exciting two-week challenge across the mountains and plains of the corridor network. The proceeds from the hike go towards developing new corridors.

For the longer term, E2A has a greater vision: It seeks to collaborate with Wilderness Foundation Africa, which has initiated a similar corridor initiative heading east of Addo Elephant National Park. In time, E2A aims to link with Addo to their Great Fish Biodiversity Corridor Assessment, which will bring them together as one, extended arc from coast to coast, incorporating all of the inland protected areas.

Examples outside of Africa

The USA's Yellowstone to Yukon (Y2Y) initiative covers 1.3 million square kilometres between Yellowstone National Park in Wyoming and the Yukon Territory in Canada. The Terai Arc Landscape links 11 protected areas across India and Nepal, while the Jaguar Corridor Initiative (managed by Panthera) aims to link jaguar populations from northern Argentina all the way to Mexico.

Success at species level

We know from numerous assessments, IPBES and the IUCN Red Data Lists that the loss of populations and species is occurring at unprecedented rates.

However, the passionate commitment of individuals and their conservation and scientific agencies, as well as certain governments, has resulted in some stunning successes at the species level. According to the Society of Conservation Biology, between 1993 and 2020, the conservation community prevented the extinction of 48 bird and mammal species through successful conservation programmes.

Each of these stories is cause for celebration, as they provide inspiration for the next generation of scientists and conservationists. Success is also the best evidence to reassure dedicated conservation supporters that their funding contributions do indeed make a difference.

NGOs undoubtedly play a crucial role in our biodiversity conservation efforts, especially in the world's less-developed regions. These agencies, and the conservation world in general, owe a huge debt of gratitude to the millions of concerned citizens who support them. Through annual subscriptions, lump-sum donations and bequests, their generosity is often their principal source of funding. Without this charitable support, much crucial work might never get done.

What follows is a selection of species brought back from the brink. From Africa and beyond, all have resonated in some way with the broader conservation community.

African black oystercatcher (*Haematopus moquini*)

By the 1980s, the population of this coastal species had fallen to fewer than 5 000 birds, spread thinly along South Africa's 3 000-kilometre coastline. The primary reasons for the increasingly poor breeding rates included uncontrolled coastal development; irresponsible dune and beach driving; alien predators introduced onto islands, and guano collectors.

The turnaround in this striking bird's fortunes can be credited to the late Dr Phil Hockey and the FitzPatrick Institute of African Ornithology, which established the Oystercatcher Conservation Programme in 1998. Working with Birdlife South Africa and a host of provincial authorities, they introduced several measures to stem the decline in numbers. These included a ban on recreational beach driving, a stop to guano collecting, and a public awareness campaigns about the oystercatcher's plight.

Today, there are more than 7 000 birds – a population recovery that has allowed the IUCN to take them off the threatened species list.

African wild dog (*Lycaon pictus*)

While the African wild dog, also referred to as the painted wolf, remains the second most endangered carnivore on the African continent (after the Ethiopian wolf), its current standing is way better now than in the early 1980s. At that time, the species no longer occurred in 75% of its range. They numbered fewer than 4 000 individuals and were declining rather rapidly.

The wild dogs had been driven to collapse by high levels of human/animal conflict (dogs were poisoned, trapped, and shot) and disease, owing to human settlements extending into the species' natural range. However, their fortunes began to turn in the 1990s when global awareness campaigns led to intensive conservation initiatives across several countries. Botswana and Zimbabwe, in particular, had significant successes in this regard, with prominent roles played by the ecotourism and wildlife documentary sectors.

Today, wild dog populations are thought to be back up above 6 000. The species has also been restored to several protected areas where they had not been seen for decades. Today, Botswana has the largest population, followed by Zimbabwe and Tanzania.

American bison (*Bison bison*)

In 2016, the American bison joined the bald eagle as a national symbol of the USA, but it almost didn't make it into the 20th century. Before the onset of commercial hunting, the region's largest mammal was thought to have numbered more than 30 million. The expansion of large-scale agricultural projects also played a significant role in the species' collapse, and by the late 1890s, fewer than 1 000 remained.

Today, they again roam the plains of most American national parks, and according to the IUCN, the population has recovered remarkably, with numbers now close to 35 000. Although many more bison live on private land around the country, most are not regarded as part of the conservation herd.

Bald eagle (*Haliaeetus leucocephalus*)

The story of the bald eagle has become one of the most celebrated conservation successes in the USA. However, during the 1960s and 70s, the USA's other national symbol was rapidly becoming extinct. Owing to the extensive use of industrial and agricultural chemicals, including pesticides, such as DDT, habitat destruction and illegal hunting, the countrywide population had plummeted to little more than 400 breeding pairs.

Using regulations under the Endangered Species Act (ESA), along with the DDT ban in 1972, conservationists were able to bring this magnificent raptor back from the brink. It took a few decades, but in 2007, the species was removed from the list of endangered species. Today, there are more than 10 000 breeding pairs across the country.

Black robin (*Petroica traversi*)

New Zealand's black robin saga is an incredible one. By 1980, only five birds remained, and of those, only one was a mature female. Small and slight of frame, the once-common birds were hunted by the cats and rats introduced by early explorers and settlers to New Zealand's Chatham Islands. Later, habitat loss exacerbated their decline.

Conservation efforts began with capturing the remaining birds and moving them to a secure breeding area. Efforts to restore their habitat followed. The initiative was based on a foster programme that used local warbler and tit species. After years of intensive management, which required moving eggs and birds, by the early 2000s, the population had recovered to more than 200 birds.

While the tiny gene pool of the black robin and its restricted range remains a concern, the fact that it survived bears testament to the dedication and ingenuity of the conservation team.

California condor (*Gymnogyps californianus*)

The California condor is another example of a species that was literally a few individual birds away from being wiped out. By 1983, there were thought to be a mere 22 left, as numbers had plummeted owing to chemical poisoning, electrocution from power lines and habitat loss.

Conservationists set about capturing the last free-flying birds and placing them in captivity to start a breeding programme that included various zoos across the USA. Extremely controversial at the time, the programme was a resounding success. The first captive-bred birds were released back into the wilds in 1992, and today there are thought to be more than 500 of these majestic flyers soaring the skies across the western regions of the USA.

Despite the success, the condors remain on the critically endangered list, as they still face pressures. Lead poisoning from spent ammunition, and ongoing habitat loss are the primary concerns.

Giant panda (*Ailuropoda melanoleuca*)

Owing to its famous conservation story, and no doubt its cute and cuddly appearance, the giant panda is often referred to as the first, global, iconic species. The success in securing its survival certainly ranks as one of Asia's most celebrated conservation achievements – particularly for the Chinese government.

By the 1960s, the panda was already part of global folklore, primarily from exposure through zoo exhibits and the WWF's logo. However, it was only in the 1980s that the conservation community declared the giant panda as threatened with extinction owing to its population crash to some 1 000 individuals. Habitat loss, poaching and wild captures were the primary reasons. Bamboo makes up 99% of the panda's diet, so with China's population growth and accelerating development, bamboo forests and the species came under increasing pressure.

After a decade of working together on securing the species' survival, in 1992, the WWF and the Chinese government formalised a joint management plan to ensure that 60% of all giant panda habitat became protected. That move, along with successful breeding and release programmes, and a clampdown on poaching, secured the species' turn-around. However, the panda's future is by no means totally assured. Habitat loss continues to be a significant threat. Nevertheless, by 2016, giant panda numbers were approaching 2 000 and the species was removed from the endangered list.

Humpback whale (*Megaptera novaeangliae*)

Assessing the status of whale populations can be problematic due to the vastness of the oceans and the wide geographical spread of some species. For these reasons, the International Whaling Commission (IWC) and other specialist whale conservation agencies often refer to regional populations, or even so-called 'stocks' within regional populations, as these can show marked differences from ocean to ocean.

Rampant commercial whaling over centuries devastated whale populations. It is estimated that over 300 000 humpbacks were slaughtered for their oil and meat, affecting all populations in every ocean. By the 1960s, the South Atlantic populations were close to extinction, as only about 450 humpback whales remained.

Recovery started with stricter enforcement of the IWC's 1982 moratorium on all commercial whaling, and by the early 2000s, scientists began to see improvement in humpback numbers across all populations.

More recently, ship strikes, net entanglement and habitat degradation from pollution have become additional threats. Still, the IUCN Red List indicates that all humpback populations have recovered to the extent that the species status is now one of 'least concern'. Some even suggest that the humpback populations are now close to levels before commercial whaling began.

Mountain gorilla (*Gorilla beringei beringei*)

Of the species brought back from the edge of extinction in Africa, the mountain gorillas of Central Africa undoubtedly rank as the most celebrated. By the 1980s, the population had fallen to a mere 650 animals, mostly confined to the upper reaches of volcanoes in Uganda, the Democratic Republic of Congo (DRC) and Rwanda. Habitat loss, intensive poaching for the bushmeat trade, and live captures for the pet and zoo trade, all exacerbated by regional conflicts and poor management, drove the numbers down.

A little over 30 years later, the situation of the mountain gorillas is much improved. Due to global awareness through Dian Fossey's celebrated work, a well-managed ecotourism programme and extensive armed protection measures, their numbers passed the magical 1 000 level in 2019.

This success is reflected in the species' latest conservation classification: The mountain gorillas have been downlisted from 'critically endangered' to 'endangered'. However, given the restricted mountain rainforest habits that remain, the species is likely to always be dependent on strict conservation measures.

Africa's rhinos (*Ceratotherium & Diceros*)

White rhinos (*Ceratotherium simum*) suffered a precipitous collapse in numbers during colonial times. By the late 1890s, there were fewer than 100 of the southern subspecies, all of them in the Hluhluwe-Imfolozi Park. There has been a slow recovery from that time, but by the 1960s, they still numbered no more than 1 000. But then, due to the efforts of doyen conservationist Dr Ian Player and his team, Operation Rhino, a breeding and relocation programme, got underway.

The southern white rhino's recovery was spectacular, and the population peaked at some 20 000 before the present poaching crisis saw white rhino numbers dip once more. Unfortunately, current losses are probably greater than the numbers being reflected. It would seem the South African white rhino population has dropped to below 5 000 in the wild, with some suggesting it may even be as low as 4 000. There are possibly another 4 000 in Namibia, Botswana, Kenya, and Zimbabwe.

Developments as of late 2021 indicate that Botswana is being heavily targeted by poachers, only a few years after the country implemented a successful reintroduction programme. It is feared that the country may again lose all of its rhinos if drastic preventative actions are not taken.

The northern white rhino also suffered great depredation, but sadly, there has been no recovery for the subspecies. By the 1950s, only about 500 remained, and over the next couple of decades, even these few dwindled to about 15. Today only two elderly female northern white rhinos survive, and the subspecies is sadly now functionally extinct.

Black rhinos (*Diceros bicornis*), once found in their hundreds of thousands across all habitats in sub-Saharan Africa (other than rainforest regions), declined throughout colonial times from over-hunting. Never-theless, by the end of the 1960s, they still numbered some 70 000. Then, during the 1970s, a catastrophic collapse set in, driven chiefly by the demand for their horns used for ceremonial Yemeni dagger handles.

By the mid-1990s, black rhinos had disappeared from most of their original range, and a mere 2 400 remained in all of Africa. However, the tide of destruction has been stemmed. Thanks mostly to efforts such as WWF's Black Rhino Range Extension Programme, numbers have recovered to some 5 600 – 98% of which are found in just four countries: Namibia, South Africa, Zimbabwe, and Kenya. Botswana now has a fledgling population of relocated animals.

While out of immediate danger, owing to the poaching resurgence over the last 15 years, the future of Africa's rhinos remains in jeopardy.

The story of the Indian rhino (also known as the greater one-horned rhino) is also worth mentioning. By the early 1900s, trophy hunting and human/animal conflict had reduced numbers to fewer than 100 animals from a population that scientists believe may well have been in the millions only a few hundred years earlier.

It took the conservation community a long time to react, but they eventually did in 2015 with the ambitious Indian Rhino Vision 2020 protection and breeding programme. As of 2020, some 3 000 Indian rhinos roam north-east India and Nepal, making this one of Asia's most celebrated conservation successes.

Other successes

Those noted are merely a handful of examples, mostly highlighting charismatic species, the animals that keep us interested and focused due to their stand-out appearance or behaviour. They are also pivotal, as they represent the health or otherwise of entire ecosystems. By focusing on the iconic species, there is an excellent chance that many other species living alongside them in a given ecosystem or locality will benefit.

Other interesting success stories at species level include the brown pelican (*Pelecanus occidentalis*); Canada goose (*Branta canadensis*); grey wolf (*Canis lupus*), Mauritius kestrel (*Falco punctatus)*, green turtle (*Chelonia mydas*), and the echo parakeet (*Psittacula eques*).

Among plant species, there have also been some notable successes, including the Cape gorse (*Aspalathus recurvispina); Debao cycad (*Cycas debaoensis); Ginkgo (*Ginkgo biloba),* and the rosewoods of Madagascar (*Dalbergia maritima and Dalbergia louvelii*).

To keep updated at species level, it is worth monitoring the IUCN Red List's annual releases. In the 2019 list, for example, the improving status of eight bird species and two freshwater fishes are highlighted. The story of the Guam rail (*Hypotaenidia owstoni*) is especially pleasing, as it is only the second bird ever to come back from declared extinction in the wild.

In 2020, Birdlife International released the findings of a study high-lighting at least 21 bird species (in time, this may reach as many as 32) that have been saved from extinction due to ongoing conservation action. Birdlife's message is clear: Give us the financial and administrative support and we can secure the future of species.

Like the triumphs highlighted by Birdlife International, a host of other conservation agencies in Africa have achieved success. Panthera; Cape Leopard Trust; Elephants Without Borders; Elephants Alive; and Lion Recovery Fund continue to do excellent work, with specific species as their focus.

Buying out the hunters

One way of stopping hunters from killing the gene pool of so many threatened species is to pay off the industry. It's perverse to think that funding, often the scarcest component in conservation, should be used in this manner. However, while trophy hunting remains legally sanctioned, buying out the hunting operators remains a practical option for anti-hunting conservationists trying to secure the future of species, such as bears, lions, wolves, leopards, and rhinos.

Such a strategy has been successfully used in the Kitlope Valley of the Great Bear Rainforest along Canada' Pacific coast. There, for the fifth year running, the Raincoast Conservation Foundation has raised funding to buy all of the hunting licences for grizzly bears in the region. Raincoast is the concession holder but has opted not to hunt any of the species on licence in the region. They have achieved similar success in buying out hunting licences for wolves and bears in numerous other parks and reserves in Canada.

In Botswana's Okavango Delta, the Jao Concession pioneered this approach back in the late 1990s. The Kayes family and their partners, Okavango Wilderness Safaris, opted to stop trophy hunting in the region by paying out the government for the hunting licences that came with the concession, but not using the permits to shoot a single animal. Despite concerns that they would not succeed commercially without the hunters, the concession has become one of the most sought-after ecotourism destinations in the Okavango. Other concessions followed Jao's example – a process that helped rid that wetland wonder and World Heritage site of most trophy hunters.

Until trophy hunting is formally stopped, this approach will likely become a more widely used conservation option.

The integrated approach

While habitat and species protection generally represents the face of conservation efforts, the buy-in of the people living alongside conservation areas is essential. In this regard, the social and educational components of conservation, as well as significantly greater benefit-sharing, are no less significant. However, achieving success in these vital areas is tough, owing to the many disciplines involved and the complex nature of the challenges. It's likely that for these very reasons, fewer organisations tackle the full spectrum of conservation at any depth.

Wilderness Foundation Africa

Wilderness Foundation Africa serves as an excellent example of an agency that has successfully spread its focus equally. With roots in the pioneering work of Dr Ian Player and his colleague Magqubu Ntombela (both founders of the present-day organisation), Wilderness Foundation Africa (WFA) has grown from the fundraising arm of the Wilderness Leadership School (started in 1957) into a global conservation agency. Based in the Eastern Cape, South Africa, WFA also has offices in the USA and UK (the Wild Foundation and the Wilderness Foundation UK, respectively).

WFA has a strong value-driven approach and has tailored its model to recognise the changing face of conservation. Its strategy is three-pronged: species, spaces and people. The species and spaces components include initiatives ranging from large predator projects to vital ecosystem restoration programmes, and the ambitious initiative linking Addo Elephant National Park to the Indian Ocean through ecological corridors.

On the people front, the organisation has achieved notable success. It has targeted education and awareness drives around environmental knowledge, wildlife trade and leadership training for budding conservationists emerging from disadvantaged communities across South Africa.

Skills and development training at youth and community levels also remains a focus; most often through the Wilderness Leadership School, which is famed for its Nature trails that immerse participants and hikers in the natural world. The school also offers guide training courses and recreational leadership trails.

WFA also works at a political and campaign level, both locally and abroad, and often in partnerships with other leading conservation agencies, to drive awareness and legislative change. In this regard, they have programmes focusing on demand reduction for wildlife parts, have driven campaigns to end mining threats in many protected areas, and host the renowned World Wilderness Congresses every four years.

Web-based campaigns

Web-based environmental campaigns offer an additional arm to traditional, practical approaches to in-situ conservation. These can be highly effective at raising awareness, directing vital funding requirements, or simply amplifying the issues around the plight of species and habitat, to the extent that causes are taken up by the broader environmental and conservation community.

Blood Lions®

Blood Lions® is the global web-based campaign that was launched with the award-winning feature documentary film of the same name. Both the film and the campaign expose the horrors of the predator breeding industry and all the commercial spin-offs thereof, including canned or captive hunting and a host of related interactive tourism activities, such as cub-petting and 'walking with lions'.

More than 8 000 predators, but possibly as many as 10 000, are currently being held in captivity across South Africa, often under the cruellest conditions. The campaign's primary aim is twofold: To end non-conservation predator breeding, and to counter the misinformation being spread by some within the breeding and hunting fraternity.

The campaign has achieved many notable successes worldwide. These include being named joint winner for the Most Compelling Digital Story in the inaugural African Travel Week & Tourism Awards in 2019/20. The film has now been screened in more than 190 countries and at most major environmental film festivals, winning numerous awards along the way.

On the political front, the campaign and its partners are closer to realising their primary objectives. In May 2021, the South African government announced recommendations to end the predator breeding industry. While there is still much that can happen in this process, a few years back, getting to this stage was simply unimaginable.

Greta Thunberg

The 19-year-old Swedish climate activist is a stunning example of how environmental campaigns based around the web and public speaking platforms can have far-reaching impacts. Within two years, she raised the profile of the global climate crisis in ways never before imagined. Not only did Thunberg do this among school children and young adults, but the youngster made the whole world sit up and take notice. She did this by bluntly challenging global political and business leaders head-on. 'How dare you,' she scolded, 'You have stolen my dreams and my childhood with your empty words.'

She was soon invited to give keynote speeches in the UN and other major climate change forums. 'You are not mature enough to tell it like it is. Even that burden you leave to us children. But I don't care about being popular. I care about climate justice and the living planet,' she said to the astounded delegates in the UN's General Assembly.

Through her commitment to action, Thunberg has inspired the Fridays for Future school protests, and she has won numerous awards for bringing widespread climate awareness to the youth. She is already an inspirational figure to millions of teenagers and adults worldwide, and a great example of how to run a successful campaign. The environmental community could do with many more like Greta Thunberg.

'Changing the world one post at a time'

I don't know who first ventured this phrase as a prophecy, but the concept of changing the world one post at a time has become a powerful force in our digitised world. With the significant advances in technology over the last two decades, running environmental campaigns on digital and social media platforms opens up the range of options to promote change – a development that every environmental activist should celebrate.

Traditionally, it was thought that getting people into the wilderness was the most effective way to inspire involvement in conservation. While there remains plenty of credence to this, the flip side shows that digital platforms provide easier, instantaneous access to far greater numbers of people across continents. They're also an alternative to conventional in-person protests or city march, which require people to convene in specific places.

At times referred to as 'clicktivism' or 'hashtag activism', the use of technology and online networking is a dynamic process that enables the participation of everyone: From the largest corporates to house-bound individuals. Such direct access is certainly a more immediate way of raising funds for causes and programmes.

This form of activism was central to the tactics used to stop Shell, the British multinational oil and gas company, from undertaking seismic survey blasting off the coast of South Africa in December 2021. While the battle was ultimately fought on behalf of local communities, Shell faced a global wave of opposition that was notably boosted by social media. In decades past, Shell would have, in all likelihood, gotten away with their environmentally destructive exploration.

Technology allows for targeted creativity and variation – aspects that allow businesses and brands to convey specific environmental messages to particular audiences. By way of example, brands such as Patagonia and Apple have used their social media platforms and digital devices to raise awareness and significant funds for various causes. Remember how Greta Thunberg mobilised millions of people to fill the streets in more than 7 000 cities during the Fridays for Future campaign.

In many instances, technology platforms have been successfully utilised to rally large numbers of people to offer immediate assistance in emergencies, such as cleaning oil spills or rescuing beached cetaceans.

There are downsides, of course: The platforms can create unnecessary 'noise', as well as instant pathways for misinformation, lies and myths to spread. As witnessed with the 'fake news' platforms in the USA, social media can significantly amplify issues in ways that have profound implications for established institutions and the environment. However, armed with a cellphone or tablet, everyone out there can be an activist of sorts; their messages impacting globally at the click of a button. This has to be a positive for the environment.

Dealing with the Anthropocene

Although the Anthropocene and the various challenges that define it are shaping up to be humanity's greatest undertaking, there certainly have been pockets of success. Even if the big picture remains daunting, these small advances offer hope that certain sectors and countries may well be starting to come to terms with the issues at hand.

For starters, some are beginning to agree that rather than tinkering with current paradigms, fundamental and transformative change across all spectrums of our living systems is a primary requirement. In this regard, the release of the Stockholm Statement was a significant step. Issued by a group of leading economists and scientists as a unified voice of concern, it outlined their acceptance that the environmental crisis and social inequality have become serious challenges. They acknowledge that the way growth and progress are currently measured by nations and institutions has systemic failings.

And we must also pay attention to the innovative solutions achieved in specific economic and engineering arenas.

From fossil fuels to renewables

The chapter, 'Why Are We so Concerned' noted that global warming and climate change are primary features of the current environmental crisis. Fired by decades of unrestricted fossil fuel use, it is clear that in chasing success to halt the impacts, the switch to renewable energy sources will be vital.

Generally referred to as 'the energy transition', scientists believe that our success or otherwise in this regard will be a key determinant. Aside from the profound positives for the environment, this transition will also have significant knock-on impact for global geopolitical alignments and rankings, and development opportunities and access costs across the less-developed world.

Several countries and regional alliances, including the European Union, have set targets for reducing GHG emissions to zero by 2050. This is widely regarded as the absolute minimum needed to avoid catastrophe. With 30 years to go, the world is starting to see some progress.

In May 2020, the US Energy Information Administration announced a milestone that, only a decade earlier, many within the fossil fuel sector thought would be impossible: Annual renewable energy consumption in the USA had surpassed coal consumption as the primary energy source for the first time in over 130 years. As Bloomberg reported, it was an outcome that Gregory Boyce, the then-CEO of Peabody Energy Corp, never thought would happen. When testifying to the US Congress in 2010, he opined: 'Wind and solar comprise just one percent of today's US energy mix. It is unrealistic to suggest that renewables could replace conventional baseload fuels.'

The same Bloomberg article went on to note that already, in two-thirds of the world, wind and solar are the cheapest forms of power. It is projected that by 2050, 'solar and wind will power half the globe'. This would be a significant turning point in attempting to halt the current rate of global warming.

These developments in the USA follow what has already happened across much of Europe. In 2017, Sweden became the first country to legally frame its pledge of achieving carbon neutrality by 2045. They were followed by the United Kingdom, the first G7 country to set a carbon-neutral timeline. Among others, France, Denmark, Japan, Canada, and South Korea have since followed suit in joining the race for neutrality by 2050. In addition, a number of the world's largest multinationals, such as Toyota, GM and BMW, have set carbon-neutral targets.

In a similar vein, in May 2021, the G7 agreed to end all financial support for coal development. The International Energy Agency went one step further, calling for a halt to all new fossil fuel developments by the end of 2021.

Another indicator pointing to shifts in the energy sector occurred in August 2020, when Exxon Mobil was removed from the New York Stock Exchange's Dow Jones Industrial Average. The company had been listed as one of America's heavyweights for investors since 1928. Its removal leaves Chevron as the only company from the oil and gas sector still listed. This is surely a pointer that progress towards renewables is being made.

And then, in September 2020, the governor of California, USA, signed an executive order requiring all motor vehicles sold in the state to be electric or zero-emission by the year 2035. The transportation sector is the largest source of emissions in the state, so this measure will significantly reduce pollution levels and carbon emissions.

Within days of his inauguration in January 2021, Joe Biden reversed the climate denialism of the previous Trump administration. Biden issued an executive order that committed the USA to place the 'climate crisis at the centre of United States foreign policy and national security'. He also signed the USA into the Paris Agreement, the leading international treaty on climate change that binds countries to lower GHG emission levels. That statement was followed by a pledge from the USA to halve greenhouse-gas emissions by 2030, and to achieve net-zero emissions by 2050.

The World Economic Forum publishes an annual Energy Transition Index – a country-based ranking to benchmark global energy transitions. It is worth following this index to stay abreast of progress, or lack thereof.

Ecosystems and biodiversity

In September 2020, ahead of the UN Biodiversity Summit, 70 nations signed the Leaders Pledge for Nature, a 10-point plan calling for urgent action from the global community to reverse the current worldwide loss of biodiversity and habitat by 2030. Its central purpose was to create a network of political will to tackle one of the most serious aspects of the global environmental crisis. The European Union and Canada are among the signatories.

In the lead-up to that same summit, China announced its pledge to become entirely carbon neutral by 2060. To achieve this, China will need to drastically reduce fossil fuel use, particularly coal, which accounts for 58% of the country's energy consumption. According to the Global Carbon Project, China is currently the largest GHG-emitting country, producing 28% of the global total. With China's firm commitment, which includes timelines, it is hoped that other major emitters, such as the USA and India, will follow suit.

In January 2021, driven by an admission that global leaders had failed to achieve any of the Aichi Biodiversity Targets set a decade earlier, a group of 50 nations launched the High Ambition Coalition during the One Planet Summit in Paris. Aimed at bringing immediate focus to rectifying the alarming loss of ecosystems and biodiversity, the nations pledged to engage in 'an urgent year of action'.

Cynicism towards yet another such initiative is understandable, but in the hope that lessons are finally being learnt, it is also worth another shot. The nations' primary commitment is to protect at least 30% of the world's land and oceans by 2030. Only 14 African countries, excluding South Africa, were part of that initiative. Those commitments were then taken a step further in September 2021 at the IUCN's World Conservation Congress, where delegates formally approved the 30% minimum target.

In the wake of the COVID-19 pandemic, China has committed to another positive development – to close down or curb wet markets and the trade in wildlife. While many have responded to the reports with scepticism, at least the conversation is happening.

Economic paradigms

Writing in *Ecologist,* Federico Demaria, a researcher in Ecological Economics and Political Ecology at the University of Barcelona, stated that already, increased growth in the European nations is not necessary. He believes that Europe is now about 'growth for the sake of growth'.

His concern is based on the uncomfortable truth that current economic models are unsustainable. For Demaria, the question for Europe (and the rest of the world, too) should now be: 'How can we manage an economy without growth?'

Concerns with current models have also been voiced by other well-known economists, who have concentrated on specific failings. That list includes Jeffrey Sachs on poverty eradication, Thomas Piketty on income inequality and wealth distribution, and Amartya Sen, for his work on welfare economics and social justice. Along with these pioneers, Demaria points out that we have no option but to look at alternatives that improve human welfare while avoiding further environmental ruin.

Together, these economists and others worldwide are pointing out that while GDP effectively accounts for goods and services, it falls short on a range of other indicators. Their sentiments are best summed up in a statement attributed to the Organisation of Economic Co-operation and Development (OECD):

'If ever there was a controversial icon of the statistics world, GDP is it. It measures income, but not equality, it measures growth, but not destruction, and it ignores values like social cohesion and the environment. Yet governments, businesses and probably most people swear by it.'

Some arguments go as far as demanding that economies be treated as social constructs centred around environmental principles rather than being treated as financial entities that are driven by the laws of supply and demand. As expected, there is strong political opposition and pushback from the vested interests to any notion of seeking alternative economic models. However, the important point is that these processes are underway in a situation that was unlikely before the 2008 financial crisis. In the aftermath of that global upset, the financial and other sectors were bailed out, leaving citizens to carry the debt and loss burdens.

None of the broad models outlined below claim to be the perfect answer, but they do offer the promise that decision-makers are beginning to understand the deep-rooted structural faults within current paradigms.

- **Zero-growth economics**

  Sometimes called steady-state economics, de-growth or slow-growth, zero-growth models reject current systems that call for unlimited growth, as measured through exponential GDP data. While not new, the thinking has received significant impetus, given the environmental destruction as a result of economic activity over the past century and more.

  Zero-growth models place constraints on production, consumption, working hours, globalisation and the financial services sector, among other initiatives. Via a transitionary process, advocates believe that zero or slow-growth economies will end up being more stable, efficient, and certainly more equitable in the long term. Significantly, they will reduce resource extraction and produce less waste.

- **Well-being economics**

  This focuses on people and the planet rather than exponential growth targets. As the phrase suggests, well-being models are concerned about improvements that development brings to the lives of all people. Aspects such as education, health, housing and security – all factors that cannot be measured or captured through current GDP based models – are prioritised.

  Other commentators refer to well-being economics as a holistic approach that focuses on prosperity that creates just and caring societies while recognising that paradigms are needed to operate within ecological limits.

  Today, several annual reports and indices track factors such as global well-being and happiness. The global World Happiness Report 2020 seeks to 'review the science of measuring and understanding subjective well-being, and to use survey measures of life satisfaction to track the quality of lives as they are being lived in more than 150 countries'. While economic data is part of the calculation, the index includes factors such as an individuals' prospects, life expectancy, freedoms, social security, corruption, and access to all services.

  Not unexpectedly, most of the top-ranked of the 153 countries are European nations operating under what can broadly be termed as social democracies. The USA is an interesting case. It comes in as the 18th happiest nation, way lower than many of the nations they ridicule as socialist. Their ranking is also lower than Costa Rica, Ireland and Israel – countries that don't do nearly as well as the USA in GDP rankings.

Unsurprisingly, the war-torn countries of Afghanistan and South Sudan rank last, but seeing the likes of Rwanda, Botswana, and Tanzania in the bottom 10 should be discomforting for their leaders, as those countries are so often lauded for their economic growth performance.

- **Doughnut economics**

This example of a well-being model has been proposed by well-known Oxford University economist Kate Raworth. Seeking to counter growth at any cost and without adequate or appropriate consideration for the environment or social justice, Raworth proposes growth with limits and equitable outcomes. The doughnut incorporates the SDGs into its ring and accounts for the need to operate within a 'safe and just space' to avoid overshoot and inequality.

In a vote of confidence, the Amsterdam City Government in the Netherlands has become the first public authority to embrace doughnut economics. Since mid-2020, the concept has become the basis for all public policy decisions in the greater city. In adapting its economic policies, the deputy mayor asked: 'How can our city be home to thriving people in a thriving place while respecting the well-being of all people and the health of the whole planet? If this isn't the question that every government around the world needs to ask, then I don't know what is.'

Regarding resource use, over-extraction has long been highlighted as a principal concern and major threat to the environment. To reverse the trends, UNEP and the International Resource Panel (IRP) have produced the first global framework to assess the issue and offer guidelines on decoupling development from resource use and fossil fuels. Using what is referred to as the 'value-chain approach' methodology, the report focuses on reducing GHG emissions and biodiversity loss across the food, construction, and textile sectors.

More recently, in 2021, the Dasgupta Review on the 'Economics of Biodiversity' became the first-ever government-commissioned report of this nature. The review has come out strongly against current paradigms. It recommends changes across the board, including to education and finance systems, and how nations measure success. The author describes the natural world as 'our most precious asset' and how humanity has mismanaged this aspect.

Food systems

Because agricultural systems have resulted in some of the most severe impacts on the environment, health and social justice, there is a common saying among planners that suggests that if the global community 'gets it right on food, we get it right on everything else'. In essence, it means that transforming food production and supply systems is central to protecting habitat, biodiversity and health. In this regard, there are several trends and initiatives in global food systems that hold promise for the future.

Beef production, especially concerning large free-range cattle herds, has long been a primary environmental destroyer. However, with beef (and pork) consumption slowing around the world, this may well bring relief to the environment. According to the UK's *Financial Times* (*FT*), beef and pork consumption show signs that 'peak meat' is being reached. This is the result of environmental and health concerns, and meat substitutes in the form of plant-based burgers and patties are increasing. The trend is set to continue.

Turning to crops, in its report, 'Common Ground: Restoring Land Health for Sustainable Agriculture', the IUCN lays out how efforts at increasing the biodiversity of soils, principally the carbon content, through new sustainable practices, are likely to boost yields of maize, wheat and rice crops by up to 23.4%, 22.9% and 41.9% per year, respectively. These are all staple foods, and the end result brings greater food security with less water use and less pressure on the natural world. These practices are set to become integrated into the UN guidelines for sustainable agricultural practices.

Over the past few decades, a feature of food systems has been the globalisation of the entire process, including large-scale monocultures. While this has brought efficiency and higher production levels, it also comes with significantly increased environmental damage and reduced opportunities at a local level, with severe social and economic consequences. As a way of reversing these trends, the food sovereignty movement has emerged. Based on returning food production and distribution to a local or regional level, the approach is also about making culturally appropriate food choices through sustainable and traditional farm-based agriculture.

First given voice as an alternative platform alongside the 1996 World Food Summit in Rome, the move towards food sovereignty attempts to reclaim food choices and systems from the industrialised process. At times, lobbyists for multinational food producers have branded the idea of achieving food sovereignty as a political movement. This sentiment is partially correct. For those seeking reform around land ownership, labour practices and improved environmental conditions, the process of tackling these socio-economic challenges associated with food insecurity is an immensely welcome one.

Another significant development involves vertical farming, or vertical agriculture. This approach is being used in urban areas where planting and harvesting occur indoors in high-rise buildings under climate-controlled conditions. Vertical farming operates under a closed system that uses multi-stack or layered enclosures built upwards rather than outwards. The design ensures that higher productivity provides greater food security and nutritional value while reducing the need for arable land and water use.

Locally produced, vertical farming also removes many global environmental concerns around transportation and pollution, while avoiding the extended production and supply chains required by multinational corporates. In addition, because it can be done using existing old buildings, it is seen as a way of regenerating decaying inner-city precincts.

First introduced as an extension to greenhouse farming techniques, vertical farming is being applied in several pilot projects across major cities around the world, like Singapore, Tokyo and London. The US state of New Jersey is also a pioneer. South Africa has two pilot projects: One in the heavily populated urban areas of Bushbuckridge alongside the Kruger National Park, and the other outside Midrand, close to Johannesburg.

Current production worldwide includes the most popular vegetables and some fruits, such as strawberries and grapes. Still, there is potential to grow almost every crop and produce fish and other proteins. According to the Vertical Farming Institute, the value of produce will reach US$5.8 billion by 2022, and it currently has an annual growth rate of approximately 24%.

Population

There is some hope regarding the growth trends in global population levels. In 2020, *The Lancet* released their findings of a comprehensive study on population scenarios covering 195 countries and territories from 2017 to 2100. This study's principal finding projected global population peaking at 9.73 billion in 2063 before dropping to 8.79 billion by 2100. The findings also included an 'alternative scenario' that refers to a global population of 6.29 billion in 2100, if the targets on education and contraception set out in the SDGs are met.

Lower global population levels would certainly provide less strain at various levels, including food security, health and housing infrastructure and education, while also lowering pollution and emission levels. However, it is vital to note that despite the possibility of reduced population levels, humanity cannot survive without significant changes to current consumption and waste production levels, too. Even then, our chances seem doubtful.

At institutional level

Globally, our approach to the natural world at the institutional level continues to embrace the exploitation of every component as a renewable resource, or to bundle and trade in a range of offset and compensation schemes – characteristics of the neoliberal era. So, marine life and forests, for example, are harvested based on growing demand, despite sustainability concerns. Carbon is traded on open markets, like any other commodity. Some even envisage rhino horn and ivory being traded similarly.

This instrumentalist thinking is entrenched across all levels of governance and lies at the core of the global failure to respond to the environmental crisis in any meaningful way. Current thinking believes the best response is to trade our way out of trouble. To realise a shift in this thinking, fundamental change needs to take place at the institutional level. At the very least, this should focus on regulatory and legislative reform to direct governance and to embrace accountability through enforceable court processes.

While any meaningful change in this regard remains some way off, there is growing recognition that our global environmental reality dictates change as inevitable. In this process, environmental rights and protection mandates are now becoming central pillars of development paradigms. According to Open Global Rights, 149 nations have constitutions that include some provisions relating to environmental protection. The IUCN now recognises that citizens are entitled to a healthy environment, including the strongest forms of legal protection.

The next step is to turn these sentiments into a legislative and constitutional process that includes strict regulation and legal conse-quences, including the reparation of environmental damage. Ultimately, the environment and the world would be better served if everyone followed the examples of Costa Rica and Ecuador. To date, these are the only countries to have amended their constitutions to give the natural world enforceable rights. Both countries have become pioneers in an ecocentric approach to development. They should be applauded for this.

The law

In 2020, Denmark advanced the legislative cause against climate change denial, obstructionism and a lack of accountability when the country introduced groundbreaking laws that enforce carbon emission and climate change mitigation obligations on sitting governments. A failure to meet commitments and obligations mean that the Danish courts can now get involved, and law-flouting governments can be ousted.

While recognising that laws are only as good as the government in power at any time, the approach clearly demonstrates the type of leadership required across the world. Denmark's approach – based on listening to the science and input of other experts, being proactive and making sitting politicians accountable – will hopefully serve as an example to other nations.

South Africa is generally regarded as having one of the world's most progressive constitutions. However, it is light on environmental protections. Intent on rectifying this, a group of legal, environmental and social professionals have set in motion an initiative to establish the Wild Law Institute. This body will be dedicated to pioneering laws and practices that respect and prioritise the environment. It will also tackle environmental crimes and the lack of accountability among government and private sector agencies across the region.

Because current legislation and the courts fail to adequately protect 'wild species, their habitats and biological diversity', the proposed non-profit body would be an excellent addition to the region's prosecutorial options in combating rampant environmental crime.

The church

Churches have typically refrained from getting involved in environmental issues. However, in a move to be welcomed, the leaders of the Anglican Communion, the Eastern Orthodox and the Roman Catholic Church issued a joint statement in September 2021 warning of the urgent need to tackle environmental issues.

Representing close to two billion people, the churches released their statement in the period leading up to an important climate change conference. The statement also highlighted issues around poverty and the need for global cooperation.

'*Biodiversity loss, environmental degradation and climate change are the inevitable consequences of our actions, since we have greedily consumed more of the Earth's resources than the planet can endure. The people bearing the most catastrophic consequences of these abuses are the poorest on the planet and have been the least responsible for causing them,*' read part of the statement.

Facing disillusionment and even loss of membership, particularly from the younger generations, the churches' involvement in environmental issues may herald a much-needed fundamental change in attitude and approach.

Looking to the youth

Historically, one of the features defining leadership structures worldwide has been the lack of youth representation. Whether at presidential, cabinet, corporate, or even regional level, leadership has typically been in the hands of elderly males.

This disparity is particularly pronounced on the African continent, where the youth make up the largest demographic by some margin, yet it lacks appropriate representation at the leadership table.

According to the Mo Ibrahim Foundation, almost 60% of Africa's population is under 25, making it the youngest continent. Contrast this with the average age of leadership, which is well into their 60s, with some countries still carrying heads of state into their late 70s and early 80s –surely this means they are out of touch with a much younger electorate. However, this untenable situation seems to be changing.

Globally, there is no doubt that countries such as New Zealand, Finland, Costa Rica, and Chile are showing the way, with some of the youngest national leaders ever. Also, consider activists like Greta Thunberg, Malala Yousafzai, and the youth leaders from the Parkland school shooting in the USA. These and others indicate a strong crop of younger women and men who are taking the world into its next phase.

In Africa, young leaders, mostly in opposition or cabinet positions, are making waves in Rwanda, Ethiopia, Uganda, Angola, and South Africa, as they take up the challenges of the 21st century against leaders mired in thinking of the past. Often hamstrung by liberation ideologies that are no longer relevant, or compromised by their roles in overseeing the environmental, economic, and social declines during their terms, these older generations seem unwilling, or unable, to cope. In fact, many of them are populist and science-averse – a profile that fits leaders on other continents, too. Others have been party to authoritarian regimes, which certainly makes them unfit to be included in future planning.

Meanwhile, the younger generations have been born and brought up with today's environmental and social mess. Their experiences of this reality are real and relevant to the challenges of fixing the world. Many young people are also accustomed to more socially enlightened times and a more inclusive and open-minded approach to cultural and social extremes. In short, older leaders tend to reinforce or protect the status quo, while younger leaders are more likely to be agents of the change and transformation that this world so desperately needs.

We should encourage and celebrate the infusion of young leaders and social entrepreneurs who brim with fresh ideas and energy. This is exactly what the world and Africa need right now. When partnered with elders who display wisdom and caution, it could be a powerful combination for good.

9 /

INTO THE FUTURE

{ *Ian Michler* }

As Faith Popcorn so astutely asks: 'What would we do differently today if we knew everything about tomorrow?'

What broad scenarios are possible as we collectively respond to the Anthropocene's challenges? Do we muddle along under current paradigms, hoping they will get us out of trouble? Or can we engineer and navigate what Prof Mark Swilling from Stellenbosch University's Sustainability Institute refers to as a 'just transition' to a truly transformed, equitable and sustainable pattern of living? If these fail, what of collapse, a process most dare not even contemplate?

Before exploring these possibilities and some variations, the complexity factor is worth reiterating. Each challenge (addressing climate change, reforming economic models or education, halting biodiversity loss, or rethinking land-use priorities, to highlight but a few), has so many threads. They are all intertwined and cover every aspect of our living. When we accept that they all need attention, some more urgently than others, the immense complexity of this time in our history is presented in sharp relief.

Any exercise in scenario-planning that is aimed at resolving such a complex dilemma relies on many assumptions and serves only as a broad outline for achieving a more positive future. Notwithstanding the urgency, each possibility must be subjected to intense scrutiny and research.

Management agendas

'Management agendas' refer to our current paradigms: the strategies that scientists, institutions and governments are using in an attempt to manage the challenges we face, but without looking to fundamentally restructure our political and economic systems.

These initiatives focus on human ingenuity, innovation and advancing new technologies. They rely on significant outlays of capital. The aims and objectives almost always relate to achieving the sustainable development agenda, represented through the SDGs and other related platforms.

This approach is fully supported by the UN and its member states, global institutions, and the corporate world. Furthermore, these management agendas have the backing of the billionaire philanthropists, like Gates, Soros, Zuckerberg, Ma, Branson, Dangote, Motsepe, Rupert, Oppenheimer and others, who need to ensure their wealth and heritage remain intact.

Timeline on sustainable development

The concept of sustainable development has become the focus of world growth and development, but as the following timeline demonstrates, it's taken a few decades to define and implement.

1960s   The scientific community begins warning about the depletion of resources and the environmental impacts of our living patterns. It heralds the advent of the environmental movement.

1972   The UN holds the Conference on the Human Environment in Stockholm, Sweden, highlighting concerns for the environment, biodiversity, and human health. The outcome is a broad 26-principal framework recommending the 'need for a common outlook and for common principles'.

1987   The UN's World Commission on Environment and Development (established in 1983) releases its seminal work, 'Our

Common Future', often referred to as The Brundtland Report. The notion of sustainable development, or sustainability, enters the policymaking lexicon. It is defined as 'development which meets the needs of current generations without compromising the ability of future generations to meet their own needs'. In addition to galvanising developmental thinking behind a common concept, policymakers begin referring to the links between environmental degradation and social inequality brought about by economic policies.

1992   The Rio Summit in Rio de Janeiro hosts the UN's Conference on Environment and Development. An important component of the Rio Summit is the parallel Earth Summit, held by civil society and NGO groups over the same period. The understanding of what sustainability embraces begins to reach a far wider audience. The result is Agenda 21 and the Rio Declaration, placing humans at the centre of the debate.

2000   The UN launches its Eight Millennium Development Goals and sets 2015 as the deadline to reach global commitments to reduce poverty, hunger, disease, illiteracy, race, gender discrimination and environmental degradation.

2002   The World Summit on Sustainable Development is held in Johannesburg, South Africa. This follow-up to the Rio Summit focuses on hastening progress regarding the implementation of Agenda 21. Parties also commit to working in public/private partnerships.

2015   The 17 Sustainable Development Goals (SDGs) succeed the Millennium Development Goals and become the global face of the drive to achieve sustainability.

2016   The Stockholm Statement is released by 13 prominent economists, introducing principles around inequality and the environment, which had been excluded in past initiatives. The Paris Agreement, a legally binding treaty on climate change, comes into force in the same year, and 196 countries sign on. With this commitment, governments seem to signal their understanding that growth, development and human living is severely threatened if global warming is not limited to below 2°C.

2021   The UN Biodiversity Conference is held in Kunming, China. It aims to commit the nations of the world to end habitat destruction and biodiversity loss. Achieving this is central to humanity having any hope of a sustainable future.

Each of the events listed has raised awareness around the challenges and has laid out a conceptual framework for action by the global community. In so doing, some headway on specific challenges has been made. Still, history shows that none of them, on their own or collectively, has successfully promoted and instigated the necessary widespread, fundamental change.

Shortcomings include vagueness in defining concepts, poor implementation and regulation, and a lack of timelines prior to the advent of the SDGs. The harshest critics simply view sustainable development as a contradiction in terms – a convenient cover for the status quo.

The Sustainable Development Goals (2015)

The 17 SDGs comprise six environmental goals and 11 economic and social goals. Together, they have become the face of current approaches to tackling sustainability. In 2015, they were adopted by all UN member states as the focus of Agenda 2030, a collective 15-year plan to achieve them. Agenda 2030 includes the commitments made by member states, and acts as the roadmap for explaining each goal, exploring ways for their implementation, and reviewing processes for achieving the goals. As the name suggests, 2030 is the deadline set for a full review of the targets.

Only time will tell whether the goals will be met or missed, and if they are realistic or not. In the meantime, and despite the drawbacks and weaknesses, they can be celebrated on one count: They represent one of the very few occasions that every nation has reached consensus on such a significant issue.

Africa has Agenda 2063; its own interpretation and action plan relating to the SDGs. This plan aims to transform the continent to fulfil its economic and political potential.

The green economy

UNEP launched its Green Economy Initiative in 2008. The collective objective is to provide analysis and policy support for investment in green sectors, while greening those not yet environmentally sensitive. Its agendas appear as various public and/or private partnerships, all developed within the sustainable development narrative, and all resembling the environmental objectives set out in the SDGs.

While there is no universally accepted definition, UNEP describes a green economy as one that is 'low carbon, resource-efficient and socially inclusive'. A green economy seeks to prioritise investment in sectors that reduce carbon emissions and pollution, and to prevent biodiversity and ecosystem loss while enhancing non-fossil fuel energy options.

One of the most visible of these public/private partnerships is the Green Economy Coalition, which has a vision to seek prosperity for all through a 'fair, green economic future'. The coalition has five principles forming its agenda: well-being, justice, planetary boundaries, efficiency, sufficiency and good governance.

The circular economy

The growing demand for resource extraction is increasingly impacting on the environment. According to the WEF and UNEP, it now exceeds 100 billion tons (92 billion tonnes), most of which ends up as emissions or waste. Because of the scale that extraction has reached, global economies and social conditions have become overly reliant on these resources, as well as vulnerable to fluctuations in commodity prices.

The concept of circular economies seeks to reverse this process by promoting regeneration and restoration rather than the current linear process of what the WEF refers to as the 'take, make and waste system'.

Some view this circular approach as the polar opposite of planned obsolescence.

Circular economies also promote a transition to renewable energy, while waste eradication is a priority through designs that allow for the break-up and re-assembly of products for re-use. Other schools of thought associated with the circular economy include biomimicry, cradle-to-cradle design, and natural capitalism.

Ecomodernism

The ecomodernist agenda overlaps significantly with the green economy. It emerged in the early 2000s as an extension, or arm, of the broader environmental movement.

Ecomodernists accept that significant environmental damage is being inflicted by current living paradigms and that resource extraction levels are unsustainable. However, they reject the notion that continued economic growth inevitably leads to environmental destruction. Instead, the focus is on enhancing science and technology to overcome environmental challenges and withdrawing from current extraction levels without reducing living standards. They also promote increased urbanisation as a way to protect the natural world.

There is a particular focus on scaling up technology in the agriculture sector – large-scale intensification, genetically modified crops, synthetic foods, desalination, and intensive aquaculture, for example. The objectives would be met in the energy sector by switching to nuclear and renewables.

The Ecomodernist Manifesto was published in 2015 by a range of prominent scientists and economists. The authors stated:

'We affirm one long-standing environmental ideal, that humanity must shrink its impacts on the environment to make more room for nature, while we reject another, that human societies must harmonise with nature to avoid economic and ecological collapse.'

The Stockholm Statement

The Stockholm Statement was released in September 2016 by leading economists, including a Nobel prize winner and several former World Bank chief economists. They met to discuss the global challenges faced by policymakers and to seek consensus on a new way forward. For many, the statement is an acknowledgement that current paradigms cannot engineer the structural change needed to achieve the goals of sustainable development. This is particularly so regarding the environmental crisis and social inequality. In this respect, it is the most constructive comment on current paradigms and offers a way forward.

The statement lays out a 10-point template to replace what the authors referred to as 'traditional economic thinking', as it 'no longer applied'. They highlight many of the themes already discussed in this and other chapters:

- Gross Domestic Product and growth rates are not the best indicators, and well-being factors must be accounted for.
- Development must be inclusive, and the inequalities seen in our societies are reflective of failed policies.
- Environmental sustainability must become a requirement and not be seen as an option.
- There is a need to balance reliance on markets with state and community involvement.
- Cultural values and social norms are vital aspects of planning and must be included in policy implementation.

There have been similar proposals by other scientists and economists, all calling for change to certain aspects of current paradigms. In August 2020, a group of 100 economists, led by Jeffrey Sachs and Joseph Stiglitz, two of the most well-known development economists, called for an end to the 'carbon economy'. Robert Reich, one of the signatories to the statement, wrote in *The Guardian*:

'The carbon economy amplifies racial, social and economic inequalities, creating a system that is fundamentally incompatible with a stable future.'

Included was a call for governments and the financial community to end their support for the fossil fuel industry and to promote fairer, equitable economic systems.

Will the Fourth Industrial Revolution be any different?

For all the hubris, it's moot whether the 'green' versions of our economic activity have any chance of bridging the tension between the scope and pace of developmental aspirations and the ecological limits of the planet. Phrased another way: is it possible to pay off our environmental and social debts by increasing utilisation of the natural world while also spending more on technology?

There is no doubt that these management agendas will make some headway in dealing with current global challenges. In the USA, for example, the 'Green New Deal', which is being promoted by the Democrats, receives plenty of plaudits for attaching poverty reduction and anti-discrimination legislation to its broader environmental aims of restructuring the energy sector. However, it can be argued that this and all other 'deals' are undermined by the same critical concern: They operate within the current economic and political paradigms and the way of living that has landed us in this mess in the first place. After all, these systems are clearly efficient at entrenching inequality, cultural disruption and polarisation, while promoting unlimited growth that destroys the environment.

Furthermore, as decision-makers embrace the much-touted Fourth Industrial Revolution, let's not forget that it heralds a technologically-geared era – one that the WEF describes as bringing great promise but also significant peril. On the upside are improved efficiencies and productivity across almost every economic sector; even greater comprehensive global connectivity and reach, and access to information, bringing increasing levels of convenience. But, on the downside, we enter an era seeking to rid the economic sphere of labour while bringing huge rewards to the engineers, entrepreneurs, and owners driving the revolution. Can this be tenable in a world already suffering from growing levels of inequality and accessibility for the disadvantaged? Can we entertain a situation in which, in all likelihood, inequality will grow?

As noted, all indicators show that Earth is already dangerously denuded and that, at a planetary level, we are beyond some limits and now operating in overdraft. We are at least a decade down the line since implementing these management agendas, but evidence clearly indicates their objectives are not being achieved. Lack of investment, legislation, enforceability and accountability play into this. So, too, does the continued emphasis on humanity's developmental path rather than understanding that this cannot occur without environmental, social, and ethical sustainability.

Some critics go further, suggesting that the sustainable development agenda simply enforces the current capitalist model. It merely promotes tinkering with the system rather than calling for profound, transform- ative structural change. Could the management agendas be strategic denialism on a grand scale?

A transitionary process

What happens if, for example, the impediments are overcome, and the SDGs and the more enlightened thinking that is embodied in the Stockholm Statement become realistic platforms for transformation?

A second scenario, one that can be broadly referred to as a 'transi- tionary process', recognises that current systems are ill-equipped to deal with the challenges of the Anthropocene. It embraces the need for fundamental and far-reaching structural change to economic and political structures and to existing global institutions in order to achieve sustainability. It proposes that the most effective way of doing this is through a transitionary process over time. New political and governance systems must genuinely represent the people, and an entirely new economic and developmental paradigm needs to have social equality and an environmental ethic at its core. A transitionary agenda also means a change in the way that nations cooperate, and a realignment of global alliances.

Given the nature of the process and its ultimate aim of totally transformed societies, it is understandable that this relatively recent field of study is still seeking consensus on many concepts and strategies.

In their book, *Just Transitions*, Prof Mark Swilling and Eve Annecke refer to the urgent need for the transition process to be a just one. They reiterate the objective of inclusive and equitable communities, along with environmental stability. For the authors, sustainability implies limits and balancing ecological and financial footprints. A just transition towards this, say Swilling and Annecke, is a process that:

'... reconciles sustainable use of natural resources with a pervasive commitment to what is increasingly being referred to as sufficiency – that is, where over-consumers are satisfied with less so that under-consumers can secure enough, without aspiring to more than their fair share'.

Swilling goes further in his book, *The Age of Sustainability; Just Transitions in a Complex World*. He refers to deep transitions, 'a series of connected and sustained fundamental transformations of a wide range of socio-technical systems in a similar direction'. This refers to the shift needed across all spectrums of our living.

Adding to the notion of a just transition, Lorenzo Fioramonti, in his book, *Wellbeing Economy*, stresses that well-being should lie at the core of the economies of transformed societies.

'Development lies not in the exploitation of natural and human resources but in improving the quality and effectiveness of human-to-human and human-to-ecosystem interactions, supported by appropriate enabling technologies.'

Such change calls for redefining our understanding and expression of growth, progress and well-being. Indeed, it embraces almost every component of our living, which means embracing zero-growth or exploring alternative options, such as doughnut economics instead of GDP-based economies. It also assumes dealing with the other inhibiting factors that are working against the transformation of our societies. In addition, all global financial and political institutions and their power relationships would have to be restructured accordingly.

Given the underlying complexity of the process, policymakers refer to 'incrementalism', a process of gradual change rather than radical shifts, as the most suitable approach to transitioning a society.

The energy transition

In the same way that the fossil fuel sector was the foundation for the past three industrial revolutions, 'the energy transition' to renewable sources of energy can, and should, become the foundation for a genuinely transformed way of living.

According to the International Renewable Energy Association (IRENA), this transition is a:

'... *pathway toward transformation of the global energy sector from fossil-based to zero-carbon by the second half of this century. At its heart is the need to reduce energy-related CO_2 emissions to limit climate change.*'

This process of decarbonisation to renewable sources is deemed urgent.

An additional tenet of the transition includes extending the switch beyond supply grids to every sphere of the economic system. All activities that have traditionally relied on fossil fuels must undergo transformation. That means that everything from vehicle manufacture, to transport systems and aviation, to the broader aspects of industry and agriculture.

In addition to the obvious environmental benefits, the energy transition must also secure access to energy for the billion-plus people currently excluded from national grids. A lack of access to power is a characteristic of the poverty trap. Removing this social blight will significantly boost economic opportunities and well-being for the poor.

The World Energy Transitions Outlook has calculated that to successfully manage and achieve this transition, annual investment spending must increase by at least 30% across the globe. This will need to total over US$131 trillion between now and 2050.

Dematerialisation and decoupling

These twin concepts are central components to structurally transforming economic and developmental paradigms. Increasingly used in sustainability debates, they also appear in the thinking of some management agendas. At times used interchangeably, they do, in fact, hold important distinctions.

Dematerialisation refers to the necessary reduction in materials (many of them non-renewable in nature) used in the current production and consumption paradigms. The need to follow this route is based on an acceptance that current patterns of overexploitation are primary reasons for habitat and biodiversity loss, climate change and many social inequalities.

Decoupling, in turn, relates to achieving economic growth and well-being, but without the concomitant increase in resource use and environmental destruction currently experienced. When implemented together, they counter the paradox of current agendas, promoting unlimited growth in a world with limited resources and planetary boundaries. Achieving this will require a thorough review of economic systems, as well as consumption and consumerism patterns.

Despite the appealing outcomes of this scenario, critics believe that the chances of a just transition taking place remain slim. Earlier, we noted the complexity of our challenges, and the polarisation that must be overcome to shift a collective consciousness and find consensus. Is the understanding and co-operation at this level attainable, and is it possible to fulfil the lifestyle aspirations and poverty reduction targets of an increasing global population? Time is also a factor: Do we have enough of it to achieve these outcomes, or are current environmental and social tensions already at breaking point?

Radical change

By definition, radical agendas call for the far-reaching and immediate transformation of societies. While often beginning with a focus on a specific aspect, they typically end up spreading quickly. Given the speed and extent of change that usually occurs, the radical approach is problematic, as it can underestimate the complexities within societies. History has shown that radical changes, as sweeping and as dramatic as they are, disrupt and ruin society as a whole.

Iraq, Zimbabwe, and Libya are good examples. These countries underwent radical transformation that ended up destroying the fabric of their living – so much so that many within the countries ask whether they are better or worse off because of the process.

In contemporary politics, radical parties are also often referred to as 'extremist' – a form of political action falling outside mainstream thinking, or the average societal values promoted by the government of the day. Current political agendas that could become more radicalised or extreme include the Yellow Vests movement in France, Al-Shabaab in Somalia and environs, and the Economic Freedom Fighters here in South Africa.

Post-sustainability and collapse

Those who believe that the sustainability agenda, which seeks to manage current challenges, has failed – specifically when it comes to the achievement of global warming and climate change mitigation targets – refer to a post-sustainability scenario, or the inevitability of collapse.

Post-sustainability

The IPCC has made it clear that if global warming results in average temperature changes passing 1.5°C, we enter the realm of catastrophe. Those who claim that we should be preparing for a post-sustainability scenario believe that it is already too late to reverse the temperature rises and the impacts of climate change, no matter what measures are now taken. This scenario argues that we are already heading through critical levels and thresholds.

According to Dr Jem Bendell, Professor of Sustainability Leadership and the Founder of the Institute for Leadership and Sustainability at the University of Cumbria, instead of focusing on managing or transitioning, we should be looking at a 'deep adaptation agenda'. By this, he means one that explores and prepares for living in an unstable and highly uncertain post-sustainability situation. Bendell believes that our systems and institutions are simply not capable of responding to the looming crisis, and that a breakdown in civilisation and an extended period of collapse is a real possibility.

This viewpoint does not currently have much support. Some argue that it's counterproductive, or even unethical. But as Bendell points out, 'collapse denial' ensures that societies do not have to confront their own downfall.

As is so often the case with highly contentious debates, the devil is in the detail – or, as is the case with responses to Bendell's assertions – it's what lies within the language. Rather than outright endorsements, his thinking gets some qualified nods. In 2019, a group of renowned scientists published their thoughts in *Nature*. Titled *Climate tipping points – too risky to bet against*, the piece spoke clearly of the threats posed by 'abrupt and irreversible climate changes' and the ensuing emergencies. All Bendell did was extend that thinking to the reality of worst-case scenarios.

Footnote: On the 1st August 2022, the PNAS released a report calling for further research into what they referred to as the 'Climate Endgame'. The authors believe that global catastrophe brought about by climate change and instability is no longer an unrealistic scenario.

Collapse

The collapse of our societies and the inevitable loss of heritage, or at the very least, the systems under which we currently live, is an outcome most of us do not want to contemplate. However, evidence shows it is a possibility that is receiving greater consideration with each passing decade.

I have been musing on sustainability issues for some time, but the irony of this scenario came into sharper focus for me about 16 years ago while spending some time with a group of Hadza people on the shores of Lake Eyasi in Tanzania.

Early one morning, I had set out with them on foot, grabbing at berries and other woodland delights along the way. Sometime later, after an attempt at bagging a hare of sorts, I watched as they hunted a vervet monkey with a perfectly made bow and arrows. Soon, and without using matches, a fire had been lit, and they cooked and ate their meal without any utensils. Before heading home, each one of them scuffed sand over the few remaining coals, leaving no trace of the morning's endeavours.

As we ambled back, I was left in no doubt as to their connectedness to the natural world, and their light footprint on its surface. Without idealising their socio-political set-up, it was clear that a humble egalitarianism permeated that band of hunters and their extended families in their small village.

Later that evening, around a campfire, I started reflecting on how this group was one of only a few true hunter-gatherers left across the continent, even the world. The San or Bushmen of the south, the Batwa of central Africa, the Inuit communities in North America, and the Andaman Islanders off India are among the few remaining groups who have historically led similar nomadic and subsistence lifestyles. Within these communities, only a few remain connected to their ancestral lands.

I contrasted this with the paradox of the world from which I come – one dominated by rapacious developmental growth, consumption, and waste, as well as inequality and political power plays at every turn. Yet, we are also involved in this frantic search for sustainability and equality – the very aspects I had witnessed that morning within the community context.

In this search of ours, there is a stark and harsh truth: The people who still have the capacity to lead truly sustainable lives, the Hadza among them, are being wiped out by the destructive ways of the system I know. Instead of listening to the Hadza and learning from them; instead of getting to understand what lies at the core of their living and how that relates to our challenge, as well as what needs to be done, our wasteful ways are simply eradicating their communities.

It is fair to say that all hunter-gatherer lifestyles will be either lost forever or absorbed into our consumerist culture within the next few decades. A genuinely sustainable way of living, and all the knowledge that we apparently yearn for, will be gone forever! Some may suggest that this is a simplified analogy. Still, I come back to the essence of our crisis and the challenges laid out earlier in this chapter: True sustainability focused on overcoming our environmental and social challenges presents itself as a complete contradiction to our current political and economic paradigms. We cannot even respect, let alone honour, those who have as a way of living that for which we claim to be striving. Is this an indication that we really can't change our ways? Is the collective momentum of humanity already too far down the only path we know?

Why do societies collapse?

Dr Luke Kemp is an existential risk researcher attached to the University of Cambridge in the United Kingdom. Much of his work is focused on the theories of how and why societies collapse. According to Kemp, collapse can be defined as:

'A rapid and enduring loss of population, identity and socio-economic complexity. Public services crumble and disorder ensues as government loses control of its monopoly on violence.'

Kemp has studied every civilisation or society (including empires), which he quantifies as a collection of people and their technologies, along with the systems and structures they develop in complex but ordered ways. These go back almost 4 000 years and include the great and famous: The Romans and Mayans, for instance – and those more obscure, like the Olmec in Mexico. Each has experienced collapse in some form. Some have disappeared permanently, while others have recovered as a transformed grouping. There is an argument that rather than total collapse, societies undergo steady but complex declines before taking on another shape or form.

In his research, Kemp has picked up many common threads. As we examine our own global challenges, these remain extremely relevant today. While he is at pains to point out that there is no conclusive reason or theory behind collapse, or a precise timeframe attached to it, the following list includes factors preceding the collapse of past societies and civilisations:

- The direct environmental impacts on habitats and biodiversity from human activities.

- External shocks, such as disease and invasion.
- Natural disasters such as climate change.
- Rising inequality that is seen or experienced within the political, economic, and social spheres, often associated with oligarchical leadership.
- The complexity and bureaucracy levels of societies reach a state where the benefits start diminishing. At that point, collapse sets in.

Regarding this last factor, Kemp turns to the thinking of historian Joseph Tainter in his book, *The Collapse of Complex Societies*. Like Kemp, Tainter refers to a society or civilisation as a collection of people and their technologies, living in complex but ordered systems. Furthermore, these societies are problem-solving entities that act ostensibly for the benefit of all who live under their structures. However, collapse sets in when there is a diminishing return on solving socio-economic complexities.

How many of these factors do we recognise as defining the Anthropocene?

Kemp warns that being a large society, or having advanced technology, may not count in our favour:

'*We may be more technologically advanced now. But this gives little ground to believe that we are immune to the threats that undid our ancestors. Our newfound technological abilities even bring new, unprecedented challenges to the mix.*'

While Kemp says that collapse is not inevitable, it is likely, given the history and our current situation.

More recently, a group of 250 scientists from universities and research institutes around the world released a statement urging governments and civil society to engage in discussions around widescale societal disruption and collapse.

'*We have experienced how emotionally challenging it is to recognise the damage being done ... It is time to invite each other into difficult conversations, so we can reduce our complicity in the harm, and be creative to make the best of a turbulent future,*' they said.

Is there any solace in the collapse scenario? Not all will agree, but for those more concerned about other species and the environment, there is perhaps comfort in knowing that biodiversity and the planet will survive. And so, too, will we. It's our current way of living, and our systems and societies that are most at risk.

In the end

No matter one's philosophical, cultural, or religious frame of reference, no one is excused or exempt from taking responsibility for the state we are in. Understanding this, along with the concept of the Anthropocene, is vital. Accepting the damage being done and the inequalities in existence are the first steps in reassessing and ultimately transforming our relationship with the planet and other communities.

As we have noted, the science is emphatic and unequivocal – whether reporting on measurements of faraway and invisible impacts, or through very real everyday experiences across the globe. We simply cannot continue within current paradigms.

Untold reports and reviews attest to this, but as a closing word, I will draw on three of the very latest to again confirm what we already know about the mess.

The 'Making Peace with Nature' blueprint was released by UNEP in 2021. Its key message contains a simple but extremely stark warning: 'Humanity's environmental challenges have grown in number and severity ever since the Stockholm Conference in 1972 and now represent a planetary emergency.'

The report adds some optimism regarding a way forward, but also highlights an urgently required shift in thinking. 'Transforming humankind's relationship with nature is the key to a sustainable future,' conclude the authors.

The Dasgupta Review: The Economics of Biodiversity, released by the UK government in early 2021, is a little less strident, but the message nonetheless carries a similar warning. Two of the highlight messages are: 'Our unsustainable engagement with nature is endangering the prosperity of current and future generations,' and 'At the heart of the problem lies deep-rooted, widespread institutional failure.'

The third is the response of UN Secretary-General Antonio Guterres to the 2022 IPCC assessment. He referred to the report as 'an atlas of human suffering and a damning indictment of failed climate leadership'.

In essence, we are being told again that our current approach is not working and that under current policies and structures, we are unlikely to be able to engineer the transformational change that is urgently required.

To begin the process, at the very least, these reports and the many other research assessments referenced in this book should be urgently incorporated into policymaking across every level of government around the world. In-house corporate and government institutional training should be mandated to include this information as part of their agendas. This research, and the untold reports detailing the state of our planet, should also become integral to education curricula, from the first year of schooling to the final year of university and beyond. This is not to suggest an intrusion into freedom of choice. It's simply common sense.

Suppose that you are one of those who continue to support the status quo, believing that humanity and the way we live will prevail. In that case, I ask you to consider this: no amount of power, status, wealth, wilful ignorance, denial, or privilege will secure anyone's status in a calamitous scenario. There are no factors that exclude you or anyone from the obligation to change.

For each one of us, our very survival and that of our families depend on being responsible towards the planet. Functioning ecological cycles, as well as healthy habitats, ecosystems and biodiversity levels drive all natural processes. These include climate regulation, soil formation, water provision, carbon sequestration and nutrient cycling, which are all vital for our existence. Approximately 50% of the global economy is based directly on biological products and natural cycles. These factors have allowed us and our families to accumulate wealth and comfort.

When we were hunter-gatherers, our existence was inextricably linked to knowing and respecting the natural world. After thousands of years of conquest and technological development, that relationship has been well and truly severed for billions of people. As an aspirational societal goal, any new paradigm must re-establish these links to the environment. This is not a yearning for a bygone era, but a logical call for what is necessary today.

In my judgement, this should come before we set about destroying our moon and other planets. For all of the ingenuity that folks such as Elon Musk, Jeff Bezos, and Richard Branson show, they embody the current system. With proceeds bestowed, and at levels of obscene wealth by paradigms that promote environmental destruction and favour structural inequality, they race to conquer horizons way beyond our current needs and challenges. In doing so, they display a rather selfish and impatient competitive urge. Is all of this necessary? Conquering new territory has always involved acquisition and pillage. Why would the space race be any different?

But it's not the desire to invent and investigate – a notable human characteristic that has propelled us to the situation today – that is the primary dilemma. Instead, it is apparent that boredom and disinterest with current challenges here on Earth, and the way we repeat the patterns of our historical ways.

I vote for sorting the mess out here before extending humanity's to-do list elsewhere.

Of uncertainties and fears

Any talk about ending eras or paradigms implies profound change, and the problem we all face is that this brings uncertainty, anxiety and even fear. Thinking about where we may be called to compromise, or what we will be asked to sacrifice, is disruptive. Naturally, we become apprehensive about what we don't know and what may unfold.

While this is absolutely acceptable – some would even say emotionally necessary – as individuals, families, communities, and nations, we somehow have to ensure these concerns do not result in strategic denial and inaction. As the scientists warn, such a scenario is even more risky and uncertain.

Finally, even if the pathway to improving our environmental record remains daunting, the destruction of the environment, and our future options to rectify are, for the most part, quantifiable. Whether we follow them or not, science and logic lay those out for us.

However, reinterpreting the meaning of being human, and our consequential relationships with each other in such a rapidly changing world requires insight in a more demanding way. This aspect concerns me. Driven by the intensity of the technological and digital development that represents the Fourth Industrial Revolution and more, do we have any grasp how this might impact our humanness?

Robotics, artificial intelligence, and the rate at which computer processing and social media develops, for example, all have profound implications on our personal development and relationships, behaviour and mental stability. This stuff is meant to free us and make our lives easier, but it has ended up controlling us and making our lives less meaningful. What are the impacts of these technological developments and the rapid change they bring on individual behaviour, as well as to the social fabric of societies? In addition, we also now contend with different realities to the extent that societies are no longer in agreement over what constitutes truth. Are we coping, or are we fraying the edges of civility?

Already, we have become what some sociologists refer to as 'the lab rats of big tech'. We date and can choose our children online; get fired and divorced by text message; bring governments down using social media networks and compete against machines for work. Soon, there may not be any schooling or work, not to mention banks and shops, or a plateful of wholesome food. We may be marrying machines, travelling by staying at home, and being able to genetically manipulate our own being. This comes on top of climate change anxiety, the stresses of increasing polarisation within communities and cultures, and looking for meaning in the maze of a post-truth world.

Do we have the emotional capacity to adapt and even transform ourselves and our cultures to meet these required new human profiles? Given the path and duration of natural evolutionary processes, is it even possible for humans to evolve a new spiritual and psychological understanding of what it is to be human in the future? Or is the exponential pace of technological advancement and the loss of what we know about our humanness occurring at a speed beyond our evolutionary and adaptive capacity?

10 /

STAYING IN TOUCH

{ *Ian McCallum & Ian Michler* }

The challenges outlined in this book are, by nature, complex and dynamic. To be effective over time, it is important to stay up to date on the debates and strategies, as well as policies being formulated and implemented. In this section, we list a range of sites and sources that will hopefully offer greater insight and benefit to your work. It is by no means a complete list.

Conservation and environmental organisations

Global

African Wildlife Foundation – www.awf.org
Birdlife International – www.birdlife.org
Blue Marine Foundation – www.bluemarinefoundation.com
Born Free Foundation – www.bornfree.org.uk
Center for Biological Diversity – www.biologicaldiversity.org
Conservation Corridor – www.conservationcorridor.org
Conservation International – www.conservation.org
Dallas Safari Club – www.biggame.org
Earthwatch Institute – www.earthwatch.org
FACE – Hunters of Europe – www.face.eu
Fauna and Flora International – www.fauna-flora.org
Global Environment Facility – www.thegef.org
Global Nature Fund – www.globalnature.org

Greenpeace – www.greenpeace.org
Humane Society International – www.hsi.org
IFAW – www.ifaw.org
International Whaling Commission – www.iwc.int
IUCN – www.iucn.org
National Audubon Society – www.audubon.org
Natural Resources Defence Council – www.nrdc.org
Nature Needs More – www.natureneedsmore.org
Oceana – www.oceana.org
One Tree Planted – www.onetreeplanted.org
Panthera – www.panthera.org
Raincoast Conservation Foundation – www.raincoast.org
Re:wild – www.rewild.org
Safari Club International – www.safariclub.org
Sea Shepard Conservation Society – www.seashepardglobal.org
Sierra Club – www.sierraclub.org
Stop Ecoside International – www.stopecocide.earth
The Global Alliance for the Rights of Nature – www.therightsofnature.org
The Jane Goodall Institute – www.janegoodall.org
The Nature Conservancy – www.nature.org
The Royal Society for the Protection of Birds – www.rspb.org.uk
The Wildlife Conservation Society – www.wcs.org
Tusk – www.tusk.org
UN Environment Programme – www.unenvironment.org
US Fish & Wildlife Service – www.fws.gov
Wetlands International – www.wetlands.org
WildAid – www.wildaid.org
Wild Foundation – www.wild.org
Women for Conservation – www.womenforconservation.org
WWF – www.worldwildlife.org

African

African Conservation Foundation – www.africanconservation.org
African Parks – www.africanparks.org
Baboon Matters – www.baboonmatters.org.za
Big Cats Initiative – www.nationalgeographic.org
Big Life Foundation – www.biglife.org
Cheetah Conservation Botswana – www.cheetahconservationbotswana.org
Cheetah Conservation Fund – www.cheetah.org
Conservation Alliance of Kenya – www.conservationalliance.or.ke
Custodians of Professional Hunting & Conservation South Africa –
    www.cphc-sa.co.za

Dian Fossey Gorilla Fund International – www.gorillafund.org
Earthlife Africa – www.earthlife.org.za
Eden to Addo – www.edentoaddo.co.za
Elephants Alive – www.elephantsalive.org
Elephants Without Borders – www.elephantswithoutborders.org
Giraffe Conservation Foundation – www.giraffeconservation.org
Integrated Rural Development and Nature Conservation – www.irdnc.org.na
International Elephant Foundation – www.elephantconservation.org
Kalahari Research and Conservation – www.krcbots.org
Kenya Wildlife Trust – www.kenyawildlifetrust.org
Landmark Foundation – www.landmarkfoundation.org.za
Lewa Wildlife Conservancy – www.lewa.org
Lion Guardians – www.lionguardians.org
Lion Landscapes – www.lionlandscapes.org
Niassa Carnivore Project – www.niassalion.org
Northern Rangelands Trust – www.nrt-kenya.org
PAMS Foundation – www.pamsfoundation.org
Peace Parks Foundation – www.peaceparks.org
Pride – www.pridelionalliance.org
Ruaha Carnivore Project – www.ruahacarnivoreproject.com
South African National Biodiversity Institute – www.sanbi.org
Save the Elephants – www.savetheelephants.org
Save the Rhino – www.savetherhino.org
Sheldrickwildlife Trust – www.sheldrickwildlifetrust.org
Soft Foot Alliance – www.softfootalliance.org
Southern African Foundation for the Conservation of Coastal Birds –
     www.sanccob.co.za
South African Shark Conservancy – www.sharkconservancy.org
Southern Tanzania Elephant Program – www.stzelephants.org
The Cape Leopard Trust – www.capeleopard.org.za
The Endangered Wildlife Trust – www.ewt.org.za
Tsavo Trust – www.tsavotrust.org
WESSA – www.wessa.org.za
Wild Bird Trust – www.wildbirdtrust.com
Wild Entrust – www.wildentrust.org
Wilderness Foundation Africa – www.wildernessfoundation.com
Wildlife Act – www.wildlifeact.com
Wildlife Direct – www.wildlifedirect.org
Wild Shots Outreach – www.wildshotsoutreach.org
Zambian Carnivore Programme – www.zambiancarnivores.org

Youth Agencies

Earth Guardians – www.earthguardians.org
Future Coalition – www.futurecoalition.org
Hip Hop Caucus – www.hiphopcaucus.org
Kids Rights – www.kidsrights.org
Roots & Shoots – www.rootsandshoots.org
Sunrise Movement – www.sunrisemovement.org
The Youth Café – www.theyouthcafe.com
UK Youth Climate Coalition – www.ukycc.com
Youth 4 African Wildlife – www.youth4africanwildlife.org
Youth4Conservation – www.youth4conservation.co.za
Youth4Nature – www.youth4nature.org
Zero Hour – www.thisiszerohour.org

The Anthropocene

General

Anthropocene – www.anthropocene.info
Anthropocene – www.anthropocenemagazine.org
Carbon Disclosure Project (CDP) – www.cdp.net/en
Center for Global Development – www.cgdev.org
Doughnut Economics Action Lab – www.doughnuteconomics.org
EU Environment – https://ec.europa.eu/environment/index_en
Earth Overshoot Day – www.overshootday.org
Environmental Defense Fund – www.edf.org
Environmental News Network – www.enn.com
Faith Popcorn's Brain Reserve – www.faithpopcorn.com
Globaia – https://globaia.org/anthropocene
Global Footprint Network – www.footprintnetwork.org
Global Wellness Institute – https://globalwellnessinstitute.org/industry-research/
        happiness-wellbeing-index
Grist – www.grist.org
International Institute for Sustainable Development – www.iisd.org
International Renewable Energy Agency – www.irena.org
International Resource Panel – www.resourcepanel.org
Just Transition Knowledge Portal – www.tips.org.za
Learn Biomimicry – www.learnbiomimicry.com
National Academy of Sciences – www.nasonline.org
One World – www.oneworldgroup.co.za
Our World in Data – www.ourworldindata.org

Renewable Energy World – www.renewableenergyworld.com
Stockholm Resilience Centre – www.stockholmresilience.org
Sustainability for All – www.activesustainability.com
Sustainability Institute – www.sustainabilityinstitute.net
Sustainable Development Goals – www.sustainabledevelopment.un.org
Treehugger – www.treehugger.com
The Anthropocene Project – www.theanthropocene.org
The Donella Meadows Project – www.donellameadows.org
The Embedding Project – www.embeddingproject.org
UN Economic and Social Council – https://www.un.org/ecosoc/en/home
UN Environment Programme – www.unenvironment.org
UN Global Compact – https://www.unglobalcompact.org/what-is-gc/mission/
    principles
UN Global Issues Overview – https://www.un.org/en/global-issues
Yale Environment 360 – www.e360.yale.edu
Women's Environment & Development Organization – www.wedo.org
World Business Council for Sustainable Development – www.wbcsd.org
World Centric – www.worldcentric.com
World Economic Forum – www.weforum.org
World Inequality Database – https://wid.world/news-article/2020-regional-
    updates
World Overshoot Day – www.overshootday.org
World Resources Institute – www.wri.org

Biodiversity and ecosystem services

Chemical Watch – www.chemicalwatch.com
Conservation Capital – www.conservation-capital.com
Global Forest Watch – www.globalforestwatch.org
Intergovernmental Science-Policy Platform on Biodiversity and Ecosystem
    Services (IPBES) – www.ipbes.net
IUCN Red List of Threatened Species – www.iucnredlist.org
IUCN Species Survival Commission – https://www.iucn.org/commissions/
    species-survival-commission
Laboratory for Anthropogenic Landscape Ecology – www.ecotope.org
Nature Serve – www.natureserve.org
New York Declaration on Forests – www.forestdeclaration.org
Rainforest Action Network – www.ran.org
Regime Shifts Database – www.regimeshifts.org
UN Environment Programme World Conservation Monitoring Centre –
    www.unep-wcmc.org

Food

Association for Vertical Farming – www.vertical-farming.net
Cambridge Sustainable Food – www.cambridgesustainablefood.org
International Food Policy Research Institute – www.ifpri.org
IPES Food – www.ipes-food.org
Farmers Footprint – www.farmersfootprint.us
Food and Agriculture Organization of the United Nations – www.fao.org
Global Agriculture – www.globalagriculture.com
The EAT – Lancet Commission on Food, Planet, Health – www.eatforum.org
The Global Food Security Index – https://impact.economist.com/sustainability/project/food-security-index

Population and urbanisation

Global Infrastructure Hub – www.gihub.org
Migration Data Portal – www.migrationdataportal.org
Population Matters – www.populationmatters.org
Resite – www.resite.org
United Nations Population – www.un.org/en/development/desa/population/publications/database/index.asp

Climate change

Applied Centre for Climate & Earth Systems Science (ACCESS) – www.access.ac.za
350 – www.350.org
Carbon Brief – www.carbonbrief.org
Center for Climate and Energy Solutions – www.c2es.org
Climate Action Tracker – www.climateactiontracker.org
Committee on Climate Change – www.ccc.org.uk
Global Carbon Project – www.globalcarbonproject.org
International Energy Agency (IEA) – www.iea.org
International Solar Energy Society – www.ises.org
Intergovernmental Panel on Climate Change – www.ipcc.ch
NASA Global Climate Change – www.climate.nasa.gov
National Oceanic and Atmospheric Administration – www.noaa.gov
Real Climate – www.realclimate.org
The Green Economy Coalition – www.greeneconomycoalition.org
United Nations Climate Change – www.unfccc.int

Important reports

Agenda 2030 Spotlight, 'Spotlight on Sustainable Development Report by the Reflection Group on the 2030 Agenda for Sustainable Development' – https://www.2030spotlight.org/sites/default/files/contentpix/spotlight/pdfs/Agenda-2030_engl_160713_WEB.pdf

A tale of two continents, Fighting inequality in Africa – https://www.oxfam.org/en/research/tale-two-continents-fighting-inequality-africa

A New Global Partnership – https://sustainabledevelopment.un.org/content/documents/8932013-05%20-%20HLP%20Report%20-%20A%20New%20Global%20Partnership.pdf

Common Ground – https://www.iucn.org/theme/ecosystem-management/our-work/agriculture-and-land-health/common-ground-report

Financing for Sustainable Development Report 2021, 'Inter-agency task force on financing for development' – https://developmentfinance.un.org/sites/developmentfinance.un.org/files/FSDR_2021.pdf

Food, Planet, Health – https://eatforum.org/eat-lancet-commission

Global Assessment Report on Biodiversity and Ecosystem Services – https://ipbes.net/global-assessment

Global Biodiversity Outlook – https://www.cbd.int/gbo5

Global Environment Outlook – https://www.unep.org/resources/global-environment-outlook-6

Global Resources Outlook – www.resourcepanel.org

Global Material Resources Outlook to 2060 – www.oecd.org

Global Risks Report 2021 – https://www.weforum.org/reports/the-global-risks-report-2021

Human Development Report – http://hdr.undp.org/en/2020-report

Inequality in a Rapidly Changing World – https://www.weforum.org/reports/the-global-risks-report-2020

Intergovernmental Panel on Climate Change (Reports) – https://www.ipcc.ch/reports/

Intergovernmental Panel on Climate Change (Africa) – https://www.ipcc.ch/report/ar5/wg2/africa

International Renewable Energy Agency, 'World Energy Transitions Outlook: 1.5°C Pathway' – https://www.irena.org/publications/2021/Jun/World-Energy-Transitions-Outlook

International Resource Pane, Reports – https://www.resourcepanel.org/reports

International Resource Panel, 'Building biodiversity' – https://www.resourcepanel.org/reports/building-biodiversity

International Resource Panel, 'Resource Efficiency and climate change' – https://www.resourcepanel.org/reports/resource-efficiency-and-climate-change

IPBES, 'Global assessment report on biodiversity and ecosystem services' – https://ipbes.net/global-assessment

IUCN Red List of Threatened Species – https://www.iucn.org/resources/conservation-tools/iucn-red-list-threatened-species

The KPMG survey of sustainability reporting 2020 – https://assets.kpmg/content/dam/kpmg/xx/pdf/2020/11/the-time-has-come.pdf

Living Planet Report 2018 – https://www.footprintnetwork.org/content/uploads/2018/10/LPR-2018-full-report.pdf

Living Planet Report 2020 – https://livingplanet.panda.org/en-za

Millennium Assessment Reports – http://www.millenniumassessment.org/en/index.html

One Planet Network & IRP 2021 – https://www.resourcepanel.org/sites/default/files/documents/document/media/report_unea5_catalysing_science-based_policy_action_on_scp_-_task_group_irp-one_planet.pdf

Our Future on Earth – https://drive.google.com/file/d/1chEx2Aewehp1_0nXYnERwUViJI6qR2hi/view

Slum Almanac – https://unhabitat.org/sites/default/files/download-manager-files/Slum%20Almanac%202015-2016_PSUP.pdf

Special Report on the Ocean and Cryosphere in a Changing Climate – https://www.ipcc.ch/srocc

Sustainable Development Report 2021, 'The decade of action for the Sustainable Development Goals' – https://sdgindex.org/reports/sustainable-development-report-2021

The Economics of Biodiversity, The Dasgupta Review – https://assets.publishing.service.gov.uk/government/uploads/system/uploads/attachment_data/file/957291/Dasgupta_Review_-_Full_Report.pdf

The Global Transition to Green and Fair Economies – https://www.greeneconomycoalition.org/assets/reports/GEC-Reports/1037-GEC-Barometer-Phase2-A4-V8j-WEB.pdf

The Future of Food and Farming – http://www.eracaps.org/sites/default/files/content/foresight_report.pdf

The State of Food Security and Nutrition in the World 2019 – https://www.fao.org/3/ca5162en/ca5162en.pdf

Sustainable Development and Human Well-being – https://happiness-report.s3.amazonaws.com/2020/WHR20_Ch6.pdf

UN Department of Economic and Social Affairs – https://www.un.org/en/development/desa/population/publications/pdf/policy/World_Population_Policies_2019_Highlights.pdf

UNEP, 'Making peace with nature: A scientific blueprint to tackle the climate, biodiversity and pollution emergencies' – https://www.unep.org/resources/making-peace-nature

UNEP & IRP, 'Catalysing science-based policy action on sustainable consumption and production' – https://www.resourcepanel.org/reports/catalysing-science-based-policy-action-sustainable-consumption-and-production

United in Science – https://ane4bf-datap1.s3-eu-west-1.amazonaws.com/wmocms/s3fs-public/ckeditor/files/United_in_Science_ReportFINAL_0.pdf?XqiG0yszsU_sx2vOehOWpCOkm9RdC_gN

World Happiness Report 2020 – https://worldhappiness.report/ed/2020

World Population Prospects 2019 – https://www.un.org/development/desa/publications/world-population-prospects-2019-highlights.html

WWF, 'The loss of nature and the rise of pandemics: Protecting human and planetary health' – https://wwfint.awsassets.panda.org/downloads/the_loss_of_nature_and_rise_of_pandemics___protecting_human_and_planetary_health.pdf

Web-based platforms

Africa Geographic – www.africageographic.com

Anthropocene Magazine – www.anthropocenemagazine.org

Blood Lions – www.bloodlions.org

Centre for Environmental Rights – www.cer.org.za

Compassionate Conservation – www.compassionateconservation.net

Conservation Action Trust – www.conservationaction.co.za

Conservation Mag – www.conservationmag.org

Earth Justice – www.earthjustice.org

Earth Times – www.earthtimes.org

Eco Atlas – www.ecoatlas.co.za

Ecologist – www.theecologist.org

Environmental Investigation Agency – www.eia-international.org

For the Love of Wildlife – www.fortheloveofwildlife.org.au

Fridays For Future – www.fridaysforfuture.org

George Monbiot – www.monbiot.com

Global Alliance for the Rights of Nature – www.therightsofnature.org

Global Forest Watch – www.globalforestwatch.org

Global Wildlife Conservation – www.globalwildlife.org

International Association for the Study of the Commons – www.iasc-commons.org

IUCN – www.iucn.org

IUCN Africa Protected Areas Congress – https://www.iucn.org/sites/default/files/2022-07/apac-kigali-call-to-action-final_0.pdf

IUCN Protected Areas – https://www.iucn.org/theme/protected-areas

IUCN Red List – www.iucnredlist.org

LionAid – www.lionaid.org

Mongabay.com – www.news.mongabay.com

National Geographic – www.nationalgeographic.com

Nature – www.nature.com

Rainforest Alliance – www.rainforest-alliance.org

ReWild Africa – www.rewildafrica.com
Rewilding Europe – www.rewildingeurope.com
Scientific American – www.scientificamerican.com
Shannon Elizabeth Foundation – www.shannonelizabeth.org
Stop Poaching Now – www.stoppoaching-now.org
Stop Rhino Poaching – www.stoprhinopoaching.com
The Lancet – www.thelancet.com
The Tyee – www.thetyee.ca
The Wildlife Society – www.wildlife.org
The Wild Things Initiative – www.wildthingsinitiative.com
True Nature Foundation – www.truenaturefoundation.org
UN Environment Programme – www.unenvironment.org
Untold Africa – www.untoldafrica.com
UNESCO – www.whc.unesco.org
Union of Concerned Scientists – www.ucsusa.org
United Nations Environment Network – www.unenvironment.org
WellBeing International – www.wellbeingintl.org
Wild Law Institute – www.wildlaw.net

Tourism and travel

Global Sustainable Tourism Council – www.gstcouncil.org
Responsible Travel – www.responsibletravel.com
SATSA – https://satsa.com/satsa-animal-interaction-guidelines-holding-statement
Sustainable Travel International – www.sustainabletravel.org
The International Ecotourism Society – www.ecotourism.org
Travelyst – www.travelyst.org
UN World Tourism Organization – www.unwto.org
World Travel & Tourism Council – www.wttc.org

Academic sites

Directory of Open Access Journals – www.doaj.org
Elsevier – www.elsevier.com
Google Scholar – www.scholar.google.com
Research Gate – www.researchgate.net
Science Daily – www.sciencedaily.com
Science Direct – www.sciencedirect.com
Scientific Research – www.scirp.org
Society for Conservation Biology – www.conbio.org
Wildlife Conservation Research Unit – www.wildcru.org

Guide training schools

African Guide Academy – www.guidetrainingcourses.com
Bhejane Nature Training – www.bhejanenaturetraining.com
Bushwise Field Guides – www.bushwise.co.za
EcoTraining – www.ecotraining.co.za
Lowveld Trails – www.lowveldtrails.co.za
Nature Guide Training – www.natureguidetraining.com
Pathfinders Africa – www.pathfindersafrica.com
The Nature College – www.thenaturecollege.com
Tracker Academy – www.trackeracademy.co.za
Wilderness Leadership School – www.wildernesstrails.org.za

'One falsehood spoils a thousand truths'

This proverb originates with the Ashanti people of Ghana and reflects on precisely why reading to stay informed is vital. What follows is a list of books, in alphabetical order by author, that may well enhance an understanding of the issues covered in this book.

Author	Title	Publisher
Abhijit V. Banerjee & Esther Duflo	*Poor Economics: The surprising truth about life on less than $1 a day*	Penguin, 2012
Pius Adesanmi	*You're not a country, Africa*	Penguin, 2011
Nnimmo Bassey	*To Cook a Continent: Destructive Extraction and Climate Crisis in Africa*	Pambazuka, 2012
Duncan Brown	*Wilder Lives – Humans and our Environments*	University of KwaZulu-Natal Press, 2019
Dr Lee Berger	*Almost Human: The Astonishing Tale of Homo Naledi and the Discovery That Changed Our Human Story:*	National Geographic Society, 2017
Mike Berners-Lee	*There is no Planet B*	Lancaster University, 2019
Thomas Berry	*The Great Work; Our Way into the Future*	Bell Tower, 1999
Edited by Robert Bly	*News of the Universe*	Sierra Club Books, 1995
Edited by Peter Burdon	*Exploring Wild Law, The Philosophy of Earth Jurisprudence*	Wakefield Press, 2011
Rachel Carson	*The Silent Spring*	Houghton Mifflin, 1962
Jerry A. Coyne	*Why Evolution is True*	Oxford Landmark Science, 2009
Jared Diamond	*Collapse: How societies chose to fail or succeed*	Penguin, 2011
Jared Diamond	*Guns, Germs and Steel*	W.W. Norton, 1997

Author	Title	Publisher
Edited by Ben Collen, Jonathan E. M. Baillie, Sarah M. Durant	*Biodiversity Monitoring and Conservation: Bridging the Gap Between Global Commitment and Local Action*	2013
Susan Clayton & Gene Myers	*Conservation Psychology – Understanding and Promoting Human Care for Nature*	Wiley, 2015
Cormac Cullinan	*Wild Law*	Green Books, 2011
Dr Adam Cruise	*It's Not About the Bats: Conservation, the coronavirus and how we must re-set our relationship with nature*	Tafelberg, 2021
Charles Darwin	*On the Origin of Species*	Classics of World Literature
Charles Darwin	*The Voyage of The Beagle*	Classics of World Literature
Richard Dawkins	*Science in the Soul*	Random House, 2017
Richard Dawkins	*The Greatest Show on Earth*	Free Press, 2008
Richard Dawkins	*The Selfish Gene*	Oxford University Press, 1976
Kathleen Dean Moore & Michael P. Nelson	*Moral Ground; Ethical Action for a Planet in Peril*	Trinity University Press, 2010
Federico Demaria	*Degrowth: A Vocabulary for a New Era*	Routledge, 2014
Frans de Waal	*Are We Smart Enough to Know How Smart Animals Are?*	Granta Books, 2017
Frans de Waal	*The Bonobo and the Atheist*	W.W. Norton and Company, 2014
Craig Dilworth	*Too Smart for Our Own Good*	Cambridge University Press, 2009
Sylvia Earle	*Sea Change – A Message of The Oceans*	Texas A&M University Press, 2020
Richard Estes	*Behaviour Guide to African Mammals*	University of California Press, 2012

Author	Title	Publisher
John Elkington	*Green Swans – The Coming Boom in Regenerative Capitalism:*	Fast Company Press, 2021
Lorenzo Fioramonti	*Wellbeing Economy*	Pan MacMillan SA, 2017
Tim Flannery	*We are the Weather Makers*	Penguin, 2007
John Fowles	*The Tree*	Little Toller Books, 2016
Al Gore	*An Inconvenient Truth*	Viking Books, 2007
Thom Hartmann	*The Last Hours of Ancient Sunlight*	Hodder, 2001
Tim Halliday	*The Book of Frogs: A Life-Size Guide to Six Hundred Species from Around the World*	Ivy Press, 2016
Yuval Noah Harari	*Sapiens: A brief history of humankind*	Vintage, 2105
David G. Haskell	*The Songs of Trees: Stories from Nature's Great Connectors*	Viking, 2017
Paul Hawken	*The Ecology of Commerce*	HarperBusiness, 1994
Kerryn Higgs	*Collision Course – Endless Growth on a Finite Planet*	MIT Press, 2014
Tim Jackson	*Prosperity Without Growth*	Routledge, 2009
Leonie Joubert	*Invaded; The Biological Invasion of South Africa*	Wits University Press, 2009
Mervyn King with Teodorina Lessidrenska	*Transient Caretakers – Making Life on Earth Sustainable*	Pan MacMillan, 2009
Jonathan Kingdon	*The Kingdon Field Guide to African Mammals*	A&C Black, 2003
Elizabeth Kolbert	*The Sixth Extinction: An Unnatural History*	Henry Holt & Co., 2014
Elizabeth Kolbert	*Under a White Sky: The Nature of the Future*	Crown Publishing Group, 2021
Brendon Larson	*Metaphors for Environmental Sustainability*	Yale University Press, 2011
Richard Leakey	*The Sixth Extinction*	Anchor, 1996
Aldo Leopold	*A Sand County Almanac*	Oxford University Press, 1949

Author	Title	Publisher
James Lovelock	*Homage to Gaia: The Life of an Independent Scientist*	Oxford University Press, 2001
James Lovelock	*The Revenge of Gaia: Earth's Climate Crisis & the Fate of Humanity*	Basic Books, 2006
Anna Lowenhaupt Tsing	*Arts of Living on a Damaged Planet: Ghosts and Monsters of the Anthropocene*	University of Minnesota Press, 2017
Wangari Maathai	*The Challenge for Africa*	Pantheon, 2009
Wangari Maathai	*Unbowed: A memoir*	Anchor, 2007
Marianna Mazzucato	*Mission Economy: A Moonshot Guide to Changing Capitalism*	Allen Lane, 2021
Ian McCallum	*Ecological Intelligence – Rediscovering Ourselves in Nature*	Fulcrum Publishing, 2008
Ian McCallum	*Untamed*	Ian McCallum, 2012
Ian McCallum	*Wild Gifts*	Ian McCallum, 1999
Bill McKibben	*The End of Nature*	Random House, 2006
Carolyn Merchant	*The Anthropocene and the Humanities: From Climate Change to a New Age of Sustainability*	Yale University Press, 2020
Carolyn Merchant	*The Death of Nature: Women, Ecology, and the Scientific Revolution*	HarperOne, 1990
Guy Middleton	*Understanding Collapse – Ancient history and modern myths*	Cambridge University Press, 2017
Todd Miller	*Storming the Wall*	City Lights, 2017
Oliver Milman	*The Insect Crisis: The Fall of the Tiny Empires That Run the World:*	W.W. Norton Company, 2022
George Monbiot	*How Did We Get into This Mess?*	Verso, 2016
George Monbiot	*The Age of Consent*	Harper Perennial, 2016
George Monbiot	*Out of the Wreckage: A New Politics for an Age of Crisis*	Verso, 2017
Jay Naidoo	*Change: Organizing tomorrow, today*	Penguin, 2017
Daniel B. O' Leary	*Escaping the Progress Trap*	Geozone Communications, 2007

Author	Title	Publisher
Naomi Oreskes & Erik M. Conway	*Merchants of Doubt*	Bloomsbury, 2010
Garth Owen-Smith	*An Arid Eden*	Jonathon Ball, 2010
Don Pinnock and Colin Bell	*The Last Elephants*	Smithsonian Books, 2019
Cassandra Phillips & Chris Moore	*Plastic Ocean*	Avery Publishing, 2011
Kate Raworth	*Doughnut Economics*	Random House, 2017
Nathaniel Rich	*Losing Earth*	MCD, 2019
Johan Rockström and Owen Gaffney	*Breaking Boundaries – The Science of our Planet*	2021
Carl Safina	*Beyond Words – What Animals Think and Feel*	Henry Holt & Company, 2015
Carl Safina	*Song for the Blue Ocean*	Holt, 1999
Ken Saro-Wiwa	*Silence Would be Treason: Last writings of Ken Saro-Wiwa*	Codesria Conseil Pour Le Developpement de La Reche, 2013
Vandana Shiva	*Biopiracy: The plunder of nature and knowledge*	South End Press, 2019
Vandana Shiva	*Staying Alive: Women, Ecology, and Development*	Zed Books, 1998
Mary Soderstrom	*Concrete: From Ancient Origins to a Problematic Future*	University of Regina Press, 2020
William Stolzenburg	*Where the Wild Things Were*	Bloomsbury, 2008
Noah Strycker	*The Thing with Feathers: The Surprising Lives of Birds and What They Reveal about Being Human*	Riverhead Books, 2014
Mark Swilling & Eve Annecke	*Just Transitions: Explorations of sustainability in an unfair world*	United Nations University Press, 2012
Mark Swilling	*The Age of Sustainability: Just Transitions in a Complex World*	Routledge, 2019

Author	Title	Publisher
Great & Svante Thunberg and Malena & Beata Ernman	*Our House Is on Fire: Scenes of a Family and a Planet in Crisis*	Penguin, 2020
Greta Thunberg	*No One is Too Small to Make a Difference*	Penguin, 2019
Christopher Tucker	*A Planet of 3 Billion*	Atlas Observatory Press, 2019
Colin Tudge	*The Variety of Life*	Oxford University Press, 2000
Jack Turner	*Abstract Wild*	University of Arizona Press, 1996
David Wallace-Wells	*The Uninhabitable Earth – A Story of the Future*	Allen Lane, 2019
Harriet A. Washington	*A Terrible Thing to Waste: Environmental racism and its assault on the American mind*	Little, Brown Spark, 2019
Rupert Watson	*Peacocks & Picathartes – Reflections on Africa's Birdlife*	Penguin Random House, 2020
Edward O. Wilson	*Biophilia*	Harvard University Press, 1986
Edward O. Wilson	*Half-Earth – Our Planet's Fight for Life*	Liveright, 2016
Edward O. Wilson	*The Diversity of Life*	W.W. Norton Company, 1999
Edward O. Wilson	*The Social Conquest of Earth*	Liveright, 2012
Jonathan White	*Talking on Water – Conversations about Nature*	Trinity University Press, 2016
Peter Wohlleben	*The Hidden Life of Trees*	Greystone Books, 2016

'Music speaks louder than words'

The above insightful phrase is thought to be another African proverb. We also know it's the title of a song performed by various artists over the years, including the American folk band of the 1960s, Peter, Paul & Mary.

Music is to love what water is to life, and no one should ever be without these vital ingredients. If you are coming to Africa, you shouldn't leave without sampling our sounds. Here are some options, in alphabetical order of the artist.

Album	Artist
Water from an ancient well	Abdullah Ibrahim
Savane	Ali Farka Toure
In the Heart of the Moon	Ali Farke Touré & Toumani Diabaté
Ali and Toumani	Ali Farke Touré & Toumani Diabaté
Dimanche A Bamako	Amadou & Mariam
Another Universe	Arno Carstens
En Mana Kuoyo	Ayub Ogada
Wango	Baaba Maal
Miri	Bassekou Kouyaté & Ngoni Ba
Every now and then	Bright Blue
Miss Perfumado	Cesaria Evora
Voz D' Amor	Cesaria Evora
True Blues	Dan Patlansky
Klassic Kramer	David Kramer
I met her by the river	Dawda Jobarteh
éVoid	éVoid
25 anos	Eyuphuro
The Best of The Black President	Fela Kuti
Beat the Border	Geoffrey Oryema
Sixty	Hugh Masekela
Home is where the music is	Hugh Masekela

Album	Artist
The Balladeer	Ismaël Lo
Afrika 4 Beginners	Jack Parow
Voëlvry die Toer (Live)	Johannes Kerkorrel & Die Gereformeerde Blues Band
The Final Journey – Live	Johnny Clegg
Third World Child	Johnny Clegg & Savuka
Scatterlings	Juluka
The Star and The Wiseman	Ladysmith Black Mambazo
Welela	Miriam Makeba
Miriam Makeba	Miriam Makeba
Tuku Music	Oliver Mtukudzi
Specialist on all Styles	Orchestra Baobab
Die Geheim van Slangfontein – Grootste Treffers	Radio Kalahari Orkes
Soro	Salif Keita
Zandisiie	Simphiwe Dana
The Best Of	Sipho 'Hotstix' Mabuse
Aman Iman	Tinariwen
Imidiwan: Companions	Tinariwen
The Mandé Variations	Toumani Diabaté
Ishumar	Toumast
Fondo	Vieux Farka Touré
Naledi Ya Tsela	Vusi Mahlasela
Everything is not quite enough	Wasis Diop
No Sant	Wasis Diop
Immigrés	Youssou N' Dour

REFERENCES

The following is a list of topics, articles, publications, and websites referred to in this book. While comprehensive, we have deliberately not presented it in an academic format, as it is intended solely for easy access and the convenience of readers wishing to delve a bit deeper into the overall subject matter.

A

Acme: 'On the importance of a date, or decolonizing the Anthropocene.' https://acme-journal.org/index.php/acme/article/view/1539/1303

Acquisition International: 'Greenwashing, social washing and other laundry matters.' https://www.acquisition-international.com/greenwashing-social-washing-and-other-laundry-matters

Africa Geographic: 'Trophy hunting in Africa is in decline, and no longer pays its way.' https://africageographic.com/stories/trophy-hunting-africa-decline-no-longer-pays-way/#

Africa Geographic: 'Large-tusked elephants are in decline, need to be protected from trophy hunting and poaching, says researcher.' https://africageographic.com/stories/large-tusked-elephants-are-in-decline-need-to-be-protected-from-trophy-hunting-and-poaching-says-researcher

Africa News: 'President Magufuli warns Tanzanians against COVID-19 vaccines.' https://www.africanews.com/2021/01/27/president-magufuli-warns-tanzanians-against-covid-19-vaccines//

African Elephant Journal: 'Investigation: The efficacy of Namibia's wildlife conservation model as it relates to African elephants.' https://africanelephantjournal.com/wp-content/uploads/2021/ 11/ Investigation-in-Namibias-conservation-model-Full-Report-LR.pdf

African Parks: www.africanparks.org

Agenda 2030: 'Transforming our world – the 2030 agenda for sustainable development.' https://sustainabledevelopment.un.org/content/documents/21252030%20Agenda%20for%20Sustainable%20Development%20web.pdf

Agenda 2063: 'The Africa we want.' https://au.int/en/agenda2063/overview

American Meteorological Society: 'Explaining Extreme Events from a Climate Perspective.' https://www.ametsoc.org/ams/index.cfm/publications/bulletin-of-the-american-meteorological-society-bams/explaining-extreme-events-from-a-climate-perspective

American Museum of Natural History: 'Arthur Holmes: Harnessing the Mechanics of Mantle Convection to the Theory of Continental Drift.' https://www.amnh.org/learn-teach/curriculum-collections/earth-inside-and-out/geologist-arthur-holmes#

Americana: 'Hunting girls: Patriarchal fantasy or feminist progress?' https://www.americanpopularculture.com/journal/articles/spring_2013/oliver.htm

An Ecomodernist Manifesto: www.ecomodernism.org

An Introduction to Complexity Theory: https://medium.com/@junp01/an-introduction-to-complexity-theory-3c20695725f8

A New Global Partnership: https://sustainabledevelopment.un.org/content/documents/8932 013- 05%20-%20HLP%20Report%20-%20A%20New%20Global%20Partnership.pdf

AP News: 'Trump spurns science on climate: 'Don't think science knows'.' https://apnews.com/article/bd152cd786b58e45c61bebf2457f9930

Australian Government Bureau of Meteorology: 'A warmer than average year for Australia, despite La Niña in successive summers.' http://www.bom.gov.au/climate/current/annual/aus/#tabs=Overview

Australian Institute of Marine Science: 'Declining coral growth.' https://www.aims.gov.au/docs/research/climate-change/declining-coral-growth.html

B

Ballotpedia – Ecomodernism: https://ballotpedia.org/Ecomodernism

Ban Trophy Hunting: https://bantrophyhunting.org/wp-content/uploads/2019/08/Dellinger_JELLVol34.pdf

BBC: 'Are we on the road to civilization collapse?' https://www.bbc.com/future/article/20190218-are-we-on-the-road-to-civilisation-collapse

BBC: 'Billions of years of evolutionary history under threat.' https://www.bbc.com/news/science-environment-52808103

BBC: 'Coronavirus: Brazil's Bolsonaro in denial and out on a limb.' https://www.bbc.com/news/world-latin-america-52080830

Bendell, J. 'Deep Adaptation: A Map for Navigating Climate Tragedy.' https://mronline.org/wp-content/uploads/2019/06/deepadaptation.pdf

Biology Letters. 'Why men trophy hunt.' https://royalsocietypublishing.org/doi/pdf/10.1098/rsbl.2016.0909

Birdlife International: 'Conservation action has prevented at least 28 extinctions since 1993.' https://www.birdlife.org/worldwide/news/conservation-action-has-prevented-least-28-extinctions-1993

Blood Lions: www.bloodlions.org

Bristow, David & Bell, Colin: *Africa's Finest.* https://africasfinest.co.za/the-book

Britannica: 'Complexity – a scientific theory.' https://www.britannica.com/science/complexity-scientific-theory

Britannica: 'Holocene epoch.' https://www.britannica.com/science/Holocene-Epoch

British Ecological Society: 'Trophy hunting and conservation: do the major ethical theories converge in opposition to trophy hunting?' https://besjournals.onlinelibrary.wiley.com/doi/full/10.1002/pan3.10160

Brookings: 'Education system alignment for 21st century skills.' https://www.brookings.edu/wp-content/uploads/2018/11/Education-system-alignment-for-21st-century-skills-012819.pdf

Bulletin of the Atomic Scientists: 'Can nuclear weapons fallout mark the beginning of the Anthropocene epoch?' https://journals.sagepub.com/doi/10.1177/0096340215581357

Business Insider: 'FAANG stands for five very successful tech companies that can move the stock market.' https://www.businessinsider.com/what-is-faang?IR=T

C

Cape Leopard Trust: www.capeleopard.org.za

Cartagena Protocol: https://bch.cbd.int/protocol

Cartmill, Matt. 'A view to a death in the morning – hunting and nature through history.' https://www.amazon.com/View-Death-Morning-Hunting-Through/dp/0674937368

Carbon Brief: 'Factcheck – How global warming has increased US wildfires.' https://www.carbonbrief.org/factcheck-how-global-warming-has-increased-us-wildfires

Carbon Brief: 'Mapped – How climate change affects extreme weather around the world.' https://www.carbonbrief.org/mapped-how-climate-change-affects-extreme-weather-around-the-world

Carbon Disclosure Project (CDP): 'New report shows just 100 companies are source of over 70% of emissions.' https://www.cdp.net/en/articles/media/new-report-shows-just-100-companies-are-source-of-over-70-of-emissions

Carnegie Endowment: 'How to understand the global political spread of political polarization.' https://carnegieendowment.org/2019/10/01/how-to-understand-global-spread-of-political-polarization-pub-79893

Center for Biological Diversity: 'Halting the extinction crisis.' https://www.biologicaldiversity.org/programs/biodiversity/elements_of_biodiversity/extinction_crisis

Center for Climate and Energy Solutions: 'History of UN Climate Talks.' https://www.c2es.org/content/history-of-un-climate-talks

Center for a Humane Economy: 'Botswana's trophy hunts of rare animals should stir action by US and the rest of the global community.' https://centerforahumaneeconomy.org/2021/03/31/botswanas-trophy-hunts-of-rare-animals-should-stir-action-by-u-s-and-the-rest-of-the-global-community

Chardonnet, Bertrand: 'Africa is changing: Should its protected areas evolve? Reconfiguring the protected areas in Africa.' https://conservationaction.co.za/wpcontent/uploads/2019/03/etudesAP_configAP_EN.pdf

Chemical Watch: 'What have the Stockholm Convention national implementation plans achieved so far?' https://chemicalwatch.com/100422/what-have-the-stockholm-convention-national-implementation-plans-achieved-so-far

Climate Change Committee: 'What is climate change?' https://www.theccc.org.uk/what-is-climate-change/what-is-causing-climate-change2

Climate Psychiatry Alliance: www.climatepsychiatry.org

Climate Psychology Alliance: 'Difficult Truths.' www.climatepsychologyalliance.org

CNN: 'It's official: Clinton swamps Trump in popular vote.' https://edition.cnn.com/2016/12/21/politics/donald-trump-hillary-clinton-popular-vote-final-count/index.html

CNN: 'There's 14 million metric tons of microplastics sitting on the seafloor, study finds.' https://edition.cnn.com/2020/10/06/world/microplastics-oceans-14-million-metric-tons-intl-hnk/index.html

CNN: 'The flat-Earth conspiracy is spreading around the globe. Does it hide a darker core?' https://edition.cnn.com/2019/11/16/us/flat-earth-conference-conspiracy-theories-scli-intl/index.html

Conference on the Human Environment: http://www.un-documents.net/aconf48-14r1.pdf

Conservation Action Trust: 'Big game hunting in Africa is economically useless.' https://conservationaction.co.za/recent-news/big-game-hunting-in-africa-is-economically-useless-iucn

Conservation Action Trust: 'In urgent need of an environmental ethic.' https://conservationaction.co.za/media-articles/in-urgent-need-of-an-environmental-ethic

Conservation Action Trust: 'Reconfiguring the protected areas in Africa.' https://conservationaction.co.za/wp-content/uploads/2019/03/etudesAP_configAP_EN.pdf

Conservation Action Trust: 'The implications of the reclassification of South African wildlife species as farm animals.' https://conservationaction.co.za/recent-news/the-implications-of-the-reclassification-of-south-african-wildlife-species-as-farm-animals

Conservation Biology: 'Effects of trophy hunting on lion and leopard populations in Tanzania.' https://conbio.onlinelibrary.wiley.com/doi/abs/10.1111/j.1523-1739.2010.01576.x

Conservation Conversation: 'Prof Craig Packer on trophy hunting.' https://www.conservationconversation.co.uk/post/prof-craig-packer-on-trophy-hunting

Conservation Corridor: 'Large-scale networks.' https://conservationcorridor.org/corridors-in-conservation/large-scale-networks/

Conservation Letters: 'Emotions and the ethics of consequence in conservation decisions: Lessons from Cecil the Lion.' https://conbio.onlinelibrary.wiley.com/doi/full/10.1111/conl.12232

Conservation Letters: 'The elephant (head) in the room: A critical look at trophy hunting.' https://conbio.onlinelibrary.wiley.com/doi/full/10.1111/conl.12565

Convention on Biological Diversity: www.cbd.int

Council to Advance Hunting and the Shooting Sports: 'The Future of Hunting and Fishing.' https://cahss.org/wp-content/uploads/2018/ 07/Future-of-Hunting-and-Fishing-Project-Pages-1-34_updated.pdf

Current Anthropology: 'The Anthropocene Divide – Obscuring understanding of social-environmental change.' https://www.journals.uchicago.edu/doi/pdfplus/10.1086/697198

D

Daily Maverick: 'Like the fossil fuel industry, trophy hunting is unsustainable.' https://www.dailymaverick.co.za/opinionista/2018-05-10-like-the-fossil-fuel-industry-trophy-hunting-is-unsustainable/#

Daily Maverick: 'Land reform and conservation meet on the banks for the Selati River.' https://www.dailymaverick.co.za/article/2021-02-15-land-reform-and-conservation-meet-on-the-banks-of-the-selati-river/?utm_source=homepagify

Doughnut Economics Action Lab: www.doughnuteconomics.org

E

Earth 2020: 'Science, society, and sustainability in the Anthropocene.' https://www.pnas.org/content/117/16/8683

Earth Magazine: 'The first complete geologic timescale is published.' https://www.earthmagazine.org/article/benchmarks-march-1913-first-complete-geologic-timescale-published

Earth.org: 'What is Tragedy of the Commons?' https://earth.org/what-is-tragedy-of-the-commons

Earth Overshoot Day: www.overshootday.org

Ecomodernist Manifesto: www.ecomodernism.org

Economic Policy Institute: 'CEO's now earn 321 times as much as a typical worker.' https://www.epi.org/publication/ceo-compensation-surged-14-in-2019-to-21-3-million-ceos-now-earn-320-times-as-much-as-a-typical-worker

Economists at Large: 'The $200million question: how does trophy hunting really contribute to African communities?'
https://www.ecolarge.com/work/the-200-million-question-how-much-does-trophy-hunting-really-contribute-to-african-communities

Edie.com: 'Greenwash: 40% of websites 'misleading' consumers on environmental credentials.' https://www.edie.net/news/7/Greenwash--40--of-websites--misleading--consumers-on-environmental-credentials

EdSurge Independent: 'The current education system is failing our students.' https://edsurgeindependent.com/the-current-education-system-is-failing-our-students-b35614943541

Ehrlich, R, P., Ehrlich, H, A.: 'Can a collapse of global civilization be avoided?' https://www.ncbi.nlm.nih.gov/pmc/articles/PMC3574335

Elephants Without Borders: www.elephantswithoutborders.org

Ellen Macarthur Foundation: 'What is a Circular Economy?' https://www.ellenmacarthurfoundation.org/circular-economy/concept

Environment and Energy Study Institute (EESI): 'Timeline of Major UN Climate Negotiations.' https://www.eesi.org/policy/international

Environmental Justice Organizations, Liabilities and Trade: 'Dematerialization.' http://www.ejolt.org/2015/09/dematerialization

Environmental Science: 'Invasive Species: How they affect the environment.' https://www.environmentalscience.org/invasive-species

Environment and Society: 'An Inconvenient Truth.' http://www.environmentandsociety.org/mml/inconvenient-truth

Environment and Society Portal, Paul J. Crutzen: 'Mister Anthropocene.' http://www.environmentandsociety.org/exhibitions/anthropocene/paul-j-crutzen-mister-anthropocene

E. O. Wilson Biodiversity Foundation: 'The 8 million species we don't know.' https://eowilsonfoundation.org/the-8-million-species-we-dont-know/#

Economics: 'The rise of neoliberalism: the cause of extreme inequality.' https://evonomics.com/rise-of-neoliberalism-inequality

F

Faith Popcorns Brain Reserve: www.faithpopcorn.com

Feola, G.: 'Societal transformation in response to global environmental change: A review of emerging concepts.' https://www.ncbi.nlm.nih.gov/pmc/articles/PMC4510318

Fioramonti, L.: 'Wellbeing Economy.' https://thenextsystem.org/sites/default/files/2017-08/LorenzoFioramonti.pdf

Food and Agriculture Organization (FAO): www.fao.org

Food and Agriculture Organization (FAO): 'The State of World Fisheries and Aquaculture 2020.' http://www.fao.org/state-of-fisheries-aquaculture

Food and Agriculture Organization (FAO): 'Climate change: unpacking the burden on food safety.' http://www.fao.org/documents/card/en/c/ca8185en

Freedom Lab: 'The need for complexity thinking.' https://freedomlab.org/the-need-for-complexity-thinking

Future of Life Institute: 'Benefits and risks of artificial intelligence.' https://futureoflife.org/background/benefits-risks-of-artificial-intelligence

G

Galbraith Kenneth John: 'How much should a country consume?' http://www.preservenet.com/flexibleworktimeGalbraithHowMuch ShouldACountryConsume.html

Global Biodiversity Outlook 5: https://www.cbd.int/gbo5

Global Carbon Project: 'Global Carbon Budget.' https://www.globalcarbonproject.org/carbonbudget/index.htm

Global Citizen: 'Extreme poverty: Everything you need to know.' https://www.globalcitizen.org/en/content/extreme-poverty-definition-statistics-rate

Global Environment Outlook 6 (GEO-6): https://www.unenvironment.org/resources/global-environment-outlook-6

Global Environment Outlook 6: 'Summary for policy makers.' https://wedocs.unep.org/bitstream/handle/20.500.11822/ 27652/ GEO6SPM_EN.pdf?sequence=1&isAllowed=y

Global Footprint Network: 'Ecological footprint.' https://www.footprintnetwork.org/our-work/ecological-footprint

Global Risks Report: 'Global Risks Report 2022.' https://www.weforum.org/reports/global-risks-report-2022

Governance and Social Development – Resource Centre: 'Defining poverty, extreme poverty and inequality.' https://gsdrc.org/topic-guides/poverty-and-inequality/measuring-and-analysing-poverty-and-inequality/defining-poverty-extreme-poverty-and-inequality

Green Economy Coalition: www.greeneconomycoalition.org

Greenhouse gases: 'Causes, Sources and Environmental Effects.' https://www.livescience.com/37821-greenhouse-gases.html

H

Harvard Business Review: 'Dematerialization and what it means for the economy and climate change.' https://hbr.org/podcast/2019/09/dematerialization-and-what-it-means-for-the-economy-and-climate-change

Harvard Business Review: 'Leaders in denial.' https://hbr.org/2008/ 07/leaders-in-denial

Harvard University Press: 'The Diversity of Life.' https://www.hup.harvard.edu/catalog.php?isbn=9780674058170

Harvey, R.: 'No place for hunting in the sixth extinction.' https://conservationaction.co.za/media-articles/no-place-for-trophy-hunting-in-the-sixth-extinction

Hattingh, Johan: 'Finding creativity in the diversity of environmental ethics.' https://www.semanticscholar.org/paper/Finding-creativity-in-the-diversity-of-ethics-Hattingh/54ff29dd6d2689ab31cbcc5f9d13bb947004d99f

Heifetz, A. R.: 'Leadership without easy answers.' https://www.hup.harvard.edu/catalog.php?isbn=9780674518582

History: '5 Presidents who lost the popular vote but won the election.' https://www.history.com/news/presidents-electoral-college-popular-vote

History: 'How did humans evolve?' https://www.history.com/news/humans-evolution-neanderthals-denisovans

History Today: 'The idea of poverty' https://www.historytoday.com/archive/idea-poverty

I

International Fund for Animal Welfare (IFAW) – Wildlife Crime Program: https://www.ifaw.org/international/programs/wildlife-crime

International Fund for Animal Welfare (IFAW): 'Zimbabwe signs wildlife conservation partnership with IFAW.' https://www.ifaw.org/ca-en/news/zimbabwe-signs-wildlife-conservation-partnership-with-ifaw

Independent: 'Major polluters spend 10 times as much on climate lobbying as green groups, study finds.' https://www.independent.co.uk/environment/climate-change-fossil-fuels-lobbying-usa-transport-renewable-energy-environment-a8452941.html

Independent: 'Teaching material calling for an end to capitalism banned from schools as Minister's brand it extreme.' https://www.independent.co.uk/news/uk/politics/capitalism-teaching-school-racism-violence-democracy-gavin-williamson-b625480.html

Inside Climate News: 'Deforestation is getting Worse, 5 years after countries and companies vowed to stop it.' https://insideclimatenews.org/news/13092019/forest-loss-rate-global-deforestation-amazon-fires-corporate-agribusiness-international-declaration

Intergovernmental Panel on Climate Change (IPCC): 'Fifth Assessment Report.' https://www.ipcc.ch/assessment-report/ar5

International Atomic Energy Agency: 'Nuclear Safety Conventions.' https://www.iaea.org/topics/nuclear-safety-conventions

Inquiries Journal: 'Nature or Culture? The Anthropocene as social narrative.' http://www.inquiriesjournal.com/articles/1643/nature-or-culture-the-anthropocene-as-social-narrative

Intelligent Economist: 'Malthusian Theory of Population.' https://www.intelligenteconomist.com/malthusian-theory

International Commission on Stratigraphy: www.stratigraphy.org

International Geosphere – Biosphere Programme: 'Great Acceleration.' http://www.igbp.net/globalchange/greatacceleration.4.1b8ae20512db692f2a680001630.html

International Institute for Environment and Development: 'Effective evaluation for the sustainable development goals.' https://www.iied.org/effective-evaluation-for-sustainable-development-goals

International Resource Panel: www.resourcepanel.org

International Society for Environmental Ethics: www.enviroethics.org

International Renewable Energy Agency: 'World Energy Transitions Outlook.' https://www.irena.org/publications/2021/March/World-Energy-Transitions-Outlook

Investopedia: 'Gini Index.' https://www.investopedia.com/terms/g/gini-index.asp

IPBES: 'Extinction Debt.' https://ipbes.net/glossary/extinction-debt

IPBES: 'The Evidence is Clear: Transformative Change Needed Now to Address Nature Crisis and Protect Human Quality of Life.' https://ipbes.net/news/new-article-science-ipbes-global-assessment-authors

IPBES: 'Nature's dangerous decline 'unprecedented'; species extinction Rates 'accelerating'.' https://www.un.org/sustainabledevelopment/blog/2019/05/nature-decline-unprecedented-report

iPhoneLife: 'The evolution of the iPhone: Every model from 2007-2020.' https://www.iphonelife.com/content/evolution-iphone-every-model-2007-2016

IPPC: 'Summary for policymakers of IPCC Special Report on Global Warming of 1.5°C approved by governments.' https://www.ipcc.ch/2018/10/08/summary-for-policymakers-of-ipcc-special-report-on-global-warming-of-1-5c-approved-by-governments

IUCN: 'Compatibility of Trophy Hunting as a Form of Sustainable Use with IUCN's Objectives.' https://www.iucn.org/news/world-commission-environmental-law/201909/compatibility-trophy-hunting-a-form-sustainable-use-iucns-objectives

IUCN: 'Ecosystem services.' https://www.iucn.org/commissions/commission-ecosystem-management/our-work/cems-thematic-groups/ecosystem-services

IUCN: 'European bison recovering, 31 species declared Extinct – IUCN Red List.' https://www.iucn.org/news/species/202012/european-bison-recovering-31-species-declared-extinct-iucn-red-list

IUCN: 'Genetic frontiers for conservation.' https://portals.iucn.org/library/efiles/documents/2019-012-En.pdf

IUCN: 'Global Invasive Species Database.' http://www.iucngisd.org/gisd/

IUCN: 'Glossary of definitions.' https://www.iucn.org/downloads/en_iucn__glossary_definitions.pdf

IUCN: 'Habitats classification.' https://www.iucnredlist.org/resources/habitat-classification-scheme

IUCN: 'Invasive species.' https://www.iucn.org/theme/species/our-work/invasive-species

IUCN: 'Issues brief: Ocean warming.' https://www.iucn.org/resources/issues-briefs/ocean-warming

IUCN Red Data Lists: 'Background and history.' https://www.iucnredlist.org/about/background-history

IUCN Red Data Lists: 'Summary statistics.' https://www.iucnredlist.org/resources/summary-statistics

IUCN Red List of Ecosystems: https://www.iucn.org/ur/node/25352

IUCN Red List Threats Classification Scheme: https://www.iucnredlist.org/resources/threat-classification-scheme

IUCN Species Survival Commission (SSC): 'IUCN calls for halt to species decline by 2030.' https://www.iucn.org/news/species-survival-commission/201910/iucn-calls-halt-species-decline-2030

IUCN Species Survival Commission Cat Specialist Group: 'Guidelines for the conservation of lions in Africa; Version 1.0, December 2018.' https://www.cms.int/sites/default/files/publication/GCLA%20%20181220%20%28E%29_0.pdf

J

Jembendell.com: 'The love in deep adaptation – A philosophy for the forum.' https://jembendell.com/2019/03/17/the-love-in-deep-adaptation-a-philosophy-for-the-forum

Jembendell.com: 'Climate science and collapse – warnings lost in the wind.' https://jembendell.com/2020/06/15/climate-science-and-collapse-warnings-lost-in-the-wind/Joubert, Leonie:

Joubert, Leonie: 'Invaded: The biological invasion of South Africa' https://www.amazon.com/Invaded-Biological-Invasion-South-Africa/dp/186814478X

Journal of African Elephants: 'Investigation into the trophy hunting of elephant in Botswana's community-based natural resource management areas.' https://africanelephantjournal.com/investigation-into-the-trophy-hunting-of-elephants-in-botswanas-community-based-natural-resource-management-areas/?

Journal of Sustainable Tourism: 'Neo-colonialism and greed: Africans' views on trophy hunting in social media.' https://resourceafrica.net/wp-content/uploads/2020/05/Mkono-2019-Neo-colonialism-and-greed-Africans-views-on-trophy-hunting-in-social-media.pdf

L

Live Science: '1st known case of coronavirus traced back to November in China.' https://www.livescience.com/first-case-coronavirus-found.html

Live Science: 'After 2 500 studies, it's time to declare animal sentience proven.' https://www.livescience.com/39481-time-to-declare-animal-sentience.html

Live Science: 'Bid to rename Homo Sapiens is called unwise.' https://www.livescience.com/15615-homo-sapiens-change.html

Live Science: 'Trophy hunting causing 'reverse evolution'.'
    https://www.livescience.com/3176-trophy-hunting-causing-reverse-
    evolution.html
Live Science: 'Greenhouse gases: Causes, sources and environmental
    effects.' https://www.livescience.com/37821-greenhouse-gases.html
Live Science: 'Holocene epoch – The Age of Man.' https://www.livescience.
    com/28219-holocene-epoch.html
Live Science: 'Pollution Facts and Types of Pollution.' www.livescience.
    com/22728-pollution-facts.html
Live Science: 'The major discoveries that could transform the world
    in the next decade.' https://www.livescience.com/next-decade-biggest-
    scientific-advances.html
Living Planet Report 2018: https://www.wwf.org.uk/sites/default/files/2018-10/
    LPR2018_Full%20Report.pdf
Living Planet Report 2020: https://livingplanet.panda.org/en-za
Los Angeles Times: 'The frightening implications of California's first million-acre
    fire.' www.latimes.com/california/story/2020-10-06/the-frightening-
    implications-california-first-million-acre-wildfire
Luke, Brian: Brutal – Manhood and the exploitation of animals.
    https://www.amazon.com/Brutal-Manhood-Exploitation-Brian-Luke/
    dp/0252074246
Lyrics translations: www.lyrtran.com/Imidiwan-ma-tennam-id-42380

M
Michler, I: 'People, poverty, and the environment'; Africa Geographic, October
    2011.
Millennium Development Goals: https://www.un.org/millenniumgoals
Millennium ecosystem assessment: www.milleniumassessment.org
Monbiot, G: 'Caught in the crossfire' https://www.monbiot.com/2020/ 11/27/
    caught-in-the-crossfire
Mongabay: 'Tropical forests' lost decade: the 2010s.' https://news.mongabay.
    com/2019/12/tropical-forests-lost-decade-the-2010s
Mountain Journal: 'A death of ethics: Is hunting destroying itself?'
    https://mountainjournal.org/hunting-in-america-faces-an-ethical-
    reckoning

N
Nagoya Protocol: https://www.cbd.Int/abs
NASA: 'A Degree of concern: Why global temperatures matter.' https://climate.
    nasa.gov/news/2878/a-degree-of-concern-why-global-temperatures-matter
NASA: 'Earth by the Numbers.' https://solarsystem.nasa.gov/planets/earth/by-
    the-numbers

NASA: 'Global temperature.' https://climate.nasa.gov/vital-signs/global-temperature

NASA: 'Graphic: The relentless rise of carbon dioxide.' https://climate.nasa.gov/climate_resources/24/graphic-the-relentless-rise-of-carbon-dioxide

NASA: 'Living Ocean.' https://science.nasa.gov/earth-science/oceanography/living-ocean

NASA: '2020 tied for warmest year on record, NASA analysis shows.' https://www.nasa.gov/press-release/2020-tied-for-warmest-year-on-record-nasa-analysis-shows

National Geographic: 'Ancient megadrought causes present-day drama.' https://www.nationalgeographic.com/science/2018/09/news-meghalayan-holocene-megadrought-archaeology

National Geographic: 'Biodiversity.' https://www.nationalgeographic.org/encyclopedia/biodiversity

National Geographic: 'Continents.' https://www.nationalgeographic.org/encyclopedia/Continent

National Geographic: 'Ginkgo trees nearly went extinct.' https://www.nationalgeographic.com/environment/article/ginkgo-trees-nearly-went-extinct-how-we-saved-these-living-fossils

National Geographic: 'Insects are vanishing at an alarming rate—but we can save them.' https://www.nationalgeographic.com/animals/2021/01/studies-confirm-alarmiang-insect-decline

National Geographic – **Invasive Species 101**: https://www.youtube.com/watch?v=gYNAtw1c7hI

National Geographic: 'Poaching animals, explained.' https://www.nationalgeographic.com/animals/reference/poaching-animals

National Geographic: 'Trophy hunting may drive extinctions, due to climate change.' https://www.nationalgeographic.com/news/2017/11/wildlife-watch-trophy-hunting-extinctions-evolution

National Geographic: 'What are mass extinctions, and what causes them?' https://www.nationalgeographic.com/science/prehistoric-world/mass-extinction

National Ocean Service: 'Why should we care about the ocean?' https://oceanservice.noaa.gov/facts/why-care-about-ocean.html

National Resources Defense Council: 'Greenhouse Effect 101.' https://www.nrdc.org/stories/greenhouse-effect-101

Natural Resources – Democratic House Committee: 'Missing the mark: African trophy hunting fails to show consistent conservation benefits.' https://naturalresources.house.gov/imo/media/doc/Missing%20the%20Mark.pdf

Nature: 'Covid curbed carbon emissions in 2020 – but not by much.' https://www.nature.com/articles/d41586-021-00090-3

Nature: 'Climate tipping points – too risky to bet against.' https://www.nature.com/articles/d41586-019-03595-0

Nature: 'First atomic blast proposed as start of the Anthropocene.' https://www.nature.com/news/first-atomic-blast-proposed-as-start-of-anthropocene-1.16739

Nature: 'Global human-made mass exceeds all living biomass.' https://www.nature.com/articles/s41586-020-3010-5

Nature: 'Global methane levels soar to record highs.' https://www.nature.com/articles/d41586-020-02116-8

Nature: 'Humans versus Earth: the quest to define the Anthropocene.' https://www.nature.com/articles/d41586-019-02381-2

Nature: 'Involve social scientists in defining the Anthropocene.' https://www.nature.com/news/involve-social-scientists-in-defining-the-anthropocene-1.21090

Nature: 'Mapping tree density at a global scale.' https://www.nature.com/articles/nature14967#

Nature: 'Protect the last of the wild.' https://www.nature.com/articles/d41586-018-07183-6

Nature: 'USA pledges to dramatically slash greenhouse emissions over next decade.' https://www.nature.com/articles/d41586-021-01071-2

Nature: 'Why deforestation and extinctions make pandemics more likely.' https://www.nature.com/articles/d41586-020-02341-1

New Scientist: 'We are killing species at 1000 times the natural rate.' https://www.newscientist.com/article/dn25645-we-are-killing-species-at-1000-times-the-natural-rate

New Scientist: 'We were warned – so why couldn't we prevent the coronavirus outbreak?' https://www.newscientist.com/article/mg24532724-700-we-were-warned-so-why-couldnt-we-prevent-the-coronavirus-outbreak

Newsweek: 'Senators who voted to convict Trump represent 18 million more Americans than those who voted to acquit.' https://www.newsweek.com/senators-who-voted-convict-trump-represent-18-million-more-americans-those-who-voted-acquit-1485972

New York Declaration on Forests: www.forestdeclaration.org

NOAA: 'Ocean Acidification.' https://www.noaa.gov/education/resource-collections/ocean-coasts/ocean-acidification

NOAA Climate.Gov: 'Climate Change: Atmospheric carbon dioxide.' https://www.climate.gov/news-features/understanding-climate/climate-change-atmospheric-carbon-dioxide

NOAA Climate.Gov: 'Climate Change: Global Sea Level.' https://www.climate.gov/news-features/understanding-climate/climate-change-global-sea-level

NPR: 'US formally begins to leave the Paris Climate Agreement.' https://www.npr.org/2019/11/04/773474657/u-s-formally-begins-to-leave-the-paris-climate-agreement

NPR: 'Drawing a line in the mud: scientists debate when the age of humans began.' https://www.npr.org/2021/03/17/974774461/drawing-a-line-in-the-mud-scientists-debate-when-age-of-humans-began

Nobel Prize.org: 'Paul J. Crutzen – Biographical.' https://www.nobelprize.org/prizes/chemistry/1995/crutzen/biographical

O

Open Democracy: 'Coronavirus spells the end of the neoliberal era. What's next?' https://www.opendemocracy.net/en/transformation/coronavirus-spells-the-end-of-the-neoliberal-era-whats-next

Open Democracy: 'What will 2020 bring? Finding our way in a more polarized world.' https://www.opendemocracy.net/en/global-extremes/what-will-2020-bring-finding-our-way-more-polarised-world

Open Mind: 'Ecology and Environmental Ethics.' https://www.bbvaopenmind.com/en/articles/ecology-and-environmental-ethics

Open Secrets.org: 'Lobbying spending reaches $3.4 billion in 2018, highest in 8 years.' https://www.opensecrets.org/news/2019/01/lobbying-spending-reaches-3-4-billion-in-18

Our Common Future: 'The Brundtland Report.' http://www.un-documents.net/our-common-future.pdf

Our World in Data: 'Humans make up just 0.01% of Earth's life – what's the rest?' https://ourworldindata.org/life-on-earth

Our World in Data: 'Environmental impacts of food production.' https://ourworldindata.org/environmental-impacts-of-food

Our World in Data: 'The Environmental impacts of food.' https://ourworldindata.org/environmental-impacts-of-food

Outdoor Life. 'Why we suck at recruiting new hunters, why it matters, and how you can fix it.' https://www.outdoorlife.com/why-we-are-losing-hunters-and-how-to-fix-it

Oxford Economics – Global Infrastructure Outlook: https://www.oxfordeconomics.com/recent-releases/Global-Infrastructure-Outlook

Overpopulation Awareness: https://www.overpopulationawareness.org/en

Oxfam International: 'Africa's three richest men have more wealth than the poorest 650 million people across the continent.' https://www.oxfam.org/en/press-releases/africas-three-richest-men-have-more-wealth-poorest-650-million-people-across

Oxford Poverty & Human Development Initiative: 'Global Multi-dimensional Poverty Index.' https://ophi.org.uk/multidimensional-poverty-index/#

P

Panthera: www.panthera.org

PBS Evolution: 'The current mass extinction.' https://www.pbs.org/wgbh/evolution/library/03/2/l_032_04.html

Peace Parks Foundation: www.peaceparks.org

PLOS Biology: 'Rarity value and species extinction: The anthropogenic allee effect.' https://journals.plos.org/plosbiology/article?id=10.1371/journal.pbio.0040415

PLOS One: 'Lion trophy hunting in West Africa: a response to Bouché et al.' https://journals.plos.org/plosone/article?id=10.1371/journal.pone.0173691

PLOS One: 'Risk and ethical concerns of hunting male elephant: behavioural and physiological assays of the remaining elephants.' https://journals.plos.org/plosone/article?id=10.1371/journal.pone.0002417

PLOS One: 'Sport hunting, predator control and conservation of large carnivores.' https://journals.plos.org/plosone/article?id=10.1371/journal.pone.0005941

PLOS One: 'The trophy hunting of African lions: scale, current management practices and factors undermining sustainability.' https://journals.plos.org/plosone/article?id=10.1371/journal.pone.0073808

PNAS: Proceedings of the National Academy of Sciences of the United States of America: 'Climate endgame: Exploring catastrophic climate change scenarios.' https://www.pnas.org/doi/10.1073/pnas.2108146119

Population Education: 'What is the demographic transition model?' https://populationeducation.org/what-demographic-transition-model

Population Matters: 'Biodiversity.' https://populationmatters.org/the-facts/biodiversity?gclid

Proceedings of the National Academy of Sciences of the United States of America: 'Critical perspectives on historical collapse.' https://www.pnas.org/content/109/10/3628

Proceedings of the National Academy of Sciences of the United States of America: 'Earth 2020: Science, society, and sustainability in the Anthropocene.' https://www.pnas.org/content/117/16/8683

Proceedings of the National Academy of Sciences of the United States of America: 'Future of the human climate niche.' https://www.pnas.org/content/117/21/11350

Proceedings of the National Academy of Sciences of the United States of America: 'Scaling laws predict global microbial diversity.' https://www.pnas.org/content/113/21/5970

Proceedings of the National Academy of Sciences of the United States of America: 'The biomass distribution on earth.' https://www.pnas.org/content/115/25/6506

Protected Planet Report 2020: https://livereport.protectedplanet.net

Psychology Today: 'What is confirmation bias?' https://www.psychologytoday.com/za/blog/science-choice/201504/what-is-confirmation-bias

Psychology Today: 'Why men trophy hunt: showing off and the psychology of shame.' https://www.psychologytoday.com/intl/blog/animal-emotions/201703/why-men-trophy-hunt-showing-and-the-psychology-shame?eml

R

Raworth, K.: 'Exploring doughnut economics.' https://www.kateraworth.com/doughnut

ResearchGate: 'Trophy Hunting: Broaden the debate.' https://www.researchgate.net/publication/336786567_Trophy_hunting_Broaden_the_debate

Reuters: 'Greenwashing is rampant in online stores consumer authorities find.' https://www.reuters.com/article/us-eu-environment-greenwashing-idUSKBN29X1Y6

Reuters: 'NZ, Taiwan top Covid performance ranking, US, UK languish.' https://www.reuters.com/article/uk-health-coronavirus-australia-lowy-idUSKBN29W30Z

Rewilding Britain: '8 Marine Rewilding Projects around Britain.' https://www.rewildingbritain.org.uk/explore-rewilding/rewilding-the-seas/8-marine-rewilding-projects-around-britain

Rio Summit: 'Agenda 21 Report of the United Nations Conference on Environment and Development.' https://www.un.org/esa/dsd/agenda21/Agenda%2021.pdf

S

Sage Journals: 'The truths and falsehoods of post-truth leaders.' https://journals.sagepub.com/doi/full/10.1177/1742715020937886

Science: 'Defaunation in the Anthropocene.' https://science.sciencemag.org/content/345/6195/401

Science: 'Growing underwater heat blob speeds demise of Arctic Sea ice.' https://www.sciencemag.org/news/2020/08/growing-underwater-heat-blob-speeds-demise-arctic-sea-ice#

Science: 'South Africa's move to allow farming of lions and other wildlife is a bad idea, scientists say.' https://www.sciencemag.org/news/2020/01/south-africa-s-move-allow-farming-lions-and-other-wildlife-bad-idea-scientists-say#

Science: 'Why so much of the world is stuck in a 'poverty trap'.' https://www.sciencemag.org/news/2017/07/why-so-much-world-stuck-poverty-trap

Science Daily: 'East Africa fish in need of recovery.' https://www.sciencedaily.com/releases/2020/02/200206184326.htm

Science Daily: 'How many species on Earth?' https://www.sciencedaily.com/releases/2011/08/110823180459.htm

Science Daily: '40% of Amazon could now exist as rainforest or savanna-like ecosystems.' https://www.sciencedaily.com/releases/2020/10/201005080859.htm

Science Direct: 'Extinction debt: A challenge for biodiversity conservation.' https://www.sciencedirect.com/science/article/abs/pii/ S0169534709001918

Science Direct: 'Confirmation bias.' https://www.sciencedirect.com/topics/ medicine-and-dentistry/confirmation-bias

Science Direct: 'Joseph A Tainter – Sustainability of complex societies.' https://www.sciencedirect.com/science/article/abs/pii/001632879500016P

Science Direct: 'Sustainable Development.' https://www.sciencedirect.com/ topics/earth-and-planetary-sciences/sustainable-development

Science Direct: 'The reduction of genetic diversity in threatened vertebrates and new recommendations regarding IUCN conservation rankings.' https://www.sciencedirect.com/science/article/abs/pii

Science Direct: 'The School curriculum as viewed by the critical theorists.' https://www.sciencedirect.com/science/article/pii/S1877042813029406

Science Direct: 'Towards a cost-benefit analysis of South Africa's predator breeding industry.' https://www.sciencedirect.com/science/article/pii/ S2351989420306983

Scientific American: 'Shop till we drop: Does consumption culture contribute to environmental degradation?' https://www.scientificamerican.com/article/our-destructive-consumer

Sherman, Z.: 'The curiosity of school: Education and the dark side of enlightenment.' https://www.penguinrandomhouse.ca/books/417331/ the-curiosity-of-school-by-zander-sherman/9780143186496

Smithsonian Magazine: 'Meet the money behind the climate denial movement.' https://www.smithsonianmag.com/smart-news/meet-the-money-behind-the-climate-denial-movement-180948204/

Smithsonian Magazine: 'Welcome to the Meghalayan Age.' https://www.smithsonianmag.com/smart-news/welcome-meghalayan-age-latest-stage-earths-454-billion-year-history-180969699

Smithsonian Magazine: 'Fifty things we've learned about our Earth since the first Earth Day.' https://www.smithsonianmag.com/smithsonian-institution/ fifty-things-weve-learned-about-earth-first-earth-day-180974716/

Smithsonian – National Museum of Natural History: 'The Age of Humans: Evolutionary perspectives on the Anthropocene.' https://humanorigins. si.edu/research/age-humans-evolutionary-perspectives-anthropocene

South African Journal of Science: 'The Anthropocene.' https://www.scielo.org.za/ scielo.php?script=sci_arttext&pid=S0038-23532019000400001&lng=en &nrm=iso&tlng=en

South African National Biodiversity Institute: 'Invasive Alien Plant Alert.' https://www.sanbi.org/resources/infobases/invasive-alien-plant-alert/.

Stockholm Convention: www.pops-gmp.org

Stockholm Resilience Centre: 'Planetary Boundaries.' https://www.stockholmresilience.org/research/planetary-boundaries.html

Stockholm Resilience Centre: 'A fundamental misrepresentation of the Planetary Boundaries framework.' https://www.stockholmresilience.org/research/research-news/2017-11-20-a-fundamental-misrepresentation-of-the-planetary-boundaries-framework.html

Stockholm Statement: https://www.wider.unu.edu/sites/default/files/News/Documents/Stockholm%20Statement.pdf

Stop Rhino Poaching: www.stoprhinopoaching.com

Sustainable Development Goals: https://www.un.org/sustainabledevelopment/sustainable-development-goals

Sustainable Development Goals: 'Natures dangerous decline 'unprecedented'.' https://www.un.org/sustainabledevelopment/blog/2019/05/nature-decline-unprecedented-report

Sustainable Development Goals: https://unstats.un.org/sdgs/report/2019/goal-12

Sustainable Development Goals: 'Goal 12: Responsible Consumption and Production.' https://www.un.org/sustainabledevelopment/development-agenda

Sustainable Development Goals: 'Green Economy.' https://sustainabledevelopment.un.org/index.php?menu=1446

Sustainable Fisheries: 'Fish Populations around the World are Improving.' https://sustainablefisheries-uw.org/fish-populations-are-improving/

Sustainability Times: 'Amazon deforestation rate is 'statistic of the decade'.' https://www.sustainability-times.com/environmental-protection/the-rate-of-deforestation-in-the-amazon-is-statistic-of-the-decade

Subcommission on Quaternary Stratigraphy: 'Working group on the Anthropocene.' http://quaternary.stratigraphy.org/working-groups/anthropocene

Survival International: 'The Hadza.' https://www.survivalinternational.org/galleries/hadza

Sustainability: 'Evaluating the Global State of Ecosystems and Natural Resources: Within and Beyond the SDGs.' https://www.mdpi.com/2071-1050/12/18/7381

Sustainability for all: 'The battle against planned obsolescence.' https://www.activesustainability.com/sustainable-development/battle-against-planned-obsolescence/

Sustainability for all: '100 companies are responsible for 71% of GHG emissions.' https://www.activesustainability.com/climate-change/100-companies- responsible-71-ghg-emissions

Swilling, M., Annecke, E.: 'Just Transitions: Explorations of Sustainability in an Unfair World.' https://unu.edu/publications/books/just-transitions-explorations-of-sustainability-in-an-unfair-world.html#overview

Swilling, M.: 'The Age of Sustainability – Just transitions in a complex world.' https://www.markswilling.co.za/2019/07/age-of-sustainability-just-transitions-in-a-complex-world/

T

The Anthropocene Project: www.theanthropocene.org

The Anthropocene Review: 'The Trajectory of the Anthropocene: The Great Acceleration.' https://journals.sagepub.com/doi/abs/10.1177/2053019614564785

The Anthropocene Working Group: http://quaternary.stratigraphy.org/working-groups/anthropocene

The Atlantic: 'How Wall Street's bankers stayed out of jail.' https://www.theatlantic.com/magazine/archive/2015/09/how-wall-streets-bankers-stayed-out-of-jail/399368

The Atlantic: 'Geology's timekeepers are feuding.' https://www.theatlantic.com/science/archive/2018/07/anthropocene-holocene-geology-drama/565628

The Conversation: 'The five corrupt pillars of climate change denial.' https://theconversation.com/the-five-corrupt-pillars-of-climate-change-denial-122893

The Conversation: 'Trophy hunting in Africa: the case for viable sustainable alternatives.' https://theconversation.com/trophy-hunting-in-africa-the-case-for-viable-sustainable-alternatives-115649

The Conversation: 'Trophy hunting will not save Africa's lions – so the UK ban on imports is a positive step for wildlife conservation.' https://theconversation.com/trophy-hunting-will-not-save-africas-lions-so-the-uk-ban-on-imports-is-a-positive-step-for-wildlife-conservation-185907

The Cryosphere: www.the-cryosphere.net

The Donella Meadows Project: www.donellameadows.org

The Earth Statement: https://www.anthropocene.info/earth-statement.php

The Ecologist: 'Why economic growth is not compatible with environmental sustainability.' https://theecologist.org/2018/feb/22/why-economic-growth-not-compatible-environmental-sustainability#

The Economics of Biodiversity: The Dasgupta Review: https://assets.publishing.service.gov.uk/government/uploads/system/uploads/attachment_data/file/957291/Dasgupta_Review_-_Full_Report.pdf

The Economist: 'Global democracy has another bad year.' https://www.economist.com/graphic-detail/2020/01/22/global-democracy-has-another-bad-year

The Green Economy Coalition: 'The Global Transition to Green and Fair Economies.' https://www.greeneconomycoalition.org/assets/reports/GEC-Reports/1037-GEC-Barometer-Phase2-A4-V8j-WEB.pdf

The Guardian: 'A warning on climate and the risk of societal collapse.' https://www.theguardian.com/environment/2020/dec/06/a-warning-on-climate-and-the-risk-of-societal-collapse?

The Guardian: 'Animals to be recognised as sentient beings in UK law.' https://www.theguardian.com/world/2021/may/12/animals-to-be-formally-recognised-as-sentient-beings-in-uk-law

The Guardian: 'Brexit stems from a civil war in capitalism – we are all just collateral damage.' https://www.theguardian.com/commentisfree/2020/nov/24/brexit-capitalism *The Guardian*: 'Climate crisis: world is at its hottest for at least 12,000 years – study.' https://www.theguardian.com/environment/2021/jan/27/climate-crisis-world-now-at-its-hottest-for-12000-years

The Guardian: 'Human destruction of nature is 'senseless and suicidal', warns UN chief.' https://www.theguardian.com/environment/2021/feb/18/human-destruction-of-nature-is-senseless-and-suicidal-warns-un-chief

The Guardian: 'Humans just 0.01% of all life but have destroyed 83% of wild mammals – study.' https://www.theguardian.com/environment/2018/may/21/human-race-just-001-of-all-life-but-has-destroyed-over-80-of-wild-mammals-study

The Guardian: 'How the oil industry has spent billions to control the climate change conversation.' https://www.theguardian.com/business/2020/jan/08/oil-companies-climate-crisis-pr-spending

The Guardian: 'Letter from economists: to rebuild our world, we must end the carbon economy.' https://www.theguardian.com/commentisfree/2020/aug/04/economists-letter-carbon-economy-climate-change-rebuild

The Guardian: 'Ocean temperatures hit record high as rate of heating accelerates.' https://www.theguardian.com/environment/2020/jan/13/ocean-temperatures-hit-record-high-as-rate-of-heating-accelerates

The Guardian: 'Oil company records from 1960s reveal patents to reduce CO^2 emissions in cars.' https://www.theguardian.com/business/2016/may/20/oil-company-records-exxon-co2-emission-reduction-patents

The Guardian: 'Proof that poverty is not failure but a trap.' https://www.theguardian.com/commentisfree/2020/jul/26/proof-that-poverty-is-not-failure-but-a-trap

The Guardian: 'Most polar bears to disappear by 2100, study predicts.' https://www.theguardian.com/commentisfree/2020/jul/26/proof-that-poverty-is-not-failure-but-a-trap www.theguardian.com/environment/2020/jul/20/most-polar-bears-to-disappear-by-2100-study-predicts-aoe

The Guardian: 'Pandemics result from destruction of nature, say UN and WHO.' https://www.theguardian.com/commentisfree/2020/jul/26/proof-that-poverty-is-not-failure-but-a-trap www.theguardian.com/world/2020/jun/17/pandemics-destruction-nature-un-who-legislation-trade-green-recovery

The Guardian: 'Plunder of the Commons by Guy Standing review – how to take back our shared wealth.' https://www.theguardian.com/books/2019/aug/19/plunder-of-the-commons-manifesto-for-sharing-public-wealth-guy-standing-review

The Guardian: 'Richest nations agree to end support for coal production overseas.' https://www.theguardian.com/environment/2021/may/21/richest-nations-agree-to-end-support-for-coal-production-overseas

The Guardian: 'Thirty years of climate summits: where have they got us?':
https://www.theguardian.com/environment/2022/jun/11/cop-climate-change-conference-30-years-highlights-lowlights

The Guardian: 'US Supreme Court rules against EPA and hobbles government power to limit harmful emissions.' https://www.theguardian.com/us-news/2022/jun/30/us-supreme-court-ruling-restricts-federal-power-greenhouse-gas-emissions

The Guardian: 'We're all climate change deniers at heart.'
https://www.theguardian.com/commentisfree/2015/jun/08/climate-change-deniers-g7-goal-fossil-fuels

The Guardian: 'World fails to meet a single target to stop destruction of nature – UN report.' https://www.theguardian.com/environment/2020/sep/15/every-global-target-to-stem-destruction-of-nature-by-2020-missed-un-report-aoe

The Hindu: 'Rhinoceros – A successful conservation story in India.'
https://www.thehindu.com/sci-tech/energy-and-environment/Rhinoceros-a-successful-conservation-story-in-India/article16978537.ece

The Humane Society International – Africa: 'South Africa: Trophy hunting by the numbers.' https://www.hsi.org/wp-content/uploads/2022/02/HSI-Africa-Trophy-Hunting-Report-05-2021.pdf

The Humane Society of the USA: 'Trophy hunting by the numbers.'
https://www.hsi.org/wpcontent/uploads/assets/pdfs/report_trophy_hunting_by_the.pdf

The Intergovernmental Panel on Climate Change: www.ipcc.ch

The Journal of Sustainability Education: 'Urban Sprawl: Definitions, data, methods of measurement, and environmental consequences.'
https://www.susted.com/wordpress/content/urban-sprawl-definitions-data-methods-of-measurement-and-environmental-consequences_2014_12

The Journal of Wildlife Management: 'Sustainability of elephant hunting across international borders in southern Africa.' https://wildlife.onlinelibrary.wiley.com/doi/10.1002/jwmg.641

The Lancet: 'Fertility, mortality, migration, and population scenarios for 195 countries.' https://www.thelancet.com/journals/lancet/article/PIIS0140-6736(20)30677-2/fulltext

The New Republic: 'The collapse of neoliberalism' https://newrepublic.com/article/155970/collapse-neoliberalism

The New Republic: 'Who politicized the environment?'
https://newrepublic.com/article/128835/politicized-environment

The New Yorker: 'The Elephant in the Courtroom.' https://www.newyorker.com/magazine/2022/03/07/the-elephant-in-the-courtroom

The New York Times: 'Denial makes the world go round.'
https://www.nytimes.com/2007/11/20/health/research/20deni.html

The New York Times: 'The tyranny of convenience.' https://www.nytimes.com/2018/02/16/opinion/sunday/tyranny-convenience.html

The New York Times: 'The Variety of Life.' https://archive.nytimes.com/www.nytimes.com/books/first/t/tudge-variety.html

The New York Times: 'What is the Green New Deal? A climate proposal explained.' https://www.nytimes.com/2019/02/21/climate/green-new-deal-questions-answers.html

The Nobel Prize: 'Amartya Sen.' https://www.nobelprize.org/prizes/economic-sciences/1998/sen/biographical

The Ocean Cleanup: 'The Great Pacific Garbage Patch.' https://theoceancleanup.com/great-pacific-garbage-patch

The Sacramento Bee: '5 of the 6 largest California wildfires in history started in the past 6 weeks.' https://www.sacbee.com/news/california/fires/article245917915.html

The Scientist: 'Predicting future zoonotic disease outbreaks.' https://www.the-scientist.com/features/predicting-future-zoonotic-disease-outbreaks-64257

The Tyee: 'Ronald Wright: Can we still dodge the progress trap?' https://thetyee.ca/Analysis/2019/09/20/Ronald-Wright-Can-We-Dodge-Progress-Trap

The Virginian – Pilot: 'Bob Dylan has a lot on his mind: 'I think about the death of the human race'.' https://www.pilotonline.com/celebrity/sns-nyt-bob-dylan-still-painting-his-masterpieces-20200614-uphkgcjlffba5dcovaurjn7knu-story.html

The Washington Post: 'A guide to the financial crisis – 10 years later.' https://www.washingtonpost.com/business/economy/a-guide-to-the-financial-crisis--10-years-later/2018/09/10/114b76ba-af10-11e8-a20b-5f4f84429666_story.html

The White House: 'Executive Order on tackling the climate crisis at home and abroad.' https://www.whitehouse.gov/briefing-room/presidential-actions/2021/01/27/executive-order-on-tackling-the-climate-crisis-at-home-and-abroad

The Wildlife News: 'Why (Mostly) Men Trophy Hunt: A Biocultural Explanation.' https://www.thewildlifenews.com/2018/11/21/why-mostly-men-trophy-hunt-a-biocultural-explanation

The World Bank: 'History.' https://www.worldbank.org/en/about/archives/history

The World Bank: 'Decline of global extreme poverty continues but has slowed.' https://www.worldbank.org/en/news/press-release/2018/09/19/decline-of-global-extreme-poverty-continues-but-has-slowed-world-bank

The World Bank: 'Principles and practice in measuring global poverty.' https://www.worldbank.org/en/news/feature/2016/01/13/principles-and-practice-in-measuring-global-poverty

Think Earth: Environmental Education. www.thinkearth.org

Time: 'World Health Organization declares COVID-19 a 'pandemic'. Here's what that means.' https://time.com/5791661/who-coronavirus-pandemic-declaration

TRAFFIC: 'Empty Shells – Abalone poaching and trade from southern Africa.' https://www.traffic.org/publications/reports/empty-shells

TRAFFIC: 'The People beyond the poaching: Interviews with convicted wildlife offenders in South Africa.' https://www.traffic.org/publications/reports/the-people-beyond-the-poaching

Transparency International: www.transparency.org

Travel-News: 'Botswana tourism now accounts for one in seven of all bucks within the financial system.' https://travel-news.net/2019/03/18/botswana-tourism-now-accounts-for-one-in-seven-of-all-dollars-in-the-economy-travel-news

Trophy Hunting & Britain: The Case for a Ban. https://appgtrophyhunting.files.wordpress.com/2022/07/final-pdf-report-britain-trophy-hunting-the-case-for-a-ban-e28093-a-report-of-the-all-party-parliamentary-group-on-banning-trophy-hunting-29-june-2022-1.pdf

U

United Nations Conference on Environment and Development (Rio Summit): https://www.un.org/esa/dsd/agenda21/Agenda%2021.pdf

United Nations: 'Inequality in a rapidly changing world (2020).' https://www.un.org/development/desa/dspd/wp-content/uploads/sites/22/2020/01/World-Social-Report-2020-FullReport.pdf

United Nations: Population data. https://www.un.org/en/sections/issues-depth/population/index.html

United Nations: 'Nature's dangerous decline 'unprecedented'; species extinction rates 'accelerating'.' https://www.un.org/sustainabledevelopment/blog/2019/05/nature-decline-unprecedented-report/

United Nations: 'Religious leaders issue joint appeal ahead of COP26.' https://unfccc.int/news/religious-leaders-issue-joint-appeal-ahead-of-cop26

United Nations: 'Social justice in an open world.' https://www.un.org/esa/socdev/documents/ifsd/SocialJustice.pdf

United Nations Office on Drugs & Crime: 'World wildlife crime report: Trafficking in protected species.' https://www.unodc.org/documents/data-and-analysis/wildlife/2020/World_Wildlife_Report_2020_9July.pdf

United Nations Department of Economic and Social Affairs: 'World population prospects.' https://www.un.org/development/desa/pd/sites/www.un.org.development.desa.pd/files/files/documents/2020/Jan/wpp2019_highlights.pdf

United Nations Environment Programme (UNEP): 'Green economy.' https://www.unenvironment.org/regions/asia-and-pacific/regional-initiatives/supporting-resource-efficiency/green-economy

United Nations Environment Programme (UNEP): 'Making Peace with
    Nature: A scientific blueprint to tackle climate, biodiversity and pollution
    emergencies.' https://www.unep.org/resources/making-peace-nature
United Nations Environment Programme (UNEP): 'Our Planet is choking
    on plastic.' https://www.unenvironment.org/interactive/beat-plastic-
    pollution
United Nations Environment Programme (UNEP): 'Rosewood conservation: A
    success story from Madagascar.' https://www.unep.org/news-and-stories/
    story/rosewood-conservation-success-story-madagascar
United Nations Environment Programme (UNEP): 'Understanding the long-
    term impact of natural resource extraction.' https://www.unenvironment.
    org/news-and-stories/story/understanding-long-term-impacts-natural-
    resource-extraction
United Nations Environment Programme (UNEP): 'United in Science – High-
    level synthesis report of latest climate science information convened by
    the Science Advisory Group of the UN Climate Action Summit 2019.'
    https://ane4bf-datap1.s3-eu-west-1.amazonaws.com/wmocms/s3fs-
    public/ckeditor/files/United_in_Science_ReportFINAL_0.pdf
United Nations Environment Programme (UNEP): 'With resource use expected
    to double by 2050, better natural resource use essential for a pollution-
    free planet.' https://www.unenvironment.org/news-and-stories/press-
    release/resource-use-expected-double-2050-better-natural-resource-use
United Nations Environment Programme (UNEP): '2017 UN World Water
    Development Report, Wastewater: The Untapped Resource.'
    https://www.unenvironment.org/resources/publication/2017-un-world-
    water-development-report-wastewater-untapped-resource
United Nations Environment Programme (UNEP) & International Resource
    Pane (IRP): 'Catalysing Science-Based Policy Action on Sustainable
    Consumption and Production.' https://www.resourcepanel.org/reports/
    catalysing-science-based-policy-action-sustainable-consumption-and-
    production
United Nations University: 'The Population Paradox.' https://unu.edu/
    publications/articles/the-population-paradox.html
University of Cambridge & Dr Luke Kemp: 'Ruin, Resilience, and the
    Rungless Ladder.' http://risk.princeton.edu/img/historical_collapse_
    production/2b_Kemp.pdf
University of Cumbria: 'International warning on societal disruption and
    collapse.' http://iflas.blogspot.com/2020/12/international-scholars-
    warning-on.html
USA Environmental Protection Agency (EPA): 'Overview of greenhouse gases.'
    https://www.epa.gov/ghgemissions/overview-greenhouse-gases

V

Visual Capitalist: 'The World's Top 50 Influencers across social media platforms.' https://www.visualcapitalist.com/worlds-top-50-influencers-across-social-media-platforms

W

Welcome to the Anthropocene: www.anthropocene.info

Wilderness Foundation Africa: www.wildernessfoundation.co.za

Working Group on the Anthropocene: http://quaternary.stratigraphy.org/working-groups/anthropocene/

World Bank: 'The World Bank in South Africa.' https://www.worldbank.org/en/country/southafrica/overview

World Economic Forum: '5 reasons why biodiversity matters – to human health, the economy and your wellbeing.' https://www.weforum.org/agenda/2020/05/5-reasons-why-biodiversity-matters-human-health-economies-business-wellbeing-coronavirus-covid19-animals-nature-ecosystems

World Economic Forum: 'A five-step beginner's guide to the energy transition.' https://www.weforum.org/agenda/2020/07/a-beginners-guide- to-the-energy-transition

World Economic Forum: 'Climate Indicators' https://intelligence.weforum.org/topics/a1G680000004Cv2EAE?tab=publications

World Economic Forum: 'From linear to circular – accelerating a proven concept.' https://reports.weforum.org/toward-the-circular-economy-accelerating-the-scale-up-across-global-supply-chains/from-linear-to-circular-accelerating-a-proven-concept

World Economic Forum: Global Risks Report 2020. https://www3.weforum.org/docs/WEF_Global_Risk_Report_2020.pdf

World Economic Forum: Global Risks Report 2021. https://www3.weforum.org/docs/WEF_The_Global_Risks_Report_2021.pdf

World Economic Forum: 'Meet the doughnut: the new economic model that could help end inequality.' https://www.weforum.org/agenda/2017/04/the-new-economic-model-that-could-end-inequality-doughnut

World Economic Forum: 'Nature Risk Rising: Why the crisis engulfing nature matters for business and the economy.' http://www3.weforum.org/docs/WEF_New_Nature_Economy_Report_2020.pdf

World Economic Forum: 'Poverty: the past, present, and future.' https://www.weforum.org/agenda/2016/01/poverty-the-past-present-and-future

World Economic Forum: 'The cost of the climate crisis? 20 million homeless every year.' https://www.weforum.org/agenda/2019/12/extreme-weather-climate-change-displaced

World Economic Forum: 'The Fourth Industrial Revolution.'
https://www.weforum.org/focus/fourth-industrial-revolution

World Economic Forum: 'The future of jobs 2020.' https://www3.weforum.org/
docs/WEF_Future_of_Jobs_2020.pdf

World Economic Forum: 'The world's e-waste is a huge problem. It's also a
golden opportunity.' https://www.weforum.org/agenda/2019/01/how-a-
circular-approach-can-turn-e-waste-into-a-golden-opportunity

World Economic Forum: 'These 12 charts show how the world's population
has exploded in the last 200 years.' https://www.weforum.org/
agenda/2019/07/populations-around-world-changed-over-the-years

World Economic Forum: 'We need to talk about artificial intelligence.'
https://www.weforum.org/agenda/2021/02/we-need-to-talk-about-
artificial-intelligence

World Economic Forum: 'Why nature is the most important stakeholder of the
coming decade.' https://www.weforum.org/agenda/2020/01/why-nature-
will-be-the-most-important-stakeholder-in-the-coming-decade

World Economic Forum: 'Why schools should teach the curriculum of the
future, not the past.' https://www.weforum.org/agenda/2018/09/why-
schools-should-teach-the-curriculum-of-the-future-not-the-past/

World Economic Forum: '17 ways technology could change the world by 2025.'
https://www.weforum.org/agenda/2020/06/17-predictions-for-our-world-
in-2025

World Health Organization (WHO): COVID-19 Dashboard.
https://covid19.who.int

World Health Organization (WHO): 'How air pollution is destroying our
health.' https://www.who.int/news-room/spotlight/how-air-pollution-is-
destroying-our-health

World Inequality Database: 'Global Inequality Data: 2020 Update.'
https://wid.world/news-article/2020-regional-updates

World Politics Review: 'Radical movements.' https://www.worldpoliticsreview.
com/issues/18/radical-movements

World Resources Institute: 'Reefs at Risk Projections: Present, 2030, and 2050.'
https://www.wri.org/resources/charts-graphs/reefs-risk-projections-
present-2030-and-2050

World Summit on Sustainable Development:
https://sustainabledevelopment.un.org/milesstones/wssd

World Travel & Tourism Council (WTTC): '2018 – Economic Impact report
on Botswana.' https://wttc.org/Research/Economic-Impact

WWF: 'IUCN Red List Update: Ongoing industrial fishing drives pelagic sharks
and rays closer to extinction.' https://sharks.panda.org/news-blogs-
updates/latest-news/iucn-red-list-update-ongoing-industrial-fishing-
drives-pelagic-sharks-and-rays-closer-to-extinction

WWF: 'Road map to zero poaching in Selous.' https://www.worldwildlife.org/ projects/road-map-to-zero-poaching-in-selous#

WWF: 'Sustainable seafood.' https://www.worldwildlife.org/industries/ sustainable-seafood

WWF: 'When infrastructure goes wrong for nature and people.' https://www.worldwildlife.org/stories/when-infrastructure-goes-wrong-for-nature-and-people

WWF: https://www.worldwildlife.org/initiatives/oceans#

Y

Yale Climate Connections: 'Plant and animal species at risk of extinction.' https://yaleclimateconnections.org/2020/03/plant-and-animal-species-at-risk-of-extinction/

Yale Environment 360: 'Living in the Anthropocene: towards a new global ethos.' https://e360.yale.edu/features/living_in_the_anthropocene _toward_a_new_global_ethos

Z

Zoological Society of London (ZSL): 'Rarity, trophy hunting and ungulates.' https://zslpublications.onlinelibrary.wiley.com/doi/full/10.1111/j.1469-1795.2011.00476.x

ACKNOWLEDGEMENTS

{ *Ian McCallum* }

I wish to acknowledge the generosity and support of the following individuals and organisations, without whom, the Tracks of Giants journey and production of this book would have been very difficult:

Neville Isdell, Robert-Jan von Ogtrop and Dylan Lewis; Andrew Muir of the Wilderness Foundation Africa and Wilderness Leadership School; Wayne Duvenage (AVIS); Werner Myburgh, Craig Beech, Alan Sparrow (Peace Parks Foundation); Grant Woodrow, Patrick Bottam-Wetham, Courtney Johnson, Rob and Lundi Burns (Wilderness Safaris), Gary van Rooyen (New Balance); Sven Kreher (Bataleurs), Louis de Waal (BIKE), Dugald and Marguerite McDonald.

For part two of the book I would like to acknowledge the support, memory and example of the following voices for the wild: My wife Sharon, Alison McCallum, Ryan Jordan, Murray and Mandy McCallum, Michelle and David Knight, Dylan Lewis, Michael Chase, Kelly Landen, Pat Mitchell, Patricia Schonstein, Don Pinnock, Deborah Calmeyer, Craig Foster, Joan Berning, Colin Bell, Francis Garrard, Carel and Janetta Benade, Alex van den Heever, Vance Martin, Andrew Muir, Margie Jacobsohn, Devon Concor, Johan van der Westhuizen, Rudi van Aarde, Quinton Martins, Helen Turnbull and not least, my co-author and friend – Ian Michler.

Finally, in memory of Garth Owen-Smith, Ian Player and Magqubu Ntombela. I would like to acknowledge the 'other than human' beings in my life – the wild animals and wild places in our world. Who and what would we be without them?

And then Ian McCallum and Ian Michler owe thanks and appreciation to the entire Tracks of Giants team. They played a significant role, one that was central to the success of the journey. Johnny Frankiskos; Anton Kruyshaw; Frank Raimondo; Mandla Buthelezi; Lihle Mabunda; Martin Peterson; Chris Bakkes; Garth Owen-Smith; Margie Jacobsohn; John Sandenberg; PJ Bestelink; Dr Michael Chase; Kelly Landen; Courteney Johnson; Rob and Lundi Burns; Billie Swanepoel; Graeme Harman; Nick Chevallier; James Brundige; Michael and TJ Holding; Simon Wood; Alan Sparrow; Dr Greg Rasmussen; David Evans; Paul Dutton; and Kenton Kirkwood.

And to our principal sponsors and supporters: you made the journey a whole lot more comfortable and enjoyable. Wilderness Foundation Africa; WILD Foundation; Avis; New Balance; Bateleurs; Mantis Collection; International SOS; Wilderness Safaris; Peace Parks Foundation; Hans Hoheisen Charitable Trust; and One World.

And then to our editors, Peter Borchert, Karin Schimke and Michelle Bovey-Wood, and Vanessa Wilson and her entire team at Quickfox Publishing for getting this job done in such a professional manner.

ACKNOWLEDGEMENTS

{ *Ian Michler* }

Family, friends, mentors and peers

Having the privilege to roam, and then grasping the opportunities, is only part of the story. The missing pieces belong to those that have played such a significant role in my work and experiences over the past 30 years or so. There are many of them. Family and friends have always been there, their endurance a great comfort. To them, as well as my mentors, peers, and work associates, I owe huge thanks and appreciation. Any list is going to be incomplete, and so I apologise in advance.

PJ and Barney Bestelink; Person Mothanka; Phuraki Ngoro; Len Samaje; Adam Kapinga; Julius Masoga; Chris Kruger (1956–2021) and Colin Bell, for setting me on my way. Then Peter Borchert, Eve Gracie, and Sarah Borchert for their unwavering support early on.

Subsequently, and over the years: Karl Ammann; Dr Jeremy Anderson; Sofia Arkelsten; Dr Guy Balme; Ken Beam; Jason Bell; Joan Berning; Dr Mark Brown; Roderick Campbell; Rob Carr-Hartley; Dr Mike Chase; Nick Chevallier; Dr Adam Cruise; Norma Cuadros; Cormac Cullinan; Dr Hamish Currie; Hendrik Daffue; Michelle Davies; Dr Audrey Delsink; Esther de Villiers; Charles Dobie; Paul Dutton; Lizzie Farren; Jeff Flocken; Peter Gava; Dr Ross Harvey; Dr Michelle Henley; Rory Hensman (1946–2013); Lindy Hensman; Calista Herndon; Dr Luke Hunter; James Isiche; Map Ives; Mark Jenkins; Courteney Johnson; Dr Mark Jones; Dereck Joubert; Louise Joubert (1959–2018); Russ Juds; Masha Kalinina; Dr Pieter Kat; Richard Knocker; Dex Kotze; Kelly Landen; Jannie Laubscher; Dominique le Roux; Wayne Lotter (1965–

2017); Christine Macsween; Mpho 'Poster' Malongwa; Vance Martin; Dr Quinton Martins; Sylvia Medina; Petra Meyr; Dr Neil Midlane; Dr Gus Mills; Dr Peter Morkel; Seako Duke Motlakatshipi; Andrew Muir; Gabriel Lucas Mushi; Prof Alejandro Nadal; Steve Njumbi; Dr Katarzyna Nowak; Donalea Patman, Sirpa Pietikäinen, Robin Pope, Eliza Powell, Christina Pretorius, Alistair Rankin; Mary Rice; Chris Roche; Dr Karen Ross; Galeo Saintz; Angela Sheldrick; Ali Shenton; Annie Sowden; Brent Stapelkamp; Clive Stockil; Barry Style (1970–2018); Rob Style; Will Travers OBE; Karen Trendier; Dr Rudi van Aarde; Alex van den Heever; Charles van Rensburg; Birgitta Wahlberg; Susie Watts; Roger Whittall, and Grant Woodrow.

To the entire *Blood Lions* team: Pippa Hankinson; Nick Chevallier; Nicola Gerrard; Lauren van Nijkerk; Jeremy Nathan; Bruce Young; Dave Cohen; Dr Andrew Venter; Dr Louise de Waal; Cath Jenkins; Janelle Barnard and Casey Pratt. And to Peter Whelan and Alan Wright from Bowmans, who fought our corner in countless legal cases, winning them all.

In New York, to Iva Spitzer and the following for their kind support and help in getting the book project going: Mark Samsky; Jason Simon; Elizabeth Unger; Jon and Lou Dembrow; Barbara Russo; Larry Kruysman; Jim Brawders; Rick Livingston; Stan Kramer; Ann Cutbill Lenane; Julie Stevens, and Robert and Elaine De Angelis. And to David Schimmel, Frits Kouwenhoven, and Steve Renn for their technical support.

Calista Herndon has been instrumental in assisting us to get this project on to pages: A huge thanks to her.

Also, to my colleagues and associates at Conservation Action Trust: Francis Garrard; Colin Bell; Don Pinnock and Charan Saunders: Your work, passion, and commitment is vital beyond any words.

More recently, at the Sustainability Institute: Prof Mark Swilling; Eve Annecke; Vanessa Von Der Hyde; Angela Coetzee; Jess Schulschenk; Eduardo Shimahara (1976–2020); Beatrix Steenkamp and Monique Beukes. And to Prof Piet Naudé, thank you for nudging me in their direction.

ABOUT THE AUTHORS

Ian McCallum is a medical doctor, psychiatrist and analyst. He is the author of two anthologies of wilderness poetry: *Wild Gifts* (1999) and *Untamed* (2012). His book, *Ecological Intelligence – Rediscovering Ourselves in Nature*, won the Wild Literary Award in 2009. In collaboration with renowned sculptor Dylan Lewis, he was the writer/ poet for the *Mail & Guardian's* award-winning 'UNTAMED' exhibition at Kirstenbosch Botanical Gardens (2010–2012). He is a former rugby Springbok and, with Ian Michler, is a co-founder of the safari organisation, Invent Africa.

* * *

Ian Michler, a graduate of the Sustainability Institute, Stellenbosch University, has spent more than 30 years working across Africa as an environmental photojournalist, wilderness guide and ecotourism consultant. He has published seven natural history and travel books on Africa and is co-author of a children's book published in the USA. His conservation and travel writing has appeared in publications across the world. He is well-known for his conservation work, including the award-winning feature documentary *Blood Lions*. He is a Director of Eden to Addo and a member of the International League of Conservation Writers. In 2019, Ian was listed as one of the 76 Influential Voices speaking up for the environment in Africa. He currently lives in Plettenberg Bay, where he runs Invent Africa Safaris (www.inventafrica.com), an inbound safari company operating in 16 countries across Africa.

* * *